MARITIME COMMERCE
AND THE FUTURE OF THE PANAMA CANAL

Panama Canal viewed from 40,000 feet. National Geographic Society

Maritime Commerce
and
the Future
of the Panama Canal

By

NORMAN J. PADELFORD

and

STEPHEN R. GIBBS

Department of Ocean Engineering
Massachusetts Institute of Technology

Introduction by

Alfred H. Keil
Dean, School of Engineering
Massachusetts Institute of Technology

 M.I.T. / Report No. MITSG 74-28
SEA GRANT PROGRAM / Index No. 74-328-Npt

CORNELL MARITIME PRESS, INC.

CAMBRIDGE   1975   MARYLAND

Library of Congress Cataloging in Publication Data

Padelford, Norman Judson, 1903-
    Maritime commerce and the future of the Panama Canal.

    (Report - Massachusetts Institute of Technology, Sea Grant Program ; MITSG 74-28)
    "Index no. 74-328-NPT."
    Includes bibliographical references and index.
    1. Panama Canal. 2. Shipping—Panama Canal.
I. Gibbs, Stephen R., 1947-   joint author. II. Title. III. Series: Massachusetts Institute of Technology. Sea Grant Program. Report - Massachusetts Institute of Technology, Sea Grant Program ; MITSG 74-28.
HE537.8.P33   386'.444   75-2305
ISBN 0—87033—202-3

SSo

Printed and Bound in the United States of America

TABLE OF CONTENTS

LIST OF ILLUSTRATIONS

PREFACE

This book has been written as a portion of the M.I.T. Sea Grant Program in the field of marine commerce and engineering.

Our goal has been to make a fresh investigation of the operation of the Panama Canal with a view to ascertaining its capability for handling ocean commerce over the next thirty years.

In preparing the study we have looked closely at the operation of the waterway today. We have examined trends in cargo movement, and in shipbuilding. We have studied the limits of capacity of the Canal. We have considered the fundamentals of toll policy and sought to develop a toll strategy for the future. We have weighed alternatives for enlarging the Canal. And we have ventured into the field of policy to consider steps to modernizing treaty relationships with the Republic of Panama, believing that the larger picture of engineering, technological change, economics, and decision-making are all tied in with effective handling of Canal questions in the years ahead.

We have sought to anticipate the area of change that lies ahead, and to suggest that by capitalizing upon technological innovation the Canal can promote expanding markets and growing industry.

By giving a broad spectrum of trends and pragmatic possibilities, a base is provided for assisting the business community and the public in forming judgments of what manner of ships to employ on Canal trade routes and what manner of changes to make at the Canal itself.

There are questions of judgment whether the United States should lay out the sums of money that will be required to enlarge the capacity of the waterway, and the degree to which considerations of national defense interests will play a part in this. We have not attempted to touch these questions, feeling that they demand a special expertise we do not have. They will, however, be involved in deciding what the country should do with the Canal for the future.

We have been aided in our study by numerous officers of the Panama Canal Company who have taken hours to discuss with us problems of running and modernizing the waterway. We express our gratitude to them warmly, including Governor David S. Parker, President of the Panama Canal Company; Sidney Kaufman, Chief of the Executive Planning Staff; Hugh A. Norris, Deputy Chief; Captain Donald A. Dertien, USN (ret.), Director of the Marine Bureau; Colonel A.L. Romaneski, Director of the Engineering and Construction Bureau, Philip L. Steers, Jr., Comptroller; Gerard Welch, Chief of the Marine Traffic Control System Development Office; Robert Lessiack, Deputy Comptroller; Donald Schmidt, Chief Economist; Thomas M. Constant, Secretary of the Panama Canal Company; and Mrs. Hazel Murdock of the Washington Office.

Colleagues on the faculty at M.I.T. have been a source of help in many ways. In particular, Dean Alfred H. Keil of the School of Engineering first suggested this study to us, and has assisted with counsel and financial support. Professor Ira Dyer, Head of the Department of Ocean Engineering, gave us encouragement, advice, comments, and release from academic duties when the going became difficult. Dean A. Horn, Executive Officer of the M.I.T. Sea Grant Program, has been a constant help on administrative matters. Professors Philip Mandel, Alaa Mansour, John W. Devanney III, C. Chryssostomidis, and Henry A. Marcus aided us at many points along the way with information relating to shipping, transport, and marine commerce.

This research and study was supported jointly by a fund from the NOAA Office of Sea Grant, U.S. Department of Commerce, Grant No. NG-43-72, from the Henry L. and Grace Doherty Charitable Foundation, Inc., and from the Massachusetts Institute of Technology. This support enabled us to visit the Zone on several occasions, to develop computer programs relating to cargo and traffic, and to bring the results of the study to publication. We are also indebted to the editors of the *Journal of Maritime Law and Commerce* for permission to reproduce parts of an article that originally appeared in their columns. We also express thanks to the National Geographic Society for use of their aerial photograph of the Isthmus.

Thanks are due to James H. Wakelin, Jr., former Assistant Secretary of Commerce and Chairman of the President's Task Force on Oceanography, for suggestions relating to Chapters VII and VIII, as also to Colonel John P. Sheffey, formerly Executive Director of the Atlantic-Pacific Interoceanic Study Commission, and Special Adviser to the Office of Interoceanic Canal Treaty Negotiations, Department of State. We are also indebted to Dr. Immanuel J. Klette of the Battell Laboratory, author of *From Atlantic to Pacific: A New Interoceanic Canal*, for reading the manuscript and offering many helpful suggestions on the treatment of various parts. The critiques and comments of these authorities have aided us substantively in the task of authorship.

We express appreciation to Gordon Stewart Lingley, formerly with the Military Sea Transport Office at the Canal Zone, and to Lim H. Tan of Singapore for insights into the impact of superships on Canal traffic demand, and for a study of the land- and mini-bridge developments upon Canal commerce, during their periods as graduate students in ocean engineering at M.I.T. Particular thanks are due to Eleanor Baker for typing the manuscript with exceptional excellence. We also express our appreciation to our wives for their advice and help throughout the months of authorship.

NORMAN J. PADELFORD
STEPHEN R. GIBBS

Cambridge, Massachusetts

INTRODUCTION

The Panama Canal has been in operation for sixty years. In these years the world has changed much. More than fourscore nation states are now on the world scene that did not exist when the Canal was opened to navigation in 1914. International commerce has expanded from a few hundred million tons a year to over 2,700,000,000 metric tons, much of it moved between nations and continents by ocean shipping.

Postwar patterns of business are changing many traditional relationships and practices. Registrations of nearly a quarter of the world merchant fleet are now placed in countries other than where their true owners are situated in order to gain entrance into sheltered markets, or to obtain the benefits of low fees or less expensive labor. Multinational companies, joining firms and operations in different countries, are becoming widely used in corporate life to promote international business.

More importantly, from our point of view, a technological revolution is sweeping the world mercantile fleet. Ship sizes are increasing progressively. There are today, for instance, over a thousand vessels that are too large to be admitted to the Panama Canal locks, and nearly twice as many more that can go through the locks only if they are less than fully loaded. Dry and liquid bulk carriers are being constructed in Europe and Japan that are over 300,000 tons in capacity, too large for accommodation in the narrow, relatively shallow waters of the interoceanic passageway. The small general cargo freighters of yesteryear are giving way to large, highly specialized types of vessels.

Before 1970 practically the only specialized types of vessels generally known were oil tankers and ore and bulk carriers. Today Lloyd's Register of Shipping lists 21 different types of ocean vessels, including refrigerator ships, containerships, roll-on roll-off ships (RO/RO), oil and ore carriers, oil and dry bulk and ore ships (OBO), special petroleum products ships, lighter-aboard ships (LASH), automobile carriers, and others. As more specialized ships are being built, a downward trend is occurring in the use of general cargo vessels with their greater labor intensity in the handling of cargo.

Containerships are a revolutionary change in maritime commerce made possible by the advent of the sealed modular container. The fast turn-around time of these vessels in port, their efficient manner of stowing containers above as well as below decks, and the low pilferage and breakage of boxes sustained while en route, thereby lowering insurance charges, appeal to shippers. Furthermore, the big containerships can take the place of as many as five general cargo freighters due to their efficiency of loading, thus effecting significant savings in the use of shipping. The container revolution is not only a novelty in cargo transport; it is an innovative change in cargo handling as well. Moreover, the speed of new ships enables them to meet faster delivery schedules. Some containerships run by Sea-Land Lines, for instance, can hold 33 knots at sea, an unheard-of speed heretofore, save among naval vessels and a few passenger liners.

The tendency for growth in the size of tankers is well known. This is exemplified by the increasing number of tankers in the world fleet of 300,000 deadweight and above. These vessels cannot enter the locks of the Panama Canal because of their length, beam or draft, and indeed were designed exclusively for use on all-ocean routes as from the Persian Gulf to Europe and North America. Intermediate-size tankers of up to 100,000 deadweight can be accommodated with certain configurations. Transits by tankers that can barely squeeze into the locks are a daily feature of Panama Canal operations.

The average size of other ships has been growing as well. Not one dry bulk or combined carrier of up to 80,000 tons capacity existed in 1965. Today there are over 100 ore/oil carriers of 125,000 deadweight and above. With the appearance of very large vessels, a traffic bypassing the Panama Canal is developing for coal.

The Merchant Marine Act of 1970 inaugurated a restructuring of the United States merchant marine. Liberalized construction and operating subsidy differentials aim to make the shipbuilding industry more capital-intensive and to launch an average of 30 ships a year. The variety of types of vessels that are to be built, including containerships, roll-on roll-off carriers, liquefied natural gas ships (LNG), and the like, will stress rapidity of loading and unloading, automated facilities, deck lifts, and low transportation costs.

The next generation of ships will see vessels built to take hundreds of truck trailer rigs and cars that can be driven directly onboard and off. Freight can thus be delivered directly to inland cities. Such ships, along with specialized automobile carriers, refrigerated cargo ships, and special petroleum product ships are already operating to and from American ports. Some experts foresee an entire fleet of LNG vessels carrying up to 9.5 million cubic meters of liquefied gas a year into Western Europe, Japan, and the United States by 1980.

These are among some of the innovations that are transpiring in ocean shipping due to inputs of new engineering knowledge and techniques. They are revolutionizing the carriage and handling of cargo. More changes will occur as needs demand further innovations.

Throughout these changing times and circumstances, the Panama Canal has adhered to its original purpose of serving world commerce. It strives to get vessels from one ocean to another with the least delay, efficiently, at moderate tolls, and without discriminating among users.

Its locks, however, with their fixed dimensions impose limitations on the capacity of the Canal.

A development that will have an important bearing upon the future of the interoceanic canal and the trade that funnels through it is that of the land- and mini-bridge systems being fostered by United States railroads to move containers across the continent on fast, unitized trains, synchronized with ship arrivals and departures for overseas. Already, weekly services have been instituted from West Coast ports to speed deliveries to the East Coast. The mini-bridge concept, involving one ocean and two continents, has appeal for high-priority cargoes where delivery time is at a premium in reaching high-intensity markets, as in the electronics and automotive industries. Thus far, the ocean shipping companies have been able to compete timewise with the land-bridge between Asia and Europe by introducing high-speed containerships. The land- and mini-bridge systems do offer shippers an alternative to the Panama Canal, competing on rates up until now, and the advantages of the single bill of lading.

The question that is raised in this connection is whether the United States Government should assist the railroads to improve their service, including improving trackage, acquiring new rolling stock, and speeding the operation of trains, rather than enlarging the Canal at Panama in order to have a fully competitive system.

Another development flowing out of the unit-load innovation and the production of the wide-bodied jet planes is the rising competition between overseas air freight and containerships. Air freight now carries only about five percent of U.S. overseas commerce. The larger payloads becoming possible with the wide-bodied planes will afford a fresh dimension of rivalry between sea and air for palletized freight that has a high urgency for delivery abroad. This competition could become increasingly serious as liner freight rates continue to rise.

This is a timely moment for the appearance of a fresh, independent study of the Panama Canal, particularly since the senior author, Professor Norman Padelford, draws on a lifetime of experience, having written the most authoritative book on the Panama Canal in 1942.

By looking at the changes in maritime commerce, and the scientific and technological innovations made possible by modern engineering techniques, the authors have brought new perspectives to bear upon the operation of the interoceanic canal and the options that are open to the United States in this area. They recognize that there are many uncertainties along the way, but are confident there is a future for rising trade and maritime transport.

ALFRED H. KEIL

Dean, School of Engineering
Massachusetts Institute of Technology

MARITIME COMMERCE
AND THE FUTURE OF THE PANAMA CANAL

CHAPTER ONE

MARITIME ADVANTAGES
OF THE INTEROCEANIC CANAL

When the Panama Canal was opened to navigation in 1914, it introduced a shortcut that was hailed as a major boon to the ocean-shipping community. Distances of 6,000 miles and more were saved on some of the principal world trade routes, thereby reducing time spent at sea and affording economies to seaborne transportation between the Atlantic and Pacific Oceans.

In the years since the Canal was constructed, an increasing stream of traffic has turned this into one of the main thoroughfares of world commerce. Nearly half a million vessels have transited since 1914. Ships flying the flags of nearly every principal maritime nation move an ever enlarging tonnage of cargo through the Canal to and from the world's ports.

The oceanborne commerce of the United States has long been a primary beneficiary of the existence of the Canal. For many years United States flag shipping stood in first place in numbers of transits per year. Although vessels flying the U.S. flag made more than 1,200 transits in 1973, vessels registered in Liberia, the United Kingdom, and Japan each outnumbered them. Following after these come the shipping of Norway, Greece, Panama, Germany, the Netherlands, and Sweden. Vessels of sixty countries have employed the Canal in one year, attesting to the broad usefulness of the waterway to world commerce.[1]

Practically every country fronting on or adjacent to the Atlantic and Pacific Oceans shares to an extent in the more than 126 million long tons of cargo a year that now moves through the Canal.

Role of Canal in United States Foreign Commerce

The volume of United States foreign trade passing through the Panama Canal has increased steadily in the postwar period, as seen in Table 1. One of the primary reasons for building the Panama Canal was to promote United States ocean commerce. Table 1 and Figure 1 show the percentage of total United States oceanborne foreign commerce passing through the Panama Canal. This percentage has grown from 10.7 to 17 percent in the past 14 years.

Table 2 gives the breakdown by commodity type of the United States foreign commerce passing through the Panama Canal each year and its total estimated value. The value of cargo passing through the

1

Table 1*

Total U.S. Oceanborne Foreign Trade, and U.S. Foreign Trade Through the Panama Canal
(millions of tons)

	1958	1959	1960	1961	1962	1963	1964	1965	1966	1967	1968	1969	1970	1971
Total U.S. Oceanborne Foreign Trade	253.3	267.0	277.9	272.4	296.8	311.6	332.8	371.3	392.3	387.6	418.6	426.1	473.2	456.9
U.S. Oceanborne Commerce Through Panama Canal	27.2	28.9	34.8	37.5	40.5	35.5	40.7	44.1	48.6	53.1	57.8	63.9	74.8	77.9
Panama Percentage of Total U.S. Commerce	% 10.7	10.8	12.5	13.8	13.6	11.4	12.2	11.8	12.4	13.6	13.8	15.0	15.8	17.0

*United States Maritime Administration, Annual Report of Maritime Administration for Fiscal Year 1972, Washington, D.C., 1973. "A New Wave in American Shipping," p. 90. See also Panama Canal Company, Annual Reports, Tables 19, 20, respective years.

Table 2*

U.S. Foreign Trade Through the Panama Canal by Cargo Type and Dollar Value
(millions of long tons; billions of dollars)

	1958	1959	1960	1961	1962	1963	1964	1965	1966	1967	1968	1969	1970	1971
Total Dollar Value of U.S. Ocean Foreign Trade	$20.9	22.8	24.7	24.7	25.9	27.5	30.0	32.4	36.4	36.6	41.1	41.7	49.7	50.7
Tons of U.S. Foreign Panama Canal General Cargo Tonnage	8.6	9.1	10.1	10.8	12.0	12.0	13.3	14.5	16.0	18.4	17.6	18.9	19.0	20.6
Tons of U.S. Foreign Dry Cargo Through Panama Canal	15.5	16.6	20.9	22.9	23.5	18.6	23.8	24.6	25.3	26.4	32.2	37.7	47.7	47.6
Liquid Bulk Tons Through Panama Canal	2.9	3.4	3.6	3.7	4.9	5.0	4.8	5.9	5.5	6.7	6.7	6.2	8.9	9.3
Dollar Value of U.S. Panama Canal Cargo	$ 3.6	3.8	3.8	4.9	5.6	5.6	5.8	6.7	9.2	10.7	12.0	14.5	15.2	17.0
Percentage of Total U.S. Trade Dollar Value - Panama Canal	%17.1	16.7	15.3	19.8	22.7	20.4	19.2	20.7	25.3	29.3	29.3	34.8	30.5	33.5

*Panama Canal Company, Annual Reports, respective years.

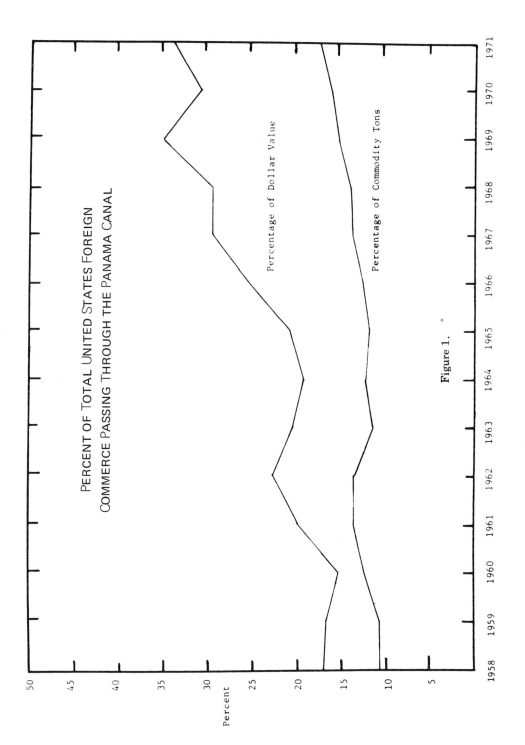

PERCENT OF TOTAL UNITED STATES FOREIGN
COMMERCE PASSING THROUGH THE PANAMA CANAL

Percentage of Dollar Value

Percentage of Commodity Tons

Figure 1.

Percent

1958 1959 1960 1961 1962 1963 1964 1965 1966 1967 1968 1969 1970 1971

5 10 15 20 25 30 35 40 45 50

Canal has almost doubled since 1950 and has grown even faster than tonnage volume.

The growth in tonnage and in value is due primarily to expanding trade between the United States East Coast and Asia. In the past 10 years the growth of Japan's economy has been phenomenal. The prospects are bright for continued growth of United States trade through the Canal with Japan, China and Australia, provided the energy crisis does not lead to a major recession.

Roughly 66 percent of all the cargo moving through the Canal comes from or goes to ports of the United States.[2] This indicates how important United States trade is for the well-being of the Canal operation. Japan ranks as the largest originator and receiver of United States trade through the Canal, followed by the United Kingdom, and West Germany.

While the Canal transited only 17 percent of the United States foreign trade in 1971, this represented approximately 33.5 percent of the total value of foreign seaborne United States trade that year. Commodities transiting the Canal as part of United States oceanborne foreign trade had a high average value compared to overall United States oceanborne foreign commerce. The lower average for overall trade was due largely to the volume of crude oil the United States imported into its East Coast ports from the Middle East. In 1971 foreign crude oil was inexpensive and little of this petroleum transited the Panama Canal.

The volume of United States cargo carried through the Canal and its dollar value give a rough measure of the importance of the Canal for United States foreign commerce. The Canal's role in United States foreign trade is growing and will continue to grow. Assuming the United States railroads do not extend their portion of the East Coast United States-Asia trade beyond present levels, as much as 25 percent of all United States foreign oceanborne commercial trade may be passing through the Canal by 1980.

Distance Savings of Panama Canal

There are numerous maritime advantages of the interoceanic Canal. It is the strategic location of the Canal, situated at the narrow waist of the Americas, that gives this shortcut its great advantage for oceanborne commerce bound between the two major oceans.

The Panama Canal provides important savings in distances for shipping bound between various ports in the Atlantic and Pacific Oceans. A vessel traveling between New York and San Francisco, for instance, can save 7,860 miles by using the Canal instead of going around Cape Horn. From New York to Callao, Peru, 6,237 miles can be saved. From New York to Yokohama, Japan, 6,509 miles can be saved compared to proceeding via the Straits of Magellan, although going around the Cape of Good Hope or through the Suez Canal when this is open is shorter than the Magellan route. A vessel sailing from New Orleans to Vancouver, B.C., can shorten the voyage by 8,807 miles compared to going around South America. From Hampton Roads, Virginia, to Yokohama, Japan, the Canal saves 5,666 miles compared with sailing around the Cape of Good Hope and proceeding across the Indian Ocean.

From European ports to points in the Pacific the distance advantages of the Panama Canal are similar. A ship en route from Liverpool, England, to San Francisco, can cut 5,575 miles off a voyage around South America. From London to Shanghai the Canal saves 3,892 miles compared with the Straits of Magellan. From Gibraltar to Callao, Peru, the Canal gives a saving of 3,322 miles.

Not all routes are, of course, equally affected. The distance from Bishop's Rock, southwest of England, to Melbourne, Australia, is 12,312 nautical miles by the Panama Canal. It is 10,754 miles via the Suez Canal when that is open, and 11,630 via the Cape of Good Hope. Normally, traffic from Europe to points in the Indian Ocean and beyond will go by way of Suez or the Cape of Good Hope. The Panama Canal offers an alternate route to these destinations when Suez is closed, giving the advantage of calls at ports in the New World en route. The Canal also provides a shorter, less stormy route than around Cape Horn.

Table 3 shows comparative distances between selected ports by a variety of routes. The principal savings are between ports on the Atlantic Ocean generally north of the bulge of Brazil (15°S), and points in the Pacific Ocean north of 40°S latitude, i.e., Wellington, New Zealand.

Vessels proceeding from ports in North America, the Caribbean, northeast South America, Western Europe and the Mediterranean to the West Coast of Latin America as far south as Valparaiso, and vice versa, will save distance by utilizing the Panama Canal compared with rounding the Horn.

Likewise, vessels from ports on the West Coast of North America, Hawaii, Japan, the Philippines, the East Coast of Australia and New Zealand, and from the West Coast of South America as far south as Callao, Peru, proceeding to ports in the Atlantic Ocean north of Recife, Brazil, will save distance by employing the Canal route.

Vessels leaving from ports near or below the equator in the Western Pacific i.e., Australia, New Zealand—or ports south of Callao, Peru, bound to Buenos Aires, Sao Paulo, Rio de Janeiro, or Africa south of Nigeria, have a shorter distance to go via Puenta Arenas and the Straits of Magellan than by the Canal. Much less shipping moves along this route, however, than via the Panama Canal because there are few intermediate stops along the way. In short, the Panama Canal is strategically placed for the main body of interoceanic commerce.

Table 3

Comparative Distances to Selected Ports Via Panama Canal and Alternate Routes[1]
(Left Side)

FROM	VIA*	TO					
		Los Angeles	San Francisco	Seattle (Vanc.)	Guayaquil	Callao	Val-paraiso
New York (N.Y.)	PC	4,931	5,263	6,038	2,842	3,368	4,634
	M	12,805	13,122	13,898	10,241	9,605	8,366
	S	18,004	17,490	17,205	19,934	19,927	19,019
	GH	20,247	19,733	19,442	19,740	19,733	18,825
Halifax (N.S.)	PC	5,251	5,583	6,358	3,162	3,688	4,954
	M	12,670	12,987	13,763	10,106	9,470	8,231
	S	NA**	16,964	NA	NA	NA	NA
	GH	NA	NA	NA	NA	NA	NA
Norfolk (Newport News, Va.)	PC	4,735	5,067	5,842	2,646	3,172	4,438
	M	12,751	13,068	13,844	10,187	9,551	8,312
	S	NA	NA	NA	NA	NA	NA
	GH	NA	NA	NA	NA	NA	NA
New Orleans (La.)	PC	4,357	4,689	5,464	2,268	2,794	4,060
	M	13,178	13,495	14,271	10,614	9,978	8,739
	S	NA	NA	NA	NA	NA	NA
	GH	NA	NA	NA	NA	NA	NA
Aruba (Neth. Ind.)	PC	3,590	3,922	4,697	1,501	2,027	3,293
	M	11,689	12,006	12,782	9,125	8,489	7,250
	S	NA	NA	NA	NA	NA	NA
	GH	NA	NA	NA	NA	NA	NA
Rio de Janeiro (Brazil)	PC	7,324	7,656	8,431	5,235	5,761	7,027
	M	8,109	8,426	9,202	5,545	4,909	3,670
	S	NA	NA	NA	NA	NA	NA
	GH	NA	NA	NA	NA	NA	NA
Buenos Aires (Argentina)	PC	8,342	8,674	9,449	6,253	6,779	NA
	M	7,265	7,582	8,358	4,701	4,065	2,826
	S	NA	NA	NA	NA	NA	NA
	GH	NA	NA	NA	NA	NA	NA
Bishops Rock (for European ports)[2]	PC	7,301	7,633	8,408	5,212	5,738	7,004
	M	12,890	13,207	13,983	10,326	9,690	8,451
	S	NA	15,283	14,998	NA	NA	NA
	GH	NA	18,722	NA	NA	NA	NA
Gibraltar (for Medit. ports)	PC	7,264	7,596	8,371	5,175	5,701	6,967
	M	12,223	12,540	13,316	9,659	9,023	7,784
	S	12,885	12,371	12,086	14,815	NA	NA
	GH	NA	NA	NA	NA	NA	NA
Freetown (Sierra Leone)	PC	6,933	7,265	8,040	4,844	5,370	6,636
	M	10,602	10,919	11,695	8,038	7,402	6,163
	S	16,794	16,280	15,995	18,724	18,717	17,809
	GH	16,636	16,122	15,831	16,129	16,122	15,214
Lagos (Nigeria)	PC	8,006	8,338	9,113	5,917	6,443	7,709
	M	11,205	11,522	12,298	8,641	8,005	6,766
	S	NA	NA	NA	NA	NA	NA
	GH	NA	NA	NA	NA	NA	NA

*Letter abbreviations refer to Panama Canal; Straits of Magellan; Suez Canal; Cape of Good Hope.

**NA = Not applicable.

___ Underscored figures indicate that shortest route is via the Panama Canal.

Table 3

Comparative Distances to Selected Ports Via Panama Canal and Alternate Routes[1]
(Right Side)

		TO				
Yokohama	Shanghai	Singapore	Bombay	Mel-bourne	Well-ington	
9,700	10,584	12,523	NA	9,942	8,523	Distances to Pacific Ports
16,209	16,761	16,619	NA	12,393	11,568	Relative to Distances from
13,026	12,344	10,137	8,168	12,961	14,326	New York to
15,269	14,587	12,380	11,382	12,641	14,132	Those Ports
10,020	10,904	12,843	NA	10,262	8,843	NY + 320
16,074	16,626	NA	NA	12,258	11,433	NY - 135
12,500	11,818	9,611	7,642	12,435	13,800	NY - 526
14,970	14,288	12,081	11,083	12,342	13,833	NY - 299
9,604	10,388	12,327	NA	9,746	8,327	NY - 196
16,155	16,707	NA	NA	12,339	11,514	NY - 54
13,185	12,503	10,296	8,327	13,120	14,485	NY + 159
15,270	14,588	12,381	11,383	12,642	14,133	NY + 1
9,126	10,010	11,949	NA	9,368	7,949	NY - 574
16,582	17,134	NA	NA	12,766	11,941	NY + 373
14,383	13,701	11,494	9,525	NA	NA	NY + 1357
15,762	15,080	12,873	11,875	13,131	14,625	NY + 493
8,359	9,243	11,182	NA	8,601	7,182	NY - 1341
15,093	15,645	NA	NA	11,277	10,452	NY - 1116
13,618	12,936	10,729	8,760	NA	NA	NY + 592
14,279	13,597	11,390	10,392	11,651	13,142	NY - 990
12,093	12,977	NA	NA	NA	10,916	NY + 2393
11,513	12,065	11,923	NA	7,697	6,872	NY - 4696
NA	13,348	11,141	NA	NA	15,330	NY + 1004
11,791	11,109	8,902	7,904	9,163	10,654	NY - 3478
NA	NA	NA	NA	NA	NA	NY + 3411
10,669	11,221	11,079	NA	6,853	6,028	NY - 5540
NA	NA	NA	10,272	NA	NA	NY + 2104
12,172	11,490	9,283	8,285	9,544	NA	NY - 3097
12,070	12,954	NA	NA	12,312	10,893	NY + 2370
16,294	16,846	NA	NA	12,478	11,653	NY + 85
10,819	10,137	7,930	5,961	10,754	12,119	NY - 2207
14,258	13,576	11,369	10,371	11,630	13,121	NY - 1011
12,033	12,917	NA	NA	12,275	10,856	NY + 2333
15,627	16,179	NA	NA	11,811	10,986	NY - 582
7,907	7,225	5,018	3,049	7,842	9,207	NY - 5119
13,550	12,868	10,661	9,663	10,922	12,413	NY - 1719
11,702	12,586	14,525	NA	11,944	10,525	NY + 2002
14,006	14,558	14,416	NA	10,190	9,365	NY - 2203
11,816	11,134	8,927	6,958	11,751	13,116	NY - 1210
11,658	10,976	8,769	7,771	9,030	10,521	NY - 3611
NA	NA	NA	NA	NA	11,598	NY + 3075
NA	NA	NA	NA	10,793	9,908	NY - 1600
NA	NA	NA	8,092	NA	NA	NY - 76
11,220	10,538	8,331	7,333	8,592	10,081	NY - 4049

1. Compiled from U.S. Hydrographic Office, Table of Distances. H.O. Publication 141. Washington: Government Printing Office, 1965.

2. Distances from Bishops Rock to sample Western European ports are: London, 413 nautical miles; Liverpool, 297 n.m.; Rotterdam 454 n.m.; Bergen 911 n.m.; Oslo 947 n.m.

Fig. 2. Almost 50 ships are seen here in Limon Bay on the Caribbean side waiting to transit. Panama Canal Company

A world map shows that there are what may be termed areas of advantage in the oceans on the opposite sides of the American continent. It is shorter to proceed via the Panama Canal when passing from one area of advantage to another than by any alternate route. As an example, San Francisco is closer via the Panama Canal to all Atlantic ports except those in South America south of latitude 30°S. It is also shorter to Mediterranean ports than by any other route. Many of the leading world ports are in a position to take advantage of the Panama Canal for some portion of their overseas trade.

For much of the overseas commerce of the United States, Canada, Western Europe, the Caribbean countries, northern Latin America, Japan, and, to an extent, Australia and New Zealand, use of the Panama Canal shortens sailing distance. This is what gives the Canal its true significance.

By shortening distances between ports in different oceans, the Canal saves time for shipping, and helps reduce fuel and transportation costs. For commercial ocean vessels—which made up more than 390,000 of the over 480,000 transits of all kinds that have taken place since the Canal was opened to navigation—the savings are important in economy of operation, thus yielding higher profits. This makes the Canal attractive to world commerce. Shipping is often waiting in considerable numbers at the Canal terminals for transit (fig. 2).

Time Advantages

Reductions in distances give savings in time. The days that are saved by using the Canal, as compared with the longer sea routes, mount up impressively. For instance, a vessel traveling at 15 knots can make Los Angeles from New York in 13 days by the Panama Canal compared with over a month via the Straits of Magellan. A ship traveling at 25 knots can make the 9,700-mile journey from Yokohama to New York in 17 days, compared with 25 days needed for making the 15,300-mile voyage around the Cape of Good Hope.

Table 4 gives a series of sample days required at different speeds for specific voyages. Thus, a ship bound from Seattle or nearby Vancouver, B.C., to Europe at 20 knots can make Bishop's Rock Light off southwest England in 17½ days compared with 31 days if it were to go around via the Straits of Magellan. A vessel bound from London, England, to Wellington, New Zealand, at 20 knots can make its destination in 23 sea days by the Panama Canal, or 25 days by Suez if that is open, or 27½ days if it goes around South Africa.

Savings in time enable the needs of commerce to be served by fewer ships, as well as affording faster delivery times. Faster ships save fewer days, the reductions in savings being proportionate to the increase in ship speed. Savings in miles that have to be traversed mean lowered fuel

Table 4

Days Required for Passage Between Selected Ports at Indicated Speeds
via Panama Canal and Alternate Routes

To	From											
	New York at knots			New Orleans at knots			Bishops Rock at knots			Gibraltar at knots		
	15	20	25	15	20	25	15	20	25	15	20	25
Los Angeles	13.7	10.3	8.2	12.1	9.1	7.3	20.3	15.2	12.2	20.2	15.1	12.1
Seattle (Vancouver)	16.8	12.6	10.1	15.2	11.4	9.1	23.4	17.5	14.0	23.3	17.4	13.9
Callao	9.4	7.0	5.6	7.8	5.8	4.6	15.9	12.0	9.6	15.8	11.9	9.5
Valparaiso	12.9	9.6	7.7	11.3	8.4	6.8	19.4	14.6	11.7	19.3	14.5	11.6
Yokohama P.C.*	27.0	20.2	16.1	25.4	19.0	15.2	33.5	25.1	20.1	33.4	25.1	20.1
Suez	-----			-----			30.1	22.5	18.0	22.0	16.5	13.2
Singapore P.C.	34.8	26.2	20.9	33.3	24.9	19.9	NA			NA		
Suez	28.2	21.1	16.9	31.9	23.9	19.2	22.0	16.5	13.2	13.9	10.5	8.4
Good Hope	34.4	25.8	20.6	35.8	26.8	21.5	31.6	23.7	19.0	29.6	22.2	17.8
Wellington P.C.	23.7	17.8	14.2	22.1	16.6	13.2	30.3	22.7	18.2	30.2	22.6	18.1
Suez	39.8	29.9	23.9	NA			33.7	25.3	20.2	25.6	19.2	15.3
Good Hope	39.3	29.5	23.6	NA			36.5	27.4	21.9	34.5	25.9	20.7
Magellan	32.2	24.1	19.3	32.2	24.9	19.9	32.4	24.3	19.4	30.6	22.9	18.4
Melbourne P.C.	27.7	20.7	16.6	26.0	19.5	15.6	34.2	25.7	20.6	NA		
Suez	36.0	27.0	21.6	NA			29.9	22.4	17.9	21.8	16.3	13.1
Good Hope	35.2	26.4	21.1	36.5	27.4	21.9	32.3	24.2	19.4	30.4	22.8	18.2

*P.C. refers to Panama Canal.

consumption, as well as crewing costs, thus reducing transportation costs for shipper and buyer, thereby furthering overseas trade.

Savings in Fuel Consumption

Lower distances along routes have a direct bearing upon the amounts of fuel consumed, depending upon a vessel's mechanical efficiency, its speed, tonnage, shaft horsepower, and hull form.

If we hypothesize a small general cargo vessel of 8,000 gross registered tons which would displace about 13,333 tons, such as many that pass through the Panama Canal, proceeding at 15 knots, with a shaft horsepower (SHP) of 6,610, its consumption of fuel figures as 35.4 long tons of oil per day.[3] In a 14½-day voyage from New York to San Francisco it will burn 512 tons of oil. The same ship taking a 36½-day circuit around South America would use up 1,290 tons of oil even if it encountered no heavy storms to slow up its progress. If fuel oil sells at $48 per ton, the Canal route will save roughly $37,000 in fuel costs alone.

A larger cargo vessel of 12,000 gross registered tons, running at 15 knots for the same distances, and consuming 46.4 tons per day, will save 1,018 tons of fuel oil, or $49,000, by employing the Canal route. This is a substantial saving.

Taking as a third sample, a modest-sized containership of 25,000 gross registered tons (41,667 tons displacement), operating at 20 knots, the fuel consumption will amount to approximately 179.5 tons a day. In this case, use of the Canal can save up to 2,950 tons of fuel oil over going around South America, making the fuel cost $93,000 rather than $234,000 if it were to go the longer way. Such a saving can make a major difference not only in the costs of transportation for shippers, but also in the profits of operation the vessel's owners or charterers realize. In a time of world energy shortages, the Panama Canal is seen as a valuable means of saving fuel, and thus of shipping costs. It thereby helps promote oceanborne trade.

Factors Bearing on Choice of Routes

Commercial vessels will normally take the shortest available route between their ports of departure and destination in order to save costs and time. Other factors may enter into the choice of a particular route, or for a specific voyage. These include such elements as cargoes to be picked up or delivered en route, orders from owners or charterers, draft and size limitation in ports, facilities for resupply, and the incidence of tolls upon ship earnings.

Considerations of government policy, and security en route, can affect the choice of routes in special circumstances, or for vessels in government employment. Fundamentally, the distances involved, cargoes to be delivered or had, orders from owners or charterers, and

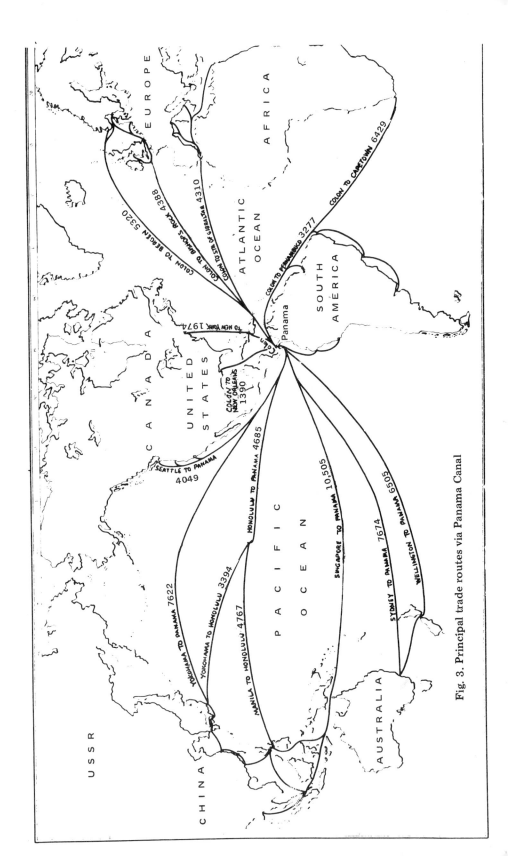

Fig. 3. Principal trade routes via Panama Canal

services available along the way, are the basic considerations shaping the courses vessels take.

For commercial, as well as for military traffic, the Canal is advantageous to the economic and national interests of the United States and others. Maintenance of this artery, free from closure or interference, is important to the economic life, and to the national security and defense of this country.

Toll charges are a factor affecting the routings of some vessels. Toll charges of $10-20,000 a voyage, depending upon a vessel's size, are not too onerous for most ocean shipping.

The incidence of tolls is relatively small for ships carrying high-unit-value commodities where time in reaching markets is often highly important and where the costs can be widely distributed. For cargoes of low-unit-priced bulk commodities, such as coal and ores, toll charges are a fairly critical item requiring close figuring. This is particularly true in a period of competition between average-size bulk carriers using the Canal and the very large supercarriers employing all-ocean routings. Efficient modern 200,000 dwt carriers can, for instance, lay down 17.8 million long tons of coal a year in Japan from Chesapeake Bay for $51.5 million less by bypassing the Canal with the long ocean voyage around the Cape of Good Hope than can 50,000 dwt vessels using the Panama Canal with its shorter sea distances, but paying tolls at both the loaded and ballast rates. Such savings are certain to be critical elements in cost accounting as the large carriers and deepwater terminals become increasingly available in the years ahead.[4]

Principal Routes Served by the Canal

The principal shipping routes passing through the interoceanic Canal are outlined in Figure 3.

The Canal is advantageous principally to shipping moving between (1) the coasts of North America, (2) the East Coast of North America and Asia, (3) the East Coast of the United States and the West Coasts of South and Central America, (4) the East Coast of North America and Oceania, (5) the West Coasts of the United States and Canada and the East Coast of South America, (6) Western Europe and the Mediterranean and the West Coasts of North and South America.

The Canal route is also beneficial to shipping moving between (7) Western Europe and Japan, (8) Western Europe and Oceania, (9) the East and West Coasts of South and Central America roughly above the equator, (10) Japan, the Philippines, China and ports in the South Pacific and the East Coast of South America along with the mid-West Coast of Africa.

The Panama Canal is marginally appealing to shipping going from the East Coast of the United States or Western Europe to points in South

Asia such as Singapore and Djkarta. Shipping schedules and intermediate ports of call are a factor in determining whether a vessel will proceed west via the Panama Canal, or go in the opposite direction via Capetown and South Africa. Vessels heading for Indian Ocean ports, as well as Perth and Melbourne in Australia, from Western Europe will normally take the Suez Canal if that is open, or proceed via the Cape of Good Hope rather than going by Panama and across the Pacific Ocean, unless they have orders or a schedule that calls for touching at North American, Caribbean, or Central American ports.

Vessels sailing between Yokohama or Shanghai and Rio de Janeiro or West African ports below the equator must cover approximately the same distance whether they proceed via the Panama Canal or the Cape of Good Hope. In these instances, factors other than distance alone guide the choice of routes.

Whatever the coordinates by which ships proceed to destinations overseas, their courses generally are fixed by schedules and by cargoes to be delivered or picked up.

For a substantial portion of the world's overseas traffic, the Panama Canal offers a conveniently-placed shortcut between the Atlantic and the Pacific Oceans. The number of vessels using the Canal each year indicates that a large amount of oceanborne commerce finds the Canal route valuable for business. The use of the Canal by ocean commercial shipping will be examined in Chapter Three.

New Developments and Old Advantages

New forms of transportation have sprung into being since the Panama Canal was opened to navigation. Air transportation has captured all but a small amount of the transoceanic passenger business, causing the express passenger liners to be laid up, sold, scrapped, or turned to the cruising trades. Increasing quantities of freight are airlifted overseas each year, although in total volume this is still not three percent of this nation's foreign trade. There are many forms of general and bulk cargo that will continue to move by water for as long as can be foreseen. These will find their way to the interoceanic shortcut on board traditional-type shipping to take advantage of the distance-time-transportation cost savings which this offers.

The supercarriers have not taken the place of the general cargo liners, containerships, tankers, oreships and reefers that are the primary beneficiaries of the Canal's presence. They are not likely to do so for a long time to come, although the availability of deepwater terminals in the United States will enhance the competitive position of the big carriers that can offer economies of scale combined with low-cost transportation. Decades will be needed to alter the patterns of shipping limited quantities of many raw materials, tropical products, manufactures, and other items shipped between many ports. For these, the average-sized cargo vessel that can get into shallow ports easily, load relatively limited quantities of cargo, and distribute it to a variety of ports quite inexpensively will ply the seaways and have need of the interoceanic short-cut. Canal planners must, nevertheless, contemplate a day when the advantages of a short water route should be extended to the large ships unable to pass through the Canal locks. Such a day may arrive before the present generation of supercarriers have seen their end.

The land- and mini-bridge systems using rail transport across the United States are a particularly notable competition for the Panama Canal (see Table 5). The operation of the land- and mini-bridge systems will be discussed further in Chapter Seven. Between Japan and the East Coast of the United States, use of the railroads can save 2,000 miles and possibly four days. This type of movement is called mini-bridge. Between Japan and Europe the land-bridge can save 1,000 miles, but may take a day longer, even allowing for a day's delay time at the Canal.[5] Land-bridge costs must, of course, be added onto ocean freight charges, along with port transshipment fees. Rail charges for containers on an 80-car unitized train are estimated to be $250 or more a container, amounting to about 8.3 mills per ton mile as compared with 1.2 mills per ton mile on an express containership moving at 30 knots.

Counting ocean transportation, port transfer charges, and transcontinental rail freight, the costs for delivering a 20 x 40-foot container in Rotterdam from Yokohama are figured as amounting to $431.88 using the U.S. land-bridge versus $166.48 using a containership running directly by the all-sea Panama Canal route.[6] "Provocative marketing techniques exercised by proponents of the United States land-bridge route, Seatrain Lines of New York in particular, have tended to disguise the economics of the system."[7] Between Japan and New York it is figured that mini-bridge delivery will cost $178.06 more per container, although present rates have been set about equal in order to capture a market.

To shippers and customers of highly competitive merchandise the mini-bridge operation does have a four-day delivery advantage over the all-water route that can be significant. Missing a connection at the West Coast transshipment port, or delay en route across the continent by rail, can wipe out the advantage, or come close to it, however (see Tables 6 and 7).

Ocean shipping has been able to retain the major share of the container cargo by putting on modern containerships that combine the advantage of fast sea delivery with avoidance of transshipments in ports, the possibilities of missing connections, being held up by U.S. dock strikes, having cargoes wrongly routed, and delays or tie-ups in crossing the continent.

The interoceanic shortcut offers strong advantages in this competition. At the present time, unit trains are reported to be making weekly departures between New York and Oakland, Long Beach and Seattle on transcontinental runs. Most of the traffic borne by these trains is carried on mini-bridge routings.

Table 5

Panama Canal vs. Land-Bridge:
Comparison of Nautical Miles and Transit Times*

Route	Land Bridge		Panama Canal	
	Miles	Days	Miles	Days
Yokohama-New York[1,2]				
Yokohama-Los Angeles	4,800	9.0		
Los Angeles-New York rail	3,000	5.0		
Yokohama-New York			9,700	17.5
Canal delay time				1.0
Total	7,800	14.0	9,700	18.5
Yokohama-Europe[2]				
Yokohama-Los Angeles	4,800	9.0		
Transfer[3]		2.0		
Los Angeles-New York rail[4]	3,000	5.0		
Transfer[3]		2.0		
New York-Europe	3,700	7.0		
Yokohama-Europe			12,500	23.0
Canal delay time				1.0
Total	11,500	25.0	12,500	24.0

NOTES: [1]No provision made for port time since it is common to both routes.

[2]Sea time assumes 23-knot ship or 552 nautical miles per day.

[3]Assumes optimum situation of direct transfer between ship and an awaiting unit train.

[4]Transit time based on Atchison, Topeka and Santa Fe Railroad proposal.

*From Interoceanic Canal Studies, 1970, Interoceanic Canal Study Commission, Washington, D.C., 1970, p. IV-120.

Table 6*

Comparison of Costs for Land-Bridge and Panama Canal Routes:
Yokohama-Europe
20x40-foot Container

Land-Bridge

Yokohama-Los Angeles - 9 days @ $6.52	$ 58.68
Port transfer charge	30.00
Ship delay - 2 days @ $4.39	8.78
Proposed ATSF rail charge special unitized train	
Los Angeles to New York City - 5 days	250.00
Port transfer charge	30.00
Ship delay - 2 days @ $4.39	8.78
New York-Rotterdam - 7 days @ $6.52	45.64
Total cost per container - 25 days	$431.88

All-Sea Panama Canal Route

Yokohama-Rotterdam - 24 days @ $6.52	$156.48
Panama Canal tolls	10.00
Total cost per container	$166.48
Difference - land-bridge excess	$265.40

NOTE: In comparison with the direct sea route, ships
will have port time at either end of the land-
bridge. An allowance of 2 days at each port
to arrive, discharge cargo and depart was assumed.

*Interoceanic Canal Studies, 1970. Report of the President's
Interoceanic Canal Study Commission. Washington, 1970,
p. IV-123.

Table 7**

Comparison of Costs for Mini-Bridge and Panama Canal Routes:
Yokohama-New York
20x40-foot Container

Mini-Bridge

Yokohama-Los Angeles	- 9 days @ $6.52	$ 58.68
Los Angeles-New York rail	- 5 days	250.00
	14 days	$308.68

All-Sea Panama Canal Route

Yokohama-New York - 18.5 days @ $6.52	$120.62
Panama Canal tolls	10.00
	$130.62
Difference - mini-bridge excess	$178.06

**Ibid., p. IV-124.

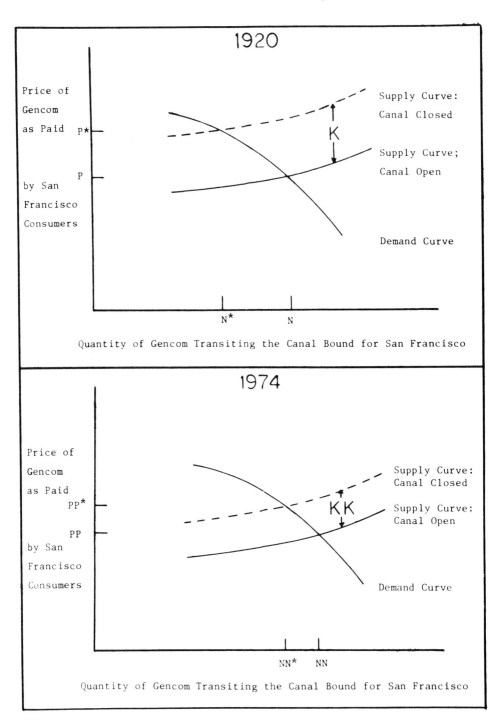

Fig. 4. Quantity of "Gencom" transiting the Canal

The land-bridge is not positioned to offer fast, inexpensive delivery of general broken-lot cargo, nor to transport heavy bulk cargoes. Thus, shippers continue to enjoy the advantages for which the Panama Canal was built.

Extending the Maritime Advantages of the Canal

When the Panama Canal opened for navigation, it represented a technological leap ahead in international transportation, extending the advantages of ocean shipping by the introduction of the interoceanic shortcut. Since that time, other modes of transportation have introduced new means of carrying goods and passengers and mail. They surpass ocean shipping through shortening time of travel and introducing new conveniences, as by air transport, but at greater cost. The large bulk carriers, on the other hand, have been increasing their efficiency and lowering the costs of transportation through introducing economies of scale, automation, and improved mechanical efficiency, but they can only be used where deep ports are available and they require large volumes of cargo to make their employment economical.

The development of these new modes and their effect on the cost of oceanborne shipping can be visualized with the aid of Figure 4. This depicts the supply and demand curve for a fictitious general commodity which can be called "gencom" which could be grain, lumber, crude oil or etc. The fictitious commodity "gencom" is used instead of grain, coal, etc., because the supply and demand curves for any particular commodity passing the Canal are not known. "Gencom" could have been any commodity carried in trade through the Panama Canal in 1920 on any trade route. Assume it moved on a route from New York to San Francisco as an example. In 1920 N tons of "gencom" were traded and they cost P dollars per ton to the consumer who purchased it.

Assuming the Canal had been out of service in 1920, "gencom" would have had to be carried around the Horn in the small, slow ships of the period or moved by rail across the continent. Use of these modes would have cost more than using the Canal. This situation would have resulted in an upward shift of the supply curve by the amount of the additional cost of shipping (K in Figure 4). Since the cost would have been higher, fewer consumers would have purchased it, and the volume traded would have been N* sold at price P*.

For the 1974 figure "gencom" was selling at price PP and NN tons were moved through the Canal and sold in San Francisco. Had the Canal been turned over to Panama that year and Panama had refused to let "gencom" transit, suppliers would have been forced to seek other alternatives. But in 1974 the alternatives included superships sailing around the Horn, air freight, pipelines and transcontinental unit trains. None of these alternatives existed in 1920 to any appreciable extent. The new modes of cargo transport were cheaper, relatively speaking, than the alternatives which existed in 1920. The added cost of transport, KK in Figure 4, would have been smaller than the added cost in 1920, K in Figure 4, and the new supply curve of "gencom" as experienced by San Francisco consumers would have risen less than it did in 1920 under similar "no Panama Canal" conditions. The selling price of "gencom" would have risen to PP*, a smaller rise than in 1920.

Particular commodity movements will exhibit the behavior of "gencom" to a greater or lesser degree depending on their likelihood for diversion to the new modes of transportation and on the market factors which determine the proportion of added transportation costs borne by the supplier and consumer.

The purpose of this discussion is to illustrate the fact that the price advantage offered by the Panama Canal to individual cargo shipments has been decreasing over time. For cost and time considerations the Canal is contributing relatively less in 1974 to the promotion of international commerce than it did in 1920 from the individual shipper's viewpoint.

Failure to account for this fact may result in a misallocation of resources in the construction of additional capacity, such as a set of third locks or a sea-level canal.

In a sense, the Canal has been losing ground to the jet planes, the jumbo carriers, overland pipelines, the trucking industry, and the minibridge innovation. At the same time, the Canal has been contributing more to world trade through transiting larger amounts of cargo each year and passing heavier volumes of traffic, and so long as use of the Canal remains the least-cost alternative, the Canal will continue to be heavily utilized.

A considerable margin of excess capacity was incorporated into the Panama Canal when it was constructed. The locks were built larger than ships then on the seas or on the architects' drawing boards. Ample water supplies were at hand for the volume of traffic that presented itself and have remained ample for over 50 years. It is now obvious that there are limits to what the Canal can accommodate. These limits are set by the size of the lock chambers, the quantities of fresh water available for use in the lockages, and the sheer numbers of vessels that can be put through within a day and year. Modern-day supercarriers cannot squeeze into the locks because of their physical size and draft. In several dry seasons it has been necessary to restrict the allowable draft of transiting ships due to the lack of water to support traffic demand at the locks. Studies foresee a point when the Canal will reach ultimate capacity after completion of all programmed improvements in channel deepening, additions to water supply, installation of more locomotives on the lock walls, better lighting in the Cut, and so forth.

The key to the continued usefulness of the Canal will be its ability to gauge the economic needs of oceangoing shipping and to mesh these with its own capabilities so that commerce can continue to prosper.

Notwithstanding what the newer modes of transportation have been accomplishing, the Canal, as Governor Leber cautioned in 1970, "is not about to go out of business." There will continue to be traffic which has a pressing need for use of the waterway, as well as traffic that can be siphoned off by other means of transportation.[8]

The increasing cost of energy will make employment of the Canal attractive to shippers, for it will reduce the competitive position of modes of transport that are energy-intensive and whose costs will rise as the costs of fuels go up. The very large bulk carriers, which are too big for the locks, moving on all-ocean routes and long-distance jet cargo planes use more energy than the standard-size cargo vessels that make up the greater part of the traffic using the Canal. As the energy shortage is likely to be of long duration, it is reasonable to assume that the maritime advantages of the Panama Canal will not be superseded in the foreseeable future.

We shall consider in Chapter Seven alternatives for extending the maritime advantages of the Canal. Meanwhile, the Canal will continue to be useful to the oceanborne commerce of nations up to the limits of its capacity.

The most likely manner of removing the limitations that now exist, and extending the maritime advantages of the interoceanic canal, appears to be replacement of the present lock canal with a sea-level waterway through which both larger shipping can pass and larger numbers of vessels per day and year can be transited. This is a logical step in improving the usefulness of the Canal when the time is right. Appropriately designed and constructed this could serve the needs of commerce for another century.

CHAPTER ONE FOOTNOTES

1. Years mentioned are fiscal years ending June 30th unless otherwise stated.

2. This figure must be carefully interpreted as it says nothing about how much the United States benefits from U.S. cargoes transiting the Panama Canal. The profits reaped by suppliers and receivers of commodities moving in trade are determined by the terms of trade which are the details of supply and demand. For example, until 1974 the United States benefited from inexpensive foreign oil. The terms of trade have now changed and oil exporters are reaping the benefits.

3. The figures are arrived at by using the formulas $SHP = .00345x(\text{displacement})^{2/3} \times (\text{speed})^3$, and the tons of fuel consumed per day $= SHP/186.6$. This is an empirical formula arrived at by naval architects.

4. Stewart G. Lingley and Norman J. Padelford, "Effect of Supershipbuilding on Canal Demand." M.I.T. Sea Grant Program, Interoceanic Canal Project. Draft Report No. 10, March 1973. Ship operating costs were figured at $6,350 a day for the 50,000 dwt carriers and $13,250 per day for the very large ships. It is figured that the smaller ships going via the Panama Canal can make the 19,200-mile round trip in 57 days, allowing four days in port, while the larger vessels will require 89 days for the 30,600-mile circuit via Good Hope. They will, on the other hand, carry more than four times the amount of coal per trip and avoid paying Canal tolls costing $48,000 a round trip for the smaller ships.

5. *Interoceanic Canal Studies, 1970.* Report of the President's Interoceanic Canal Study Commission. Washington, 1970, p. IV-120.

6. *Ibid.,* p. IV-123.

7. R.F. Gibney, "Shipping Lines Are Winning on Europe/Far East Run," *Sea-trade,* March 1973, pp. 41-45.

8. *Panama Canal Traffic, Capacity, and Tolls.* Hearings before Subcommittee on Panama Canal, Committee on Merchant Marine and Fisheries, U.S. House of Representatives, 91st Congress, 2nd Session, April 22, 1970, Serial No. 91-25, p. 3.

CHAPTER TWO

TRANSITING THE PANAMA CANAL

There are two ways in which the interoceanic canal should be viewed. One is in the large as from an airplane far above the waterway; the other from the deck of a vessel passing through the Canal where the manner of operation can be seen from close up.

The Broad View

Seen from 40,000 feet up on a clear day, with Panama City and the slender Bridge of the Americas across the Canal at one's feet below, the Panama Canal reaches across the Isthmus like a dark blue ribbon set on a rich green carpet. From this vantage point, when the skies permit, one can see the entire waterway laid out from Pacific to Atlantic, interrupted here and there with flecks of clouds that will at some point release their tropical showers to sustain the works of man beneath (see Frontispiece and Figure 5).

Northward from Panama Bay

Stretching from the deep blue waters of Panama Bay, where shipping coming in from the Pacific rides at anchor awaiting its turn to transit, the Canal marches through a wide channel past Balboa Heights, the Canal's headquarters, northward to the slender spines of Miraflores and Pedro Miguel Locks before reaching the upthrust hills of the Continental Divide. These cross the Canal in a generally right-angle direction. The Divide, a massive bulwark erected by nature, no longer blocks the flow of oceanborne commerce as it once did. It has been made to bend to the will of man.

From the gentle curves of Gaillard Cut through the Continental Divide the Canal turns northwesterly toward the large expanse of Gatun Lake. At the far end of this, in the distant haze, the Canal meets the tongue of land at Gatun that joins it via the Gatun Locks to Limon Bay. Beyond this, barely visible, lie the waters of the Caribbean stretching out to meet the Atlantic Ocean.

Southward from the Atlantic

Viewed in reverse from far above the Atlantic entrance to the Canal and the port cities of Colón and Cristobal, the prominent features in the foreground are the massive three-step Gatun Locks that raise and lower vessels 85 feet from sea level to summit lake, and the mile-long Gatun Dam that holds back the Chagres River and Gatun Lake. Behind these works lie the 163 square miles of Gatun Lake holding the water needed to operate the Canal locks. Just beyond Gamboa Reach at the southwestern extremity of the Lake can be seen coming in from the east the Chagres River. This mighty river pours an average yearly flow of 200 billion cubic feet of water into Gatun Lake from the runoff waters of the Madden Lake-Continental Divide watershed. But for the natural hydrological system that drops an average of 130 inches of rainfall a year in this area and the myriad streams that channel this toward the waterway, the lock canal could not pass the thousands of ships that file through it each year.

Beyond the confluence of the Chagres River with the Canal are seen the ridges of the Continental Divide through which the builders of the

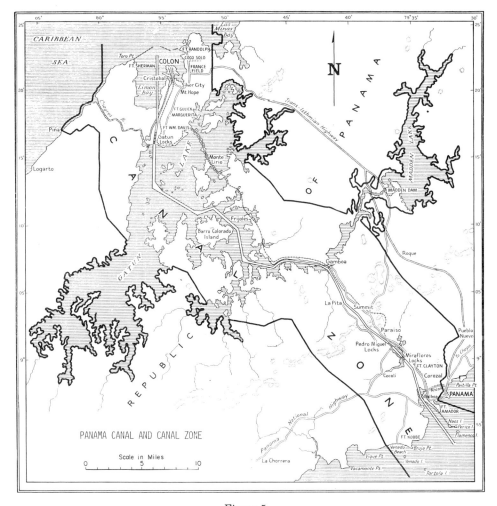

Figure 5.

Canal—Stevens, Goethals, Gaillard and their cohorts—drove the steam shovels that excavated a total of 240 million cubic yards of earth for Gaillard Cut. This great engineering feat is seen to pierce the mountains like a knife wedge. Finally, in the distance fifty miles away lies Ancon Hill, and just beyond it, Panama City, capital of the Republic of Panama.

Only thus viewed from afar, and in the whole, can the magnitude of the dream men held for generations of the "mountains divided, the oceans united" be grasped. Seen from such a height, the Canal impresses one as being like a slender reed. Yet there it stands sixty years after the venerable S.S. *Ancon* made the historic voyage opening the waterway to navigation on August 15, 1914, and after nearly a half million other vessels have followed in its wake (fig. 6).[1]

What was done with the brawn and sweat of thousands of workers, and the driving vision of a handful of great leaders, has stood the test of time. The Canal operation has been interrupted seriously only in 1915 when slides at Gold Hill closed the watercourse to traffic for a few months until American engineering was able to remove the landslide and cut the edges of the hills back enough to prevent further closure. Since then a ceaseless vigil, continued dredging, lowering the slopes of the hills, widening the Cut, and periodic maintenance of all mechanical elements of the locks, has kept the Canal in excellent working order.

Notwithstanding the continual use, vessels are locked through in practically the same time today as in the first year when the numbers were in the hundreds rather than thousands.

The Canal has become not only a marine highway between the oceans; it has become as well a link between continents and nations as traffic has funneled an unending flow of oceanborne commerce through the waterway.

To comprehend the Canal operation as a going concern, it must be seen at water level, as from the deck of a transiting ship.

Preparing for Transit

Passage through the Canal requires close cooperation between personnel aboard vessels, authorities on shore, and attending tug masters, especially at the approaches to the locks. The behavior of vessels must be watched with minute care, and the masters, officers and personnel aboard them must be ready to respond to the requests of Canal pilots and the orders of Lockmasters to avoid harm to vessels or locks.

The procedure for transiting the Canal, and the law relating to it, are fairly elaborate.[2]

Arrival at Terminal

A vessel must communicate with the Port Captain's Office at Balboa by radio or through its agents 48 hours before its arrival at the Canal to allow for arrangements to be made for its boarding, assigning of pilots,

Fig. 6. Opening of the Panama Canal, S.S. *Ancon* passing Cucaracha Slide, August 15, 1914. Panama Canal Company

and scheduling of transit. On arrival, it proceeds to an anchorage in Limon Bay at the Atlantic end, or to the Bay of Panama at the Pacific terminal.

Boarding, Inspection, and Clearance

Vessels are boarded by Canal representatives before being allowed to pass into the Canal. Their papers are inspected. Documents regarding cargo, passengers, and health must be filed. Tolls are computed, including measurements of the ship if needed, and arrangements made for payment of the tolls before a vessel is allowed to enter the Canal proper.

The boarding party may be one or more officers of the Panama Canal who perform the functions of customs, quarantine, and immigration inspection, along with admeasurement for determining tolls.[3]

Clearance is granted by the Port Captain of Balboa or Cristobal, as the case may be, after the authorities are satisfied that all necessary papers have been furnished, are in proper order, that the vessel has complied with the laws relating to shipping, and that tolls or other charges have been paid or secured.[4]

The law gives the Governor of the Canal Zone and his representatives authority to control the movements of vessels from the time they arrive at one terminal until they are cleared for sea at the other.[5] This is similar to practice in major ports of the world.

Measurement and Payment of Tolls

Vessels are as a rule subject to payment of tolls to help defray the costs of operating and maintaining the Canal. Different classes of vessels pay different amounts, but within each classification vessels of all nationalities pay on an equal basis.

Tolls are assessed upon what is termed Panama Canal net measurement tonnage which is the total internal capacity of a ship measured on the basis of 100 cubic feet per ton, minus space provided for propelling power, navigational areas, public rooms, fuel, ship's stores, water ballast, and crew accommodation.

The rate for laden ships is fixed at 90 cents per net ton, and 72 cents per net ton for vessels in ballast.[6] Measuring a vessel under Panama Canal Rules is a laborious task. This can be done at a Canal terminal. But for the sake of saving time, the rules allow certificates of measurement to be issued by Collectors in the largest seaports of the United States, and by properly designated officials abroad.[7]

Once a vessel has been given a Panama Canal Tonnage Certificate, a record of its tonnage is kept at the Canal. Remeasurement then becomes necessary only after structural changes are made that affect the earning capacity of the ship. If such changes have been made between transits, remeasurement is made before clearance is granted.

Fig. 7. Senior Canal pilot on bridge of large ore carrier. The large radio in his right hand is used for communication with assisting tugs and towing locomotives on the lock walls. The small radio is for communication with the three other pilots aboard, two of whom are visible on the specially constructed scaffolds on the forward portion of the ship.

Panama Canal Company

Tolls must be paid in United States dollars, or secured by bonds or deposits at approved banks, before the vessel may proceed to the locks.[8] For Government-owned and operated vessels, credits are taken in lieu of cash payment with settlements made between Federal agencies in Washington.

Reception of Pilots and Guards

When the boarding formalities are completed, the vessel is cleared for transit. Pilotage is compulsory with a Canal pilot being in full control of a vessel.[9]

In time of national emergency, or if it is otherwise felt to be necessary for insuring the safety of a ship or the Canal, or assuring the compliance with the laws and obligations of the United States, a vessel may be required to receive an armed guard.[10] The law allows the authorities to control and inspect vessels, secure them, remove any personnel if need be, and even to take possession of them. The powers are exercised within the Canal Zone by the Governor with the approval of the President of the United States.

Guards may be posted wherever the Governor indicates. Customarily they are stationed on the bridge, in the pilot house, radio room, engine room, fore and aft on deck, and along the sides. They have authority to take whatever measures may be needed to prevent or stop unlawful actions. In time of war or threatened danger this is very important. [11]

Pilotage and Scheduling of Transits

Role of Canal Pilot

When a vessel enters the Canal waters, control of its navigation and movements is placed under the hands of a Canal pilot. It is the duty of the ship's Master to be on the bridge when entering or leaving the locks, and when going through the Cut, to inform the pilot of individual peculiarities in the handling of the ship. It is also his responsibility to see that the pilot's orders are carried out. If the Master or another person gives an order contrary to that of the pilot, or fails to conform to the orders of the pilot, and an accident occurs, the Master is responsible, as, in general, in harbor situations. The ship may be libeled pending settlement of the costs or claims. [12]

Pilots employ walkie-talkie radios to communicate with each other on the same or different ships, with attending tugs, lockmasters, locomotive operators, and the Marine Traffic Control Office (fig. 7).

The pilot's role is particularly important as a vessel is approaching, moving through, and leaving the locks. It is also critical in the Cut where wind and fog can affect the navigation of a vessel.

Two pilots are generally put on board large vessels. Four pilots are used on the large ore carriers and tankers with one stationed on each wing of the bridge and two forward near the bow. More may be employed if need be.

Pilots may be as variable in their personalities and qualifications as the ships are in their size and handling characteristics. The most skillful and experienced pilots are assigned to the largest size ships.

Historically, obtaining skilled pilots for Canal operations has been easy for the Company due to the high wages and many fringe benefits. Now that the United States merchant marine is being revitalized, the pool of available masters has shrunk. The present pinch is expected to be temporary, as Panamanians, Norwegians, and others have proved to make excellent pilots.

Scheduling Transits

The scheduling of transits is done by the Navigation Division of the Canal Company through the Marine Traffic Control Office located at Balboa. Vessels at the Atlantic terminal are directed by the Cristobal Marine Traffic Office acting in communication with Balboa.

Passenger vessels carrying more than 50 passengers have priority in dispatching to the "extent consistent with efficient operation" of the Canal.[13] Transits are as a rule scheduled as nearly as possible in line with the order in which ships have arrived at the terminals, although vessels may be dispatched in whatever order and at whatever time is deemed best in the interests of safe and efficient operation of the Canal.

In scheduling transits the Marine Traffic Control Center has to give consideration to the wide variety of types and conditions of vessels seeking transit, the nature of the cargoes being transported, the orders some vessels have, and the circumstances in the Canal.[14] Where possible, small vessels are locked through with larger ships in order to save water and increase capacity.

With an average of 40 and more oceangoing vessels arriving for transit each day, schedules are made up so that insofar as possible one vessel will be arriving at a lock approach shortly after another has left in order to minimize lost time between lockages. With a full day's complement this means busy hours for those who work the locks and control the movements of the towing locomotives. When a vessel is delayed in getting away from its anchorage, or has an accident along the way, such as grounding or scraping its side in the locks, this can cause difficulties for schedulers and following vessels. Radio communication on multiple channels between schedulers, lockmasters, pilots, towboats, control towers, and the Port Captains is a great help in straightening out tangles when they do arise. Fortunately, the number of serious accidents or long delays has always been small due to the careful precautions that are taken all along the line.

Dispatches are now made on a 24-hour basis to handle the traffic demand. The locks are worked around the clock. Vessels of over 85-foot beam are usually put through in the daytime, the others later. Vessels can anchor at Balboa, Cristobal, Gatun Lake, Gamboa, and tie up at Gatun, Pedro Miguel and Miraflores as required and as directed.

Proceeding through the Canal

Vessels generally are directed to proceed into the Canal as soon as the Canal pilot is aboard. Moving from Limon Bay, at the Atlantic end of the Canal, a vessel first passes through a dredged channel seven miles long to Gatun.

Transiting the Gatun Locks

As a vessel approaches the locks, whether at Gatun at the Atlantic end, or at Miraflores on the Pacific, a team of Canal linehandlers is taken on board from a launch to handle the cables that are attached to the towing locomotives on the lock walls.

At the Gatun Locks a vessel is raised, or lowered as the case may be, in three consecutive chambers a total of 85 feet to the level of Gatun Lake (fig. 8). The chambers at all of the locks are nominally 1,000 feet long, 110 feet wide with rubber fendering at each end, and have 42 feet of water over the sills. Transiting a vessel at Gatun takes approximately one hour. The time is somewhat less for small vessels and considerably more for large ships that have little room to spare.

When all is in order, a chain fender is lowered in front of the first lock gate and the vessel is pulled into the lowest chamber. There the lock gates are closed behind it, valves are opened allowing water to flow down from above into the chamber until the vessel rises to the level of the second chamber. The gates in front of it are then opened and it is towed by the locomotives into the second chamber. There the same procedure is followed to raise it to the level of the third chamber and of Gatun Lake. Normally, two electric locomotives are employed on each side of a vessel to move it through the locks. These run on a track and cog rail with speed controlled to maintain cable tension and pull. More locomotives are used for the largest ships.

One of the largest commercial ships to transit the Canal has been the T.S.S. *Tokyo Bay*, a 36,000-gross-ton containership of British registry. The dimensions of this ship, 950-feet-long, 106-foot-beam, allowed less than two feet of clearance on each side. Experience has shown that these are about the maximum dimensions that can be accepted for commercial vessels (fig. 9).[15]

Within the lock areas movements are directed by the pilot in coordination with the lockmaster. The lockmaster is in direct contact with the operator of the lock gates and water valves in the control tower.

Within the lock tower a control board displays the positions of the gates, chains, water control valves, and water level in each chamber.

(*Text continues on page 35.*)

Fig. 8. Gatun Locks viewed from Limon Bay with Gatun Lake in the background. Panama Canal Company

Fig. 9. T.S.S. *Tokyo Bay* in lock chamber with inches to spare. Panama Canal Company

Fig. 10. Gaillard Cut with Pedro Miguel Locks, Miraflores Lake, Miraflores Locks, and the Pacific Ocean in view.
Panama Canal Company

(Continued from page 31.)

Operation of the locks is controlled by levers on this board. These are designed to forestall accidental opening of the valves before the gates are closed. The fender chains which prevent vessels striking the lock gates weigh more than 12 tons. They are capable of stopping a 10,000-ton ship going at four knots within 70 feet if, as has occasionally happened, one should strike them. The chain mechanisms are time-consuming to maintain. Due to the elaborate precautions taken elsewhere, few ships have ever hit the chains. Their main purpose is psychological to prevent pilots from approaching the locks too fast.

The water for lockage operations comes from Gatun Lake through culverts or tunnels in the lock walls. Each through lockage consumes approximately 52 million gallons of water. Only the large expanse of Gatun Lake, plus Madden Lake and the Chagres River, together with the prolific tropical rainfall, provide the water needed.

Gatun Lake and Gamboa Reach

When a vessel clears the third chamber of the Gatun Locks, it moves into Gatun Lake under its own power. The channel across this summit lake runs in a southwesterly direction for 21 miles. At the southern end vessels enter Gamboa Reach, an excavated channel that connects with Gaillard Cut just beyond the confluence of the Chagres River at Gamboa.

Gaillard Cut

Gaillard Cut, eight miles long, is where the Canal passes through the Continental Divide, and where slides were for a long time a hazard to navigation (fig. 10). These have now been largely conquered as the engineers have cut back the slopes of Gold Hill and Contractor's Hill at the height of the pass. Slides are still possible nevertheless. As recently as late 1972, 400,000 cubic yards of bank slid into the Cut after three weeks of heavy rain and narrowed the navigable channel to 400 feet. Rapid work on the part of Company forces minimized delays to shipping.

Bends in the original 300-foot-wide channel made it necessary to control the movements of vessels very carefully at this point. When deep-draft ships and those longer than 700 feet were in the Cut, there were places where it was difficult to pass. Passes and meets were restricted to straight, clear sections of the Cut. When vessels that were difficult to maneuver were transiting, one-way traffic had to be utilized to ensure safety.

With the channel now widened to 500 feet, and the sharpest bends reduced, most vessels can move easily in both directions, subject to careful piloting. The increased size of transiting ships and the sharpness of the bends still make for tricky navigation. Artificial lighting now illuminates portions of the Cut at night, assisting navigation after dark.

Large and unwieldy ships are generally accompanied through the Cut

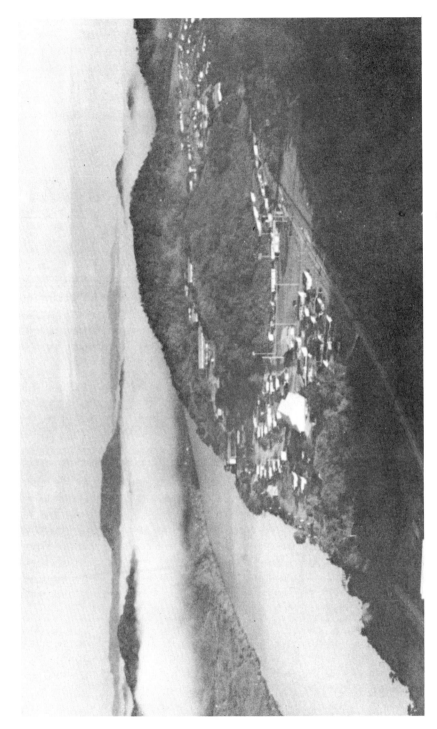

Fig. 11. Fog descending into the Cut at evening. Panama Canal Company

by a Canal tugboat following astern, ready for action if currents or gusts of wind cause a vessel to veer off course toward a bank or into the path of another ship. A small amount of push applied to a vessel at the stern on the channel side, supplementary to the rudder, is usually sufficient to cause it to nose away from the bank.

Fog is still a problem at the Cut, tying up navigation through the Cut on an average of 65 nights a year. Pilots pull off and anchor at Gamboa, going southbound if advised to by the Navigation Division (fig. 11). New lighting and signaling are a help, but pilots still feel uncertain about navigating the Cut in the fog. Torrential rains which can drastically cut visibility also tie up traffic.

Widening the Cut has contributed materially to a speeding up of transits. Previously traffic had to be scheduled so it would move in one direction for several hours. Now it is possible to move most traffic continually in both directions, save when a flight of locks is out for servicing, or when there has been some tie-up due to an accident. Clear-Cut traffic is still given to very large ships and those loaded with flammable or dangerous cargoes. Otherwise, shipping moves continuously around the clock in both directions, but pilots have to be careful on meeting other vessels in the Cut lest the wake from one affect the course of others.

Pedro Miguel and Miraflores Locks

Moving south out of Gaillard Cut, a vessel passes through the excavated valley of the Rio Obispo and Rio Grande, two small streams that flow from the Continental Divide toward the Pacific. At the end of this valley the vessel reaches the Pedro Miguel Locks. This lowers, or raises, a vessel in one chamber 31 feet with the same procedures being used that were described for Gatun. From here a vessel southbound traverses Miraflores Lake, a small artificial body of water, to the two-tiered Miraflores Locks. These locks, again uniform in dimensions with the Gatun and Pedro Miguel Lock chambers, contain two chambers that lower, or raise, a vessel an average of 54 feet to or from sea level. This is the final lockage at the Pacific end of the waterway.

Pacific Terminal and Channel to Sea

From this point a ship passes three miles out to Balboa Harbor through a channel similar to the approach to the Gatun Locks on the Atlantic side. On the starboard side southbound is the unused channel excavated for the Third Locks in 1941-42.

Beyond Balboa the right-of-way extends five miles to the Pacific Ocean past Naos, Perico, and Flamenco Island. A causeway connects the mainland with these islands cutting off a silt-laden crosscurrent that would require continual dredging.

After a vessel passes Flamenco Island, it discharges the Canal pilot into a waiting launch and is cleared for sea, thus completing the transit of the Canal.

Transit of the 50.5-mile-long Canal, from deep water to deep water, normally takes about ten hours. The overall time spent in Canal Zone waters varies, but currently averages 17 hours per transit. The times are roughly the same whichever direction a vessel is going.

Speed within the Canal is carefully regulated. The maximum speed allowed anywhere is in Gatun Lake where vessels may move up to 18 knots. In the approach channels 12 knots is the limit. Within the Cut vessels may not exceed 8 knots. This latter is essential for safety and to prevent wash from vessels eroding the banks or setting up wake that might disturb the navigation of vessels going in the opposite direction.[16]

Navigation Problems in the Canal

Little difficulty is experienced by vessels in the approach channels. These are straight, giving the pilot a clear view ahead and a sufficiently wide path in which to proceed when passing other vessels. Navigators know what to expect in these channels and have relatively little trouble either with currents, or with winds save under hard blows. The same is generally true in Gatun Lake.

Fog and Wind

In Gaillard Cut it is never certain what conditions will be encountered. Slides are no longer the critical problem they once were, although minor slippages may still occur. The widening of the Cut has substantially improved navigation. There are still factors that have to be contended with, however. We have already mentioned fog at night as one of these. Wind can be a factor both in the Cut and in the locks, particularly for vessels in ballast. These are susceptible to heavy blows that can move them off course. As a former head of the Canal Pilot's Association has said, such vessels can make a pilot sweat getting them through.

Wind is a particular problem in the locks at Miraflores and Pedro Miguel when the trade winds are blowing hard. Vessels come into these locks with the wind on their quarter. This tends to push them against the walls going in both directions, or into the path of vessels coming in the opposite direction on leaving the locks. At Gatun the problem is not so serious as the prevailing winds generally blow down through the locks, although on proceeding northbound (toward the Caribbean) there can be difficulties with a strong northeasterly blow.

Getting into Locks

Maneuvering a vessel into the lock chambers is sometimes a problem. A pilot has phrased it this way: Getting a ship into a lock is something like getting a cork into a bottle top. You have to push it in, or the vessel's displacement on going into the narrow opening will push it back out. This is where pilots, chief engineers, and the electric locomotives on the walls have to cooperate.

Suction from Vessel Movement

A problem many pilots have experienced in taking vessels through the Canal is suction along the banks of the Cut and in proceeding out of the locks. This is caused by a countercurrent set up by the motion and displacement of a vessel. This tends to pull the bow over toward a bank or lock wall if the vessel is in close. The situation is now much better with the wider channel, for vessels do not need to go as close to the banks as they used to. But it still can be a problem if pilots cut the bends too closely, or when other vessels are passing. Similarly, currents are set up within the lock chambers when the engines are given power to move a vessel out of a flight of locks as the cables to the locomotives are being cast off.

Ships differ greatly in how they respond to the wheel and how much countercurrent they set up. Twin-screw ships are generally worse than single-screw for setting up suction along the banks or walls. Large ships are more notorious in this respect than small. The few transiting ships with four propellers can be the most troublesome with their outer screws close to the sides. They tend to set up powerful countercurrents along banks and lock walls.

Pilots learn to be watchful for these things and become familiar with the traits of different ships after they have taken them through the Canal, especially those that transit frequently. This, after all, is what pilots are for: to know the Canal, the effects of various conditions on the behavior of different vessels, the ways to handle them in different parts of the Canal to avoid accidents, and the regulations that are established in the interest of promoting safety for mariners and for the Canal.[17]

Present precautions are sufficient to protect the Canal and transiting vessels from most mishaps. Occasionally, vessels will scrape the sides of the lock chambers or hit the approach walls. Once in a while serious accidents occur, such as groundings or denting plates of vessels by striking the approach walls. Cases can be found of claims and counter-claims arising from accidents in the Canal. But few accidents have been serious enough to impede operation of the Canal for extended periods.

Long-Range Planning to Expedite Traffic

A lock canal requires continual attention to maintain its operating efficiency, especially in the tropics. Channels must be dredged. Lock structures and machinery must be overhauled to reduce wear and prevent their becoming fouled with marine growths and rust. Towing loco-motives can break down and wear out. Almost every mechanical feature is subject to fatigue and obsolescence and needs regular overhaul and maintenance.

As the quantity of shipping transiting the Canal has increased from a few thousand vessels a year to 15,000, serious thought has had to be given to ways of handling increasing numbers of vessels in order to maintain optimal transit time and efficient labor schedules for operators.

For the near future, three sets of improvements are underway to enhance the Canal's operating efficiency. These include (a) lock improvements, (b) navigation improvements, and (c) seeking additional supplies of water. These will be discussed in Chapter Five.

Conclusion

The opening of the Panama Canal made possible a tremendous advance in intercoastal and overseas trade. Some of this conceivably would have come irrespective of the Canal. But the presence of the waterway, with its foreshortening of distances on principal trade routes, and its speeding of movement between the Atlantic and Pacific Oceans, was a large factor in stimulating the business that has followed.

The improvements that have been made in the Canal to widen the channel, that are now underway to increase the water supply and that will be made as needed to expedite traffic by increasing the number of towing locomotives on the lock walls, will enable the Canal to absorb a good deal more traffic than it is now handling. It is estimated that it can probably keep up with demands until about the year 2000 or later as transits have been running in recent years. We will consider in a subsequent chapter the possible magnitudes of future commerce and what these may do to the need for additional capacity or a larger canal.

The United States and other maritime countries will benefit from whatever is done to speed up the process of transiting and to increase the number and size of vessels that can be put through the Canal in a given day and year. Other nations of the American hemisphere, Western Europe, Asia, and Oceania will be served by whatever advances the usefulness of the interoceanic canal. It remains one of the principal means of furthering overseas commerce.

CHAPTER TWO FOOTNOTES

1. For the history of the building of the Canal, see Miles P. DuVal, Jr., *And the Mountains Will Move,* Stanford: Stanford University Press, 1947.

2. These are summarized in an article by the author entitled: "Ocean Commerce and the Panama Canal." *Journal of Maritime Law and Commerce*, Vol. 4, No. 3, April 1973, pp. 397-423. Much of what follows is extracted from the *Journal* with the permission of the Editor.

   The laws and regulations are incorporated into the *Code of Federal Regulations,* Title 35, Panama Canal. Washington: Office of Federal Register, revised annually [hereafter cited as CFR, 35. . .]. Congress enacted, and the President approved, a special body of law for the Zone incorporated in a *Canal Zone Code* on October 18, 1962, covering legal rights, duties, powers, and obligations within the Zone (76A Stat. 1). The United States District Court for the Canal Zone is the highest tribunal in the Zone with jurisdiction over civil, criminal, and admiralty matters. Appeals lie to the Circuit Court of Appeals, 5th Circuit, and from there to the Supreme Court. The President, acting under his implied powers, issues regulations dealing with a wide variety of actions in the Zone (see CFR, 35, Secs. 6, 10). See also McConnaughey v. Morrow, 263 U.S. 39 (1923).

Key treaties are the Hay-Pauncefote Treaty of November 18, 1901, with Great Britain, 32 Stat. 1903; the Hay-Bunau-Varilla Convention of November 18, 1903, with the Republic of Panama for the Construction of a Ship Canal, 33 Stat. 2234; the General Treaty of Friendship and Cooperation with the Republic of Panama of March 2, 1936, 53 Stat. 1807; and the Treaty of Mutual Understanding and Cooperation with the Republic of Panama, January 25, 1955, 6 U.S. Treaty Series 2273.

Regulations applying to various stages of transit, powers and duties of Canal officers, responsibilities of vessels and their officers and crew, etc., are given in CFR, 35, Secs. 101-135.

3. Each vessel is required to present a number of papers and have them certified. These include: (1) the National Register of the ship; (2) Clearance from the last port and a list of ports of call in the preceding three months; (3) Crew List; (4) Passenger List; (5) Bills of Health; (6) Store List; (7) Cargo Manifest; (8) Declaration of Explosive Cargo or inflammable or combustible liquids carried; (9) Statement of Fuel Account; (10) General Plan of Vessel; (11) Ship Information Sheet; (12) Panama Canal Tonnage Certificate; (13) Report of Structural Changes since last transit (see CFR, 35, Sec. 101.9-10). In time of national emergency, the boarding officer may be accompanied by a naval officer.

4. CFR, 35, Sec. 101.13. Panamanian-flag vessels may be inspected by their own authorities for compliance with Panamanian shipping laws in accordance with an agreement signed with the Government of Panama, August 5, 1957 (8 U.S. Treaties 1413).

   A vessel may be denied passage through the Canal if "the character or condition of the cargo, hull or machinery is such as to endanger the structures pertaining to the Canal, or which might render the vessel liable to obstruct the Canal, or whose draft at any point of the vessel exceeds the maximum allowable draft in the Canal as designated from time to time by the Canal authorities" (CFR, 35, Sec. 103.2).

5. CFR, 35, Sec. 101.2.

6. CFR, 35, Sec. 133.1c. Operators of some private vessels have contended that the tolls are burdened with costs of national defense. This has been denied. See Richard R. Baxter et al., *The Panama Canal.* Working paper prepared for the Hammarskjold Forums, New York City, May 28, 1964, pp. 33-34. The U.S. Supreme Court held in Panama Canal Co. v. Grace Line, Inc., that the question of what activities in the Canal Zone should be included within the coverage of tolls is "not appropriate for judicial action" (356 U.S. 309, 317 (1958)).

7. CFR, 35, Sec. 133.32.

8. CFR, 35, Sec. 133.71.

9. The Regulations specify that, except as provided, "no vessel shall pass through the Canal or enter or leave a terminal port, or maneuver within Canal Zone

waters lying inside the Canal entrances without having a Panama Canal pilot on board." The pilot has full control of navigation until the vessel leaves the opposite terminal for the sea, unless otherwise released by the Port Captain. CFR, 35, Sec. 105.1.

10. The power to place armed guards aboard vessels was first given by Act of June 15, 1917 (40 Stat. 220). This was amplified by an Executive Order of September 5, 1939, and by Acts of August 5 and September 26, 1950 (64 Stat. 427 and 64 Stat. 1038). See *United States Code*, Title 50, Sec. 191.

11. Norman J. Padelford, *The Panama Canal in Peace and War*, New York: Macmillan, 1942, Chapter IV.

12. CFR, 35, Secs. 105, 107. Canal pilots have similar control of the movements of all vessels of war in the Canal.

13. CFR, 35, Sec. 103.9.

14. See CFR, 35, Sec. 103.8, giving Canal authorities discretion in these matters.

15. Marine Director's Notice to Shipping Agents, August 12-72. Balboa Heights, C.Z., May 19, 1972, p. 4. The maximum draft level allowed for transits is 39 feet, 6 inches; for initial transits it is 37 feet. *Ibid.*

16. CFR, 35, Sec. 111.162.

17. We are indebted to Captain Howard L. Wentworth, Searsport, Maine, for 20 years a pilot at the Canal without an accident or investigation, for observations on problems of navigating the Canal.

CHAPTER THREE

USE OF CANAL BY OCEAN SHIPPING

Standing at Gatun at the Atlantic end of the Panama Canal, or at Balboa at the Pacific terminal, lines of vessels coming from all parts of the world can often be seen moving toward the Canal, or waiting their turn to proceed into it. On the average, as many as 40 vessels a day transit the Canal. More than 14,000 ships a year are locked through the waterway at the present time. This exceeds the dreams of those who first visualized a shipway through the Isthmus of Panama and vindicates the need for a shortcut between the oceans.

The designers of the Canal looked far into the future when drawing up the specifications for the waterway. The builders constructed a system of locks to endure for a century and more. As it turned out, the work was done on a scale of sufficient proportions to serve all but the largest ships afloat today.

Vessels today are far longer, of wider beam, and more specialized in nature than when the Canal was built. Increasing numbers of those that now regularly call at the Canal practically fill the 1,000-foot-long, 110-foot-wide chambers. The standard ship designers' measure known as "Panamax," meaning the maximum dimensions a vessel can have to fit within the locks, is being exceeded each year with new ships that are too large to go in the lock chambers. Such vessels are employed on ocean routes that would not normally pass through the Canal, such as from the Middle East to Europe or Japan carrying crude oil. Their existence raises questions, nevertheless, whether a larger waterway should one day be constructed to accommodate them.

Ships that Pass in the Day and Night

The small, plodding, coal-burning freighters and other steamships that once passed through the Panama Canal are now replaced by 850-foot tankers hauling 60,000 tons of oil, and by mammoth containerships that can sustain a speed of 30 knots and more at sea loaded.

Ship traffic at the Canal has reflected the technological progress of ocean transportation from the coal-burning reciprocating steam engine era to the gas turbine and nuclear power plant. The vessels that transit the Canal have ranged from windjammers of the days of sail and small pleasure craft to the U.S.S. *Missouri*, the "Mighty Mo" of World War II fame, with a beam of 108 feet.

Particularly interesting among today's transients are the 950-foot, 106-foot-beam containerships of the T.S.S. *Tokyo Bay* and sisterships

Fig. 12. The S.S. *Arctic* carrying 60,391 long tons of Hampton Roads coal is shown here bound for Japan.
Panama Canal Company

class of British registry and other new ships of a similar size that can carry 2,000 containers or more.

It is possible that some of the large containerships built for the Europe-Asia run will be diverted to the Suez Canal when that is reopened, for they cannot operate at their full-designed draft of 44 feet through the Panama Canal. On the other hand, the Panama route has the advantage of not charging them tolls for cargo carried on open decks as does Suez.

Other users of the Canal include giant dry bulk and oil carriers like the Liberian-flagged S.S. *Melodic* that for some years carried coal from Baltimore to Japan and iron ore from Peru to Baltimore on the return voyage. The *Melodic* holds the current record of lifting 61,078 long tons of cargo through the Canal. Its sistership, the S.S. *Arctic*, is shown in Figure 12.

New to the Canal in recent years are special automobile-carrying ships, such as the Norwegian-owned *Dyvi Pacific* which carries 2,000 European-built compact cars to the West Coast of the United States, and a comparable number of Japanese-built compacts from that country to the East Coast of the United States.

Although passenger liners have as a rule given way to the jet aircraft, a few luxury cruise ships continue to be regular patrons of the Panama Canal. Among these are such familiar names as the P & O liner *Canberra*, the Holland America Line *Rotterdam*, the Norwegian America Line *Sagafjord*, and others. With the changing fortunes of American shipping, there are today no passenger ships flying the United States flag that regularly call at the Canal.

Vessels of many kinds and descriptions pass through the Canal each year with an almost infinite variety of cargo. Although there has been a marked trend toward specialized shipping such as the container and automobile-carrying vessels, refrigerated cargo vessels, lighter-aboard-ships, tankers, and dry bulk carriers, the general cargo liners still predominate in the file of shipping.

With approximately 80 percent of the world commodity transportation carried by water and 98 percent of this and other countries' foreign trade borne by ocean shipping, the outlook for an ongoing line of shipping moving through the Canal is promising for years to come.

Patterns of Ship Traffic

The records of Canal traffic show a remarkably steady growth in business, both in numbers of vessels passing through, and in cargo carried. Transits of total ocean traffic have risen from a few thousand to 14,829 in 1970. The high point for total Panama Canal traffic of all kinds was reached in 1970 when 15,523 vessels made the transit. The volume of cargo transported through the waterway has grown from nine million tons in 1920 to 127 million in 1973. Toll receipts have risen proportionately, surpassing $113 million in 1973.[1] Interesting as is the historical record shown in Table 1, the traffic patterns since 1947 are of most concern.

Table 1

Historical Traffic Statistics*

Fiscal Year	Commercial Ocean Transits	Commercial Ocean Cargo - Long Tons	Total Transits	Total Tolls and Tolls Credit Received**
1915	1,058	4,888,400	1,108	$ 4,367,602
1916	724	3,093,335	807	2,407,047
1917	1,738	7,054,720	1,937	5,628,068
1918	1,989	7,525,768	2,210	6,439,066
1919	1,948	6,910,097	2,230	6,173,028
1920	2,393	9,372,374	2,777	8,514,207
1921	2,791	11,595,971	3,371	11,276,483
1922	2,665	10,882,607	3,050	11,198,000
1923	3,908	19,566,429	4,449	17,508,701
1924	5,158	26,993,167	5,787	24,291,596
1925	4,592	23,956,549	5,174	21,400,994
1926	5,087	26,630,016	5,923	22,931,764
1927	5,293	27,733,555	6,259	24,230,027
1928	6,253	29,615,651	7,116	26,945,862
1929	6,289	30,647,768	7,197	27,128,893
1930	6,027	30,018,429	6,875	27,077,267
1931	5,370	25,065,283	6,217	24,646,109
1932	4,362	19,798,986	5,075	20,707,856
1933	4,162	18,161,165	5,040	19,621,181
1934	5,234	24,704,009	6,211	24,065,707
1935	5,180	25,309,527	6,369	23,339,239
1936	5,382	26,505,943	6,453	23,510,629
1937	5,387	28,108,375	6,695	23,147,640
1938	5,524	27,385,924	6,930	23,215,208
1939	5,903	27,866,627	7,479	23,699,430
1940	5,370	27,299,016	6,945	21,177,759
1941	4,727	24,950,791	6,623	18,190,380
1942	2,688	13,607,444	4,643	9,772,113
1943	1,822	10,599,966	4,372	7,368,739
1944	1,562	7,003,487	5,130	5,473,846
1945	1,939	8,603,607	8,866	7,266,211
1946	3,747	14,977,940	9,586	14,796,406
1947	4,260	21,670,518	6,375	17,634,361
1948	4,678	24,117,788	6,999	20,017,439
1949	4,793	25,305,158	7,361	20,617,635
1950	5,448	28,872,243	7,694	24,511,713
1951	5,593	30,073,022	7,751	23,958,879
1952	6,524	33,610,509	9,169	30,409,500
1953	7,410	36,095,344	10,210	37,530,327
1954	7,784	39,095,067	10,218	37,191,107
1955	7,997	40,646,301	9,811	35,136,529
1956	8,209	45,119,042	9,744	37,450,759
1957	8,579	49,702,200	10,169	39,653,712
1958	9,187	48,124,809	10,608	42,834,005
1959	9,718	51,153,096	11,192	46,546,620

Table 1 Continued

Historical Traffic Statistics*

Fiscal Year	Commercial Ocean Transits	Commercial Ocean Cargo - Long Tons	Total Transits	Total Tolls and Tolls Credit Received**
1960	10,795	59,258,219	12,147	51,803,032
1961	10,866	63,669,738	12,019	55,172,719
1962	11,149	67,524,552	12,106	58,347,290
1963	11,017	62,247,094	12,005	57,855,931
1964	11,808	70,550,090	12,945	62,546,390
1965	11,834	76,573,071	12,918	67,148,451
1966	11,925	81,703,514	13,304	72,594,111
1967	12,412	86,193,430	14,070	82,296,638
1968	13,199	96,550,165	15,511	93,153,649
1969	13,146	101,372,744	15,327	95,914,608
1970	13,658	114,257,260	15,523	100,909,856
1971	14,020	118,626,906	15,348	100,566,537
1972	13,766	109,233,725	15,198	101,488,689
1973	13,841	126,104,029	15,109	113,381,398
1974	14,033	147,906,914	15,269	121,316,788
Total	403,921	2,461,189,529	495,004	$2,185,505,731

*Source: Panama Canal Company, Annual Reports.

**Excludes U.S. Government Tolls Credits for Period 1915-1951.

Commercial Ocean Transits

Commercial ocean traffic at the Canal has risen more than threefold since 1947. 4,678 commercial ocean vessels passed through the waterway in 1948. The number grew to 6,524 in 1952, exceeding the high point of the era before World War II. By 1960 over 10,000 vessels a year were transiting. By 1967 the 12,000 transit mark was passed. In 1971 the number of ocean vessels transiting the Canal went over the 14,000 line.

Figure 13 shows that transits of commercial ocean vessels rose continuously from 1945 to 1971. Indeed, transits of such vessels continued the same growth pattern from 1951-1970 as seen from 1918-1930. Short periods of leveling off can be seen from time to time since 1950, but no serious decline. Economic recessions and tie-ups on the waterfronts caused intermittent fluctuations. The first significant decline occurred in 1972, although this involved a drop of only 254 transits out of more than 14,000, or less than two percent.

The record shows that the Canal has been of large and continuing importance to commercial shipping. This is the Canal's largest customer. This, furthermore, is a business that is worldwide in scope, encompassing vessels from as many as 60 different countries in a single year.

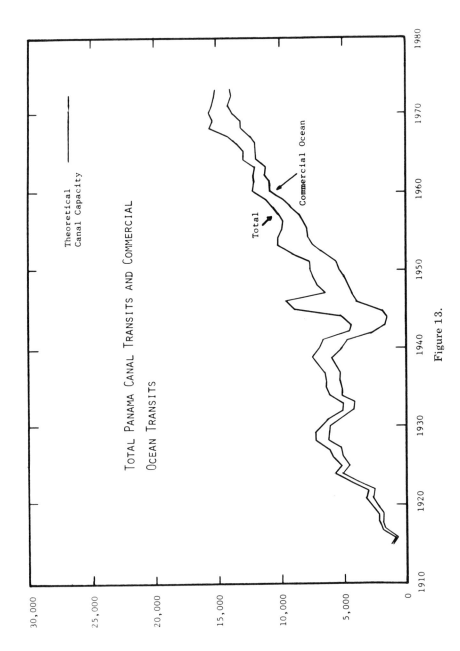

Total Panama Canal Transits and Commercial Ocean Transits

Theoretical
Canal Capacity

Commercial Ocean

Total

Figure 13.

48

Government Traffic

The top line in Figure 13 shows that there has been a considerable variation in the overall number of transits compared with commercial ocean traffic. This is explained by the varying numbers of government-owned vessels and small commercial craft that use the Canal. The government vessels—warships, military transports, tankers, etc.—are largely United States Government shipping. This class of traffic has ranged from as few as 182 transits in a year to 1,504, as shown in Table 2.

Table 2

U.S. Government Ocean Traffic at Panama Canal*

Fiscal Year	No. Transits	Long Tons Cargo	Tolls
1948	508	1,520,569	$1,755,134
1949	658	2,217,495	2,405,519
1950	443	1,429,283	1,918,785
1951	693	1,165,986	2,764,747
1952	774	3,237,311	3,383,900
1953	1,064	5,049,922	5,526,038
1954	800	2,705,380	3,862,015
1955	296	838,305	1,190,367
1956	266	1,150,121	1,215,883
1957	269	922,173	1,117,467
1958	279	791,310	972,110
1959	204	1,012,842	965,643
1960	182	804,581	818,313
1961	188	1,149,934	997,842
1962	191	1,126,418	1,028,396
1963	300	1,115,352	1,460,281
1964	285	1,177,269	1,395,548
1965	284	1,923,538	1,647,653
1966	591	3,220,190	3,446,219
1967	879	6,147,479	5,484,566
1968	1,504	8,497,221	9,206,815
1969	1,376	7,210,068	8,418,421
1970	1,068	4,410,451	6,218,541
1971	503	2,236,619	3,144,376
1972	413	1,742,303	2,651,281
1973	373	1,405,428	2,285,727
1974	248	1,743,963	1,831,561

*Compiled from Panama Canal Company, Annual Report, yearly, Table 11.

This group of shipping which forms the second ranking element of traffic changes in its composition and numbers as crises appear abroad and the need is felt for reinforcing United States interests and security.

From Table 2 it will be seen that United States Government traffic moved to peaks in the 1951-1954 and 1966-1971 periods. This was occasioned first by military buildups in the Korea-Taiwan area, and later during the war in Southeast Asia.

Although the extent of government traffic is small compared to commercial ocean shipping, the continued flow of an average of 300 transits a year helps explain the attitude of indispensability held by the United States Government toward the existence and defense of the inter-oceanic artery. It is closely identified with the security of United States interests.

There is a fairly constant traffic of approximately 90 oceangoing and 25 small Panamanian and Columbian government toll-free shipping a year. This right was given to these countries by the United States in consideration of their locations and historic concerns for an inter-oceanic connection. It will certainly be continued in any new treaty that replaces the original Canal conventions.

Small Ship Traffic

A third form of traffic distinguished at the Canal is that of small commercial and pleasure craft. These include vessels that are under 300 net tons, Panama Canal measurement, or 500 displacement tons for vessels that are assessed on this basis. These vessels are for the most part engaged in local coasting trade, or are pleasure craft, or are working vessels such as dredges and floating cranes.

This traffic averages out at around 550 transits a year. A high point for this class of users was reached in 1960 with 833 transits. Since falling back to 430 in 1963, the number of transits has been growing steadily, passing the 700 mark in 1972-1973. Considering the cargo that is carried by these small vessels (over 59,000 long tons in 1973), they play a considerable role for their size in the local economic life of the Republic of Panama and its immediate neighbors. They are therefore an important consideration to be held in view.

Commercial ocean transits at the Canal are a barometer of the state of world economic health, rising with prosperity and world economic growth, declining with its recessions and periods of slack. The traffic of United States Government-owned shipping mirrors the ups and downs in the international crisis register. Small commercial and free traffic tend to run along on a more or less even keel with here and there high and low points that are reflections chiefly of local prosperity and national pride.

Of all classes of transits, it is the commercial ocean traffic that gives the Canal the greater part of its daily and annual business. This is the traffic that has to be watched most closely for signs that the Canal is approaching the limits of its capacity, and for indications that larger locks or a sea-level waterway will be needed by a given time for accom-modating the needs of traffic.

Use of Canal by Ships of Different Nationalities

Widespread Use of Waterway by World Shipping

Vessels of many national registries transit the Canal each year. A high point was reached in 1973 when vessels flying 60 different flags were recorded passing through the Canal.[2] Table 3 shows the number of transits by vessels of different national registries in five sample years.

Shipping of the United States, the United Kingdom, Liberia, Japan, Norway, Panama, Germany, and Greece has stood in the forefront since 1960. Although the number of vessels bearing these flags has varied considerably, they nevertheless stand out from others by fairly large margins.

Today 12.3 percent of the ships transiting the Panama Canal are under the Liberian flag. This is the largest flag-of-registry user of the Canal. Japanese-flag shipping composes 11.1 percent of the total, and British-flag transits 10.7 percent. Ships flying the United States flag now provide 8.5 percent of the overall traffic, down from 26 percent in 1955.

Following these leaders come vessels from Denmark, the Netherlands, Sweden, Colombia, Italy, and France. Many of them are engaged in general cargo trades on regular schedules. While a sizable numerical gap separates the vessels flying these flags from those of the first group, their transits have generally stood above the 200-a-year mark since 1965 and displayed a rising tendency.

Many Greek, Liberian, Norwegian, and Panamanian vessels are engaged in the spot charter market carrying oil, ores, and grains. Japanese-, British-, German-, and United States-flag vessels are employed in a variety of trades, both as bulkers, container carriers, refrigerated fruit carriers (reefers), and general cargo service. The rise in Soviet-flag transits suggests a desire both to show the flag in American waters, and to expand Soviet overseas trade. With a rapidly expanding mercantile fleet, more business can be anticipated from this quarter in years to come.

The heavy users are of course the principal beneficiaries of the interoceanic shortcut. They are also the main contributors to the Canal's revenues through tolls.

Table 4 lists the comparative tolls paid by the principal user states. It is clear that the vessels of Greece, Japan, Liberia, Norway, the United Kingdom, and the United States are the best-paying customers; also that a large percentage of their vessels are going through with cargo. These leaders, it will be observed, have been at or close to the top-ranking positions from 1965 on, followed closely by the Federal Republic of Germany, which has made a very solid comeback on the seas since 1960.

Governor David S. Parker, in a statement prepared for the United States Congress in July 1973, estimated that approximately 20 percent of the world's merchant fleet of ships of 1,000 gross registered tons and over uses the Panama Canal, 4,500 out of about 25,000 ships all told. In terms of the percentages of their international oceanborne commerce

(Text continues on page 55.)

Table 3

Canal Traffic by Flags of Vessels Transiting in Selected Years*

Flag	1955	1960	1965	1970	1973	Long Tons Cargo 1973
Algeria	–	–	–	1	–	–
Argentina	1	1	1	15	8	43,380
Australia	–	–	–	2	13	143,508
Belgium	15	11	49	131	147	658,708
Brazil	10	2	3	22	35	126,969
Bulgaria	–	–	2	5	–	–
Canada	–	–	–	12	16	6,855
Chile	60	107	115	118	115	1,643,981
China, Peoples Rep.	–	–	17	–	–	–
Colombia	198	269	246	214	229	442,577
Costa Rica	31	4	–	–	20	16,256
Cuba	–	17	5	75	78	774,118
Cyprus	–	–	–	74	198	1,316,803
Czechoslovakia	–	–	–	2	–	–
Denmark	323	447	283	434	363	2,269,935
Dominican Republic	–	–	–	–	6	1,727
Germany, Fed. Rep.	375	1,296	1,186	1,108	789	4,793,020
Germany, Peoples Rep.	–	–	–	17	35	42,578
Ecuador	57	62	25	66	64	342,609
El Salvador	–	–	–	–	–	–
Ethiopia	–	–	–	6	1	–
Finland	9	15	27	66	38	189,889
France	132	167	172	247	209	926,477
Ghana	–	–	1	2	–	–
Greece	121	273	575	568	1,071	12,572,638
Honduras	428	204	268	166	99	96,639
Iceland	–	–	2	–	9	–
India	–	–	8	38	47	609,455
Haiti	–	–	1	–	–	–
Indonesia	–	–	2	–	–	–
Iran	–	–	–	2	7	74,123
Ireland	–	1	12	29	21	378,798
Israel	3	62	59	83	40	183,651
Italy	160	194	192	266	266	1,394,314
Japan	464	820	804	1,178	1,331	12,166,721
Kuwait	–	–	2	3	9	88,497
Lebanon	–	–	34	14	5	4,079
Liberia	384	997	1,118	1,601	1,685	25,937,307
Malaysia	–	–	–	–	6	156,504
Malta	–	–	–	–	–	–
Mexico	6	18	42	69	53	277,801
Morocco	–	–	–	1	3	16,045
Nauru	–	–	–	–	1	–
Netherlands	139	416	618	493	449	2,824,262
New Zealand	–	–	–	1	1	19
Nicaragua	50	77	62	34	80	140,613
Norway	904	1,167	1,446	1,323	1,190	15,991,479
Pakistan	–	–	–	–	18	139,786
Panama	551	255	518	799	959	6,629,420
Paraguay	–	–	–	1	–	–
Peru	18	83	153	180	158	1,358,499
Philippines	17	20	84	112	97	638,508
Poland	–	–	–	28	29	155,680
Portugal	–	1	–	4	–	–
Rep. China (Taiwan)	38	54	103	147	180	1,896,673

52

Table 3 Continued

Canal Traffic by Flags of Vessels Transiting in Selected Years*

Flag	1955	1960	1965	1970	1973	Long Tons Cargo 1973
Singapore	–	–	–	14	28	192,445
Somalia	–	–	–	5	30	451,601
South Africa	–	1	–	–	2	12,842
South Korea	4	9	15	77	112	757,732
South Vietnam	–	–	–	3	5	49,339
Spain	32	34	11	66	47	148,904
Sweden	207	278	388	462	419	3,083,349
Switzerland	5	11	82	8	11	62,986
Tanzania	–	–	–	1	–	–
Thailand	–	1	–	6	–	–
Tonga	–	–	–	–	2	1,203
Turkey	4	2	–	–	2	–
United Kingdom	1,145	1,295	1,339	1,591	1,378	13,279,073
United States	2,102	2,089	1,678	1,520	1,276	7,982,615
Uruguay	2	1	–	–	13	419,121
U.S.S.R.	1	3	48	104	291	1,810,738
Venezuela	–	29	17	3	2	110
Yugoslavia	1	2	17	42	45	381,072

*Compiled from Panama Canal Company, Annual Reports, for years designated, Table 13.

Table 4

Canal Tolls Paid by Leading Flag Users*

Flag State	1955	1960	1965	1970	1973
Colombia	$ 438,789	$ 787,828	$ 844,112	$ 1,042,155	$ 949,272
Denmark	1,179,766	1,762,075	1,664,459	2,282,031	2,674,397
France	597,795	929,370	800,476	1,132,603	1,138,389
Greece	545,734	505,094	3,682,461	4,600,109	8,197,346
Italy	761,236	1,141,114	1,360,631	1,696,886	1,787,311
Japan	2,299,506	4,275,435	4,377,156	8,833,601	12,854,722
Liberia	1,610,828	4,897,699	8,235,514	15,970,573	17,192,046
Netherlands	635,989	1,686,282	2,236,989	2,732,796	2,780,935
Norway	3,783,372	6,296,688	9,588,919	11,741,250	12,868,178
Panama	1,872,618	814,978	1,912,766	3,536,218	5,003,800
Sweden	856,548	1,373,825	2,308,225	3,340,520	4,073,202
United Kingdom	5,927,758	7,730,999	8,291,824	11,709,292	12,703,859
United States	10,407,307	11,414,567	10,724,351	10,288,505	9,795,713
West Germany	1,092,498	4,200,274	4,614,242	5,599,582	6,092,099

*Compiled from Panama Canal Company, Annual Reports for designated years, Table 13.

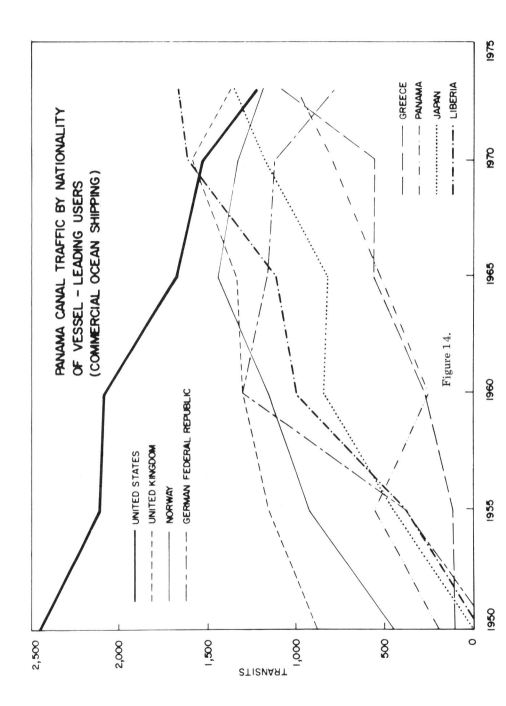

PANAMA CANAL TRAFFIC BY NATIONALITY
OF VESSEL - LEADING USERS
(COMMERCIAL OCEAN SHIPPING)

UNITED STATES
UNITED KINGDOM
NORWAY
GERMAN FEDERAL REPUBLIC

GREECE
PANAMA
JAPAN
LIBERIA

TRANSITS

2,500

2,000

1,500

1,000

500

0

1950   1955   1960   1965   1970   1975

Figure 14.

(Continued from page 51.)

passing through the Canal, some Latin American countries are proportionately more dependent on the Canal than other users. The United States is, however, the major user of the Canal in absolute terms.[3]

Decline of U.S. Shipping

Figure 14 shows the relative positions of the principal users. The decline in United States-flag transits is particularly notable compared to the rise in transits by Greek, Japanese, Liberian, Panamanian, and other shipping, and considering the marked lead United States shipping had until 1965.

The shrinking position of United States shipping has been due in part to the progressive aging and withdrawal of many wartime-built vessels and ships constructed in the early 1950s. The decline is also attributable to the costs of shipping goods in American bottoms due to the high wages paid American crews compared to those paid to foreign crews. The declining position of the United States-flag shipping is also due to lagging support at home, the disposition of many firms to ship on foreign lines, and the greater attention some lines have paid to overseas delivery arrangements.

Under the Merchant Marine Act of 1970 enacted by the United States Congress in that year the Government is undertaking to revitalize merchant shipping through constructing 30 new standardized transports a year for the next ten years.[4] It is at the same time supporting construction and operational subsidies for special-purpose vessels in order to assure U.S.-flag service on overseas routes deemed essential to the national interest.[5]

Drives mounted by the Department of Commerce to increase exports, and by the Department of the Treasury to help redress the balance of payments through devaluing the dollar, gave an advantage in the international markets to United States exports in 1972-1973, resulting in a favorable balance of trade.

With the fresh lease on life which these policies imparted to overseas commerce, the United States merchant fleet should in time be able to reverse the 20-year trend seen in Figure 14. Complementing these efforts by the Government are steps taken by some private enterprise to win trade by putting fast, highly-competitive ships built in foreign yards on the seas to rival the best others have there. Sea-Land Lines' speed-record-holding containerships on the Atlantic and the Pacific are a case in point. Although some of these vessels only occasionally transit the Canal, they are earning business for the United States that can redound to the advantage of U.S. oceanborne commerce generally.

American-Owned Ships under Foreign Flags

Several hundred vessels built in the United States have been placed under foreign registry flying the flags of Liberia, Honduras, Panama,

Table 5

Foreign Flag Ships Owned by Foreign Affiliates of Companies
Incorporated under Laws of the United States

Country of Registry	Tankers			Freighters			Bulk & Ore Carriers		
	No.	Gross Tons	Dwt Tons	No.	Gross Tons	Dwt Tons	No.	Gross Tons	Dwt Tons
Liberia	125	5,258,752	9,550,921	---	---	---	55	1,321,872	2,683,870
United Kingdom	70	3,059,974	5,590,678	17	109,003	100,583	6	78,319	117,035
Panama	87	2,004,581	3,533,315	---	---	---	4	31,438	50,357
Netherlands	18	783,662	1,346,790	---	---	---	---	---	---
Honduras	---	---	---	12	59,349	56,870	---	---	---
Germany (West)	11	334,605	548,260	---	---	---	---	---	---
Norway	10	125,677	194,203	---	---	---	---	---	---
France	9	339,503	600,936	---	---	---	---	---	---
Belgium	9	188,216	298,390	---	---	---	---	---	---
Italy	7	242,540	418,596	---	---	---	---	---	---
Venezuela	6	116,113	172,569	---	---	---	---	---	---
Canada	6	26,976	38,792	---	---	---	---	---	---
Denmark	4	61,960	101,073	---	---	---	---	---	---
Finland	4	7,999	10,878	---	---	---	---	---	---
Sweden	2	48,140	79,193	---	---	---	---	---	---
Australia	2	21,487	30,595	---	---	---	---	---	---
Uruguay	1	29,139	49,802	---	---	---	---	---	---
Argentina	1	23,566	36,169	---	---	---	---	---	---
Philippines	1	1,165	1,350	---	---	---	---	---	---

Source: U.S. Department of Commerce, Maritime Administration, Foreign Flag Ships Owned by United States Parent Companies. Ocean Going Merchant Type Ships of 1,000 gross tons and over. Washington. Report No. MAR-560-22. Revised November 9, 1971, p. 5.

and some other countries (see Table 5). The laws of these countries make use of their flags by foreign shipping desirable through simple administrative procedures that often entail liberal financial advantages as well. Control over vessels registered under the so-called Panlibhon arrangements is usually held by companies that are affiliated with parent corporations in the United States, such as the large oil companies, under conditions that permit withdrawal of the vessels to United States registry or requisition in time of national emergency.[6]

Foreign registry is employed where vessels are engaged in trades between the ports of other countries that will keep them abroad for extensive periods, as in the carriage of oil between the Middle East and Europe or Japan, or where they will not be moving between ports in the United States.

American-built vessels can be transferred to foreign registry when permission is obtained from the Maritime Administration. Vessels built abroad without government subsidy can, of course, be registered wherever their owners choose, provided they do not engage in carrying goods between United States ports.[7]

If vessels owned by affiliates of companies incorporated in the United States were to be considered along with those flying the United States flag, this country would probably still be in first place in Canal traffic.

The traffic flowing through the Panama Canal represents a broad cross section of the world community. In it are found the flags of maritime nations generally that have merchant shipping engaging in international commerce. All are treated on a basis of equality save where there are circumstances calling for special precautions, as in a time of international crisis or national emergency.

Traffic by Types of Vessels

An examination of traffic statistics covering the past 20 years shows that there has been a decided fall in transits by passenger ships and by general cargo vessels. At the same time there has been a sharp upswing in transits by dry bulk carriers and a notable growth of containership transits since 1970.

These trends are illustrated by Figure 15 and tabulated in Table 6. Table 7 gives tonnage figures for the most recent six years.

Passenger Ship Traffic

The fall-off in passenger ship business corresponds with the general shrinkage that has been taking place in ocean passenger travel as the long-distance jet planes have been supplanting the ocean liners nearly everywhere. The closing out of the Grace Lines' passenger service between the United States and the West Coast of Latin America led to a

(Text continues on page 61.)

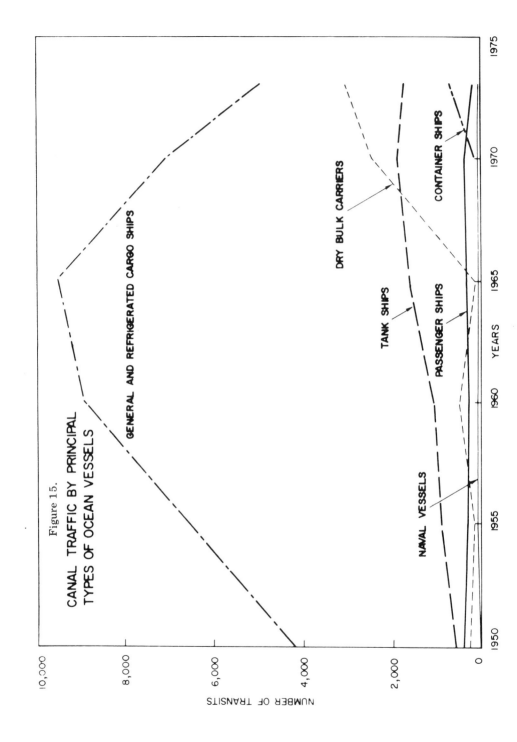

Figure 15.

CANAL TRAFFIC BY PRINCIPAL
TYPES OF OCEAN VESSELS

Table 6

Panama Canal Ocean Traffic by Principal Types of Vessels*
(Laden and Ballast)

Type	1950 No. Transits	1955 No. Transits	1960 No. Transits	1965 No. Transits	1970 No. Transits	1973 No. Transits
Combination Carriers	not listed	not listed	not listed	not listed	131	71
Containerships	not listed	not listed	not listed	not listed	137	704
Bulk Carriers (incl. ore ships)	216	124	489	165	2,438	3,059
General Cargo Ships	4,215	6,654	8,883	9,555	6,534	5,488
Refrigerated Cargo Ships	not separately listed	not separately listed	not separately listed	not separately listed	1,827	2,301
Passenger Ships	337	312	296	325	337	175
Naval Vessels	9	44	50	54	45	37
Tank Ships	665	838	1,064	1,732	1,954	1,769
Miscellaneous	16	25	23	93	251	237

*Compiled from Panama Canal Company, Annual Reports, designated years, Table 14 (after 1960).

Table 7*

Panama Canal Net Measurement Tonnage of Transiting Vessels

	1973 Tonnage	Rank	1972 Tonnage	Rank	1971 Tonnage	Rank	1970 Tonnage	Rank	1969 Tonnage	Rank	1968 Tonnage	Rank
Combination Carriers	2,025,813	6	1,702,229	6	1,941,575	7	3,500,735	6	2,482,916	6	2,265,777	6
Containerships	12,601,689	4	4,937,351	5	2,603,853	5	1,138,985	7	417,633	7	405,402	7
Dry Bulk Carriers	43,821,173	1	39,999,681	1	35,525,654	2	33,432,885	2	28,875,211	2	23,287,079	2
General Cargo Ships	35,794,315	2	38,073,609	2	42,782,019	1	40,557,106	1	38,990,422	1	42,129,424	1
Passenger Vessels	2,007,179	7	1,803,194	7	2,516,733	6	3,594,546	5	3,184,075	5	3,209,852	5
Refrigerated Cargo Ships	9,294,930	5	8,159,453	4	7,833,473	4	8,037,091	4	7,245,321	4	6,295,436	4
Tank Ships	19,603,511	3	17,171,642	3	16,864,256	3	16,997,587	3	19,060,021	3	18,098,027	3

*Compiled from Panama Canal Company, Annual Reports, Table No. 14.

(Continued from page 57.)

substantial decline in liner traffic, along with reductions in overseas service by British, French, and other companies after 1969. There is little prospect of revival in this sphere. On the other hand, an elite grouping of luxury cruise ships flying the British, Dutch, German, Norwegian and other flags regularly pass through the Canal.

Specialized Shipping

A decline in general cargo transits has been observed since 1965. The older type of general cargo vessel has for some time been giving way to newer specialized shipping—containerships, auto carriers, refrigerated cargo vessels, and bulk carriers. By the 1980s the dry bulk carriers and containerships between them may be outstripping the transits by the general purpose cargo ships and transports. Much will depend upon what happens to demand and supply in certain bulk cargoes, such as coal, grain, and ores, and to industry attitudes toward the use of modular containers. A further factor will be the competition of the transcontinental railroads in the United States for high-priority container cargoes transported across the United States in special unitized trains geared to ship arrival and departure times on both coasts—the landbridge and mini-bridge operations.

Dry Bulk Carrier Traffic

Dry bulk cargoes—coal, grain, iron and copper ore, alumina/bauxite, scrap metal, lumber, phosphates, etc.—now comprise over 48 percent of the cargo tonnage passing through the Panama Canal. It is more efficient to carry most of these cargoes in specialized dry bulk carriers than it is in the old-fashioned general cargo shipping. Many of these cargoes are susceptible to wide changes in volume due to economic and political factors. Given world demands, they are likely to increase in quantity in the next decades, barring a major economic recession or war. Vessels built to transport ores to the United States from the West Coast of South America can as well be employed to carry coal from Hampton Roads to Japan, and grain from Gulf of Mexico ports to Asia on outward-bound journeys, thereby earning freights going in both directions through the Canal.

Tanker Traffic

Tanker transits are interesting for the leveling off that has occurred since 1960. This reflects the peaking of production and new discoveries in Venezuela and California, along with the opening of new oil fields abroad—as in Indonesia, Alaska, the Gulf of Mexico and notably in the Middle East—that do not feed Canal traffic. Although tanker traffic supplied 18 percent of the cargo tonnage through the Canal in 1973, it has shown no appreciable gain since 1965. The development of new fields in Ecuador, Peru and the Upper Amazon basin may add to traffic levels as crude oil from these locations moves to the large refineries in the Caribbean—Aruba, the Virgin Islands, and the Bahamas. For the near future, the outlook is for gradually declining traffic as the older fields become exhausted, barring exceptional new discoveries.

General Cargo Traffic

It will be observed from Table 6 that general cargo shipping has over the years supplied the backbone of Canal traffic so far as numbers of transits go. This still provides the main number of transits, although a noticeable decline in numbers of these ships calling at the Canal has set in since 1965, dropping by nearly one-half. This drop-off has been compensated for by corresponding sharp increases in the numbers of transits by bulk carriers (OBO ships), containerships, refrigerated cargo ships, and tankers, many of which are of larger size and carrying capacity.

The combination of general cargo shipping, bulk carriers, tankers, and containerships seems likely to handle the greater part of the cargo moving through the Canal for the next decade at least. Table 8 shows the tonnages of cargo and the percentages of each carried through the Canal in 1973.

Table 8

Cargo Movement by Tonnages and Percentages Carried

by Varying Classes of Shipping, 1973*

Type of Vessel	Cargo Tonnage Carried (long tons)	Percentage
Bulk Carriers	61,354,000	48.7
General Cargo Vessels	31,279,000	24.8
Tankers	23,372,000	18.5
Containerships	5,930,000	4.7
Refrigerated Cargo	3,251,000	2.6
Miscellaneous	918,000	0.7
Total	126,104,000	100.0

*Data supplied by Panama Canal Company.

Within the next decade increasing quantities of bulk cargoes, both liquid and dry, may be siphoned off through competition by supercarriers operating on all-ocean routes as deepwater terminals and landing facilities are made available in the United States and abroad where they do not now exist. This is not a foregone conclusion, however, for the world energy crisis could work to the advantage of shipping that can utilize the Panama Canal with the savings in ocean distances which this makes possible. There will be business for the general cargo vessels so long as there are small ports shipping and receiving freight, and limited quantities of goods to be carried from one country and port to another (see fig. 16).

Current Trends in Canal Traffic

Contemporary Slowing of Traffic Growth

Turning to the general profile of Canal traffic, it is noticeable that there has been a leveling of transits taking place since 1968. The number of transits has slowed to a zero growth position, as shown in Table 9. The question is whether this is a temporary situation or is likely to continue for some time.

Table 9

Panama Canal Ocean Transits, 1965-1974*

1965 - 12,203	1970 - 14,829
1966 - 12,601	1971 - 14,617
1967 - 13,385	1972 - 14,238
1968 - 14,807	1973 - 14,238
1969 - 14,602	19 74 - 14,304

*Prepared from Panama Canal Company, Annual Reports, Table 11.

Several factors have been contributing to this situation. These include an increasing size, tonnage, and specialization of vessels. Political and economic forces, such as fluctuations in monetary exchanges, shortages of fuels, and labor problems along the waterfront, have also played a part.

Increasing Size and Tonnage of Vessels Transiting Canal

The sizes of vessels appearing at the Canal for transit have been increasing with the years. The average size of oceangoing commercial vessels has risen from 5,910 Panama Canal net tons in 1964 to 9,100 tons in 1973. As shown in Table 10, shipping flying the flags of several maritime states has more than doubled in average gross registered tonnage since 1955. Others have increased by somewhat less. Among the principal user states the average tonnage of transiting vessels is now 10,517 registered gross tons. If the average tonnage of vessels flying the flags of the eight largest users are plotted on a graph, as in Figure 17, it will be seen that a generally similar pattern of growth has been taking

(Text continues on page 67.)

Fig. 16. The T.S.S. *Tokyo Bay* is shown here in the right hand chamber of Pedro Miguel Locks. Panama Canal Company

Table 10

Average Registered Gross Tonnage Transiting Vessels

of Principal User States*

Flag	1955	1960	1965	1970	1973
Belgium	3,104	8,271	6,144	6,211	7,657
Chile	7,239	8,218	7,846	9,271	14,148
China, Ntl. Rep. (Taiwan)	6,960	5,780	8,267	9,886	11,137
Colombia	3,093	3,698	4,264	7,204	5,415
Denmark	4,780	5,039	7,724	6,290	9,650
France	7,014	8,672	7,223	6,946	7,642
Germany, Fed. Rep.	3,314	4,209	4,618	5,965	10,410
Greece	6,760	8,740	9,673	11,645	11,017
Honduras	2,986	4,206	1,986	2,559	4,933
Italy	7,410	8,511	10,795	9,796	10,445
Japan	7,423	7,982	8,149	11,251	13,629
Liberia	6,470	7,919	11,067	14,369	14,541
Netherlands	7,247	7,160	5,751	8,460	8,109
Norway	5,774	8,023	9,751	8,469	14,926
Panama	5,447	5,269	5,659	6,671	7,527
Peru	4,166	4,711	5,242	7,184	9,360
Sweden	5,880	7,847	9,253	10,460	14,311
United Kingdom	7,822	8,741	9,660	10,792	13,569
United States	7,595	8,146	9,282	9,103	10,392

*Compiled from Panama Canal Company, Annual Reports, Table 17.

Table 11

Increasing Beams of Vessels Transiting Canal*

Fiscal Year	Vessels 80-Foot Beam and Over	Percent of Total Ocean Transits
1969	1,795	12.3
1970	1,877	12.7
1971	1,980	13.5
1972	2,428	17.0
1973	3,204	22.5

*Figures gathered from summary comments in Panama Canal Company, Annual Reports, Chapter 1. The average size of dry cargo vessels reported on order in world shipyards in 1973 was 8,980 gross tons compared to 8,028 tons in 1965, an increase of 10.6 percent. Fairplay International Shipping Journal, Vessels on Order.

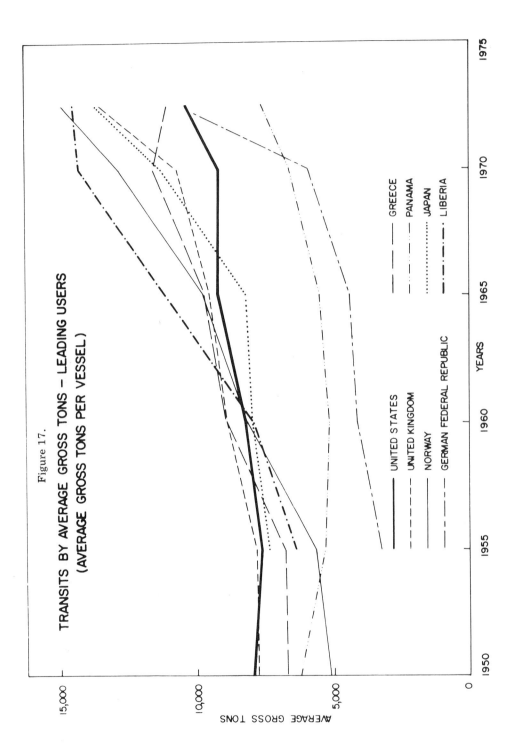

Figure 17.

TRANSITS BY AVERAGE GROSS TONS – LEADING USERS
(AVERAGE GROSS TONS PER VESSEL)

UNITED STATES
UNITED KINGDOM
NORWAY
GERMAN FEDERAL REPUBLIC

GREECE
PANAMA
JAPAN
LIBERIA

AVERAGE GROSS TONS

15,000

10,000

5,000

0

1950   1955   1960   1965   1970   1975

YEARS

(Continued from page 63.)

place since 1960, albeit with considerable variations between countries.

The growing size of shipping is also attested by the number of vessels having beams of 80-feet and over that are transiting the Canal, as noted in Table 11.

As vessels increase in size, they are of course able to carry more cargo, as well as to reduce the number of trips needed to carry given amounts of cargo in a year. It is notable that the cargo volume transported through the Canal has grown 17 percent since 1968, while the number of transits has remained virtually stationary. So long as the size of ships continues to grow in step with cargo growth, the number of transits a year can be expected to remain generally constant.

Government policy to expand exports and to enlarge overseas trade should produce further growth in traffic over the long run, but will require time to do this.

Growing Specialization of Vessels

Contributing to the leveling of transits is the improved efficiency in cargo-carrying of many of the new ships designed to handle specific commodities. Modern ships one-fourth larger in size can carry up to a third more cargo of a particular kind than the older general purpose cargo vessels. In 1963, 1.13 long tons of cargo transited the Canal for each net laden ton of ship cargo capacity. In 1973 this ratio had increased to 1.31 long tons of cargo for each net ton of capacity, indicating an improved efficiency in the use of ship cargo space.

While vessels have been becoming more specialized, and larger, total cargo has been rising at the same time. In 1969, 108.7 million long tons of cargo passed through the Canal in 14,602 transits. Cargo volume rose to 111.0 million long tons in 1972 with 14,238 transits. In 1973 the cargo load went up to 127.5 million long tons. This was carried in the same number of transits.

Twenty-two million more long tons of cargo were carried in 1973 than in 1968 in 600 fewer transits with no significant difference in the ratio of ballast to laden transits. This speaks to the improved use of space by more specialized shipping and helps explain the leveling off that has been occurring in Canal transits. The trend toward specialization is expected to continue.

Rise of Containership Traffic

The rise of containership traffic is a striking feature of contemporary oceanborne commerce. In 1973, 5.9 million long tons of container cargo went through the Canal in 702 containership transits. This was up from 2.5 million long tons in 355 containership transits in 1972, and a mere 256,788 tons in 1969 in 61 containership transits.[8]

Shipment by containerships insures safer arrivals of cargo. At the

Fig. 18. The T.S.S. *Universe Japan*, a gas turbine powered tanker is 326,560 deadweight tons and 1,133 feet long.
Gulf Oil Corporation

same time, modern containerships powered by gas turbines are able to transport cargo at nearly twice the speed of older cargo ships.

Although there has been a slackening of orders for new containerships since 1970, as seen in Table 12, this is thought to be temporary. Shipowners are being cautious lest capacity be overbuilt before trade shipments absorb the space available.

Table 12

Containerships Ordered*

Ships ordered in 1970:	205	with capacity of	241,116	20-ft boxes
" " " 1971:	95	" " "	66,741	" "
" " " 1972:	33	" " "	25,669	" "
" " " 1973:	42	" " "	39,716	" "

*World Ships on Order, quarterly.

Many ports do not yet have costly loading equipment, adequate storage space, and close-in transportation links needed to handle large quantities of containers efficiently. This will be corrected in time.

Trade reports suggest that upwards of 40 percent of general cargo is potentially containerizable.[9] Development of suitable port facilities requires both time and large investments of capital. As the facilities are expanded, added use of container shipments will follow and broken lot shipments will decline. With a rise in demand, increased calls will be made for additional containership service. The effect of this will be an inflow of orders for more bottoms. The outlook for continued and expanded containership business at the Canal is good for the coming decade.

Impact of Supercarriers on Canal Demand

Nearly 1,000 large bulk carriers, ranging from 100,000 to 500,000 deadweight tons each, have been constructed in world shipbuilding yards since 1967. These are designed to transport large quantities of liquid and dry bulk cargoes over long-distance ocean routes at low unit cost (fig. 18).

Many of the superships have been built to carry Middle Eastern, North African, and Nigerian oil to Europe, Japan, and North America, along with Indonesian oil to the West Coast of the United States and Japan. Other carriers have been constructed for carrying ores, coal, and grain. Depth limitations in ports, especially of the United States, are hampering use of these carriers for United States oceanborne commerce. When these limitations are removed, it is reasonable to expect that some of the big ships will enter into competition for the carriage of bulk cargoes now carried through the Canal in smaller craft.

According to testimony given by Governor David S. Parker to the House Subcommittee on Panama Canal, there are approximately 1,000 commercial vessels too large to transit the Panama Canal at this time. [10] Extrapolating from past trends, and considering the number of vessels now on order, [11] it is possible there may be as many as 1,850 commercial vessels too large to pass through the Canal by the year 1975. [12]

With the physical limitations of the lock chambers, the Canal can nominally accept vessels of no more than 975-foot length, 106.9-foot beam, 39.5-foot draft, and carrying no more than about 65,000 long tons of cargo.

The economies of scale which the superships can offer for low-unit-value bulk commodities, combined with automation, small crewing requirements, and lower transportation costs, will make employment of the very large carriers attractive to some businesses in place of the smaller ships that can go through the Canal. One of their virtues is that a single supership can do the hauling of several smaller carriers with as rapid turn-around time in port.

Only a sea-level waterway can handle vessels of 150,000 to 250,000 deadweight tons. If the interoceanic link is to be expanded to transit vessels of this size, this will require investing $3 to $5 billion or more, in addition to treaty payments

The cost for a sea-level canal may be no more than the outlays needed for constructing and manning two naval attack aircraft carriers of latest design. Nevertheless, the amounts involved will have to be weighed in comparison with other demands upon the public purse and the use that is likely to be made of the larger waterway. Circumstances may warrant an expenditure of the magnitude of $3-5 billion. The public will want assurances if this is called for that such a waterway will generate additional traffic to justify the expense. This may be difficult to establish far in advance.

Depending upon the size of the ships that might be employed, the quantities of liquid bulk cargoes to be transported at the time, and the storage capacities that may then be available at refineries and in ports, supertankers could theoretically transport through the Canal the 23 million long tons of oil that passed the Canal in 1973 in less than 100 transits in place of the 1,729 transits of 1973 while reaping economies of scale.

Similarly, the 58 million long tons bulk cargoes transported through the Canal in the same year in 3,059 transits could theoretically be carried in 230,000 dwt superships in only 250 transits. Although the tonnage of cargo passed would be as large, some persons might view the lower numbers of transits as hardly justifying construction of such an expensive new public work. The tonnage is the statistic of interest.

Despite the trend toward construction of very large bulk carriers, most ships in the world merchant marine today, and particularly those of the United States, are able to transit the existing interoceanic Canal.

Furthermore, the majority of new U.S.-flag ships being built under the Merchant Marine Act of 1970 will be able to transit the lock Canal. Dry cargo ships built to a configuration which will allow them to go through the Canal run around 80,000 tons, so far as American-flag ships go. It is the very large crude oil tankers, 200,000 tons and more, that will not be able to get through the present Canal or any future lock-type canal, as presently foreseen.[13]

We have looked for a relationship between expansion of the number of superships and potential Canal demand. Instead, there is a significant geographic and commodity relationship. The present physical constraints of terminals and port facilities, as well as tight supplies of fuel, point to restrictions on the use of the superships for some time to come in trades that compete with the Canal route.

The Cost of Transiting the Canal

In figuring whether it is economically advantageous to route a vessel through the Canal, toll charges are a factor that must be taken into consideration.

It is figured that under normal conditions, if the cost of operating a vessel is 20 cents per Panama Canal net ton a day, a variant with different size vessels, the cost of tolls on ships that are laden is approximately equivalent to four and one-half days' operation at sea. If a vessel can save this many days on its voyage, it is profitable to use the Canal rather than another route if one is available. A vessel in ballast can profit by using the Canal if it saves three and three-fifths days in reaching its destination. These estimates do not take into account all the commercial advantages of the time saved.

Conclusion

The Panama Canal has aided a large advance in overseas trade. By foreshortening distances on principal trade routes, it has been a factor in stimulating oceanborne commerce.

The growth of ship traffic and cargo movement in the past 60 years suggests that a further expansion of trade through the interoceanic waterway is conceivable. There are potentialities of further growth, as we shall suggest in the next chapter.[14]

With technology spurring new uses of materials and methods of production, and with worldwide demands for goods continuing to rise, opportunities exist for further growth of commerce. Whatever stimulates these trends will induce further growth of traffic at the Canal.

As we shall see in Chapter Five, there are finite limits to the physical capacity of the existing Canal in terms not only of the size of vessels that can be passed, but also in the number of vessels that can be transited in a given year.

CHAPTER THREE FOOTNOTES

1. For traffic figures, see Panama Canal Company, *Annual Reports*, Table 11.
2. Panama Canal Company, *Annual Report*, 1973, Table 13.
3. *Shipping and Canal Operations*, Hearing before the Subcommittee on Panama Canal of the Committee on Merchant Marine and Fisheries. House of Representatives, 93rd Congress, 1st Session, July 17, 1973, Ser. No. 93-19, pp. 4, 12. The statement takes account of traffic that is both going to and coming from the user states.

Percent of Selected Countries' Oceanborne Commerce

Passing Through Panama Canal

Australia	3.3%	El Salvador	66.4%	New Zealand	15.7%
Canada	6.8%	Ger. Fed. Rep.	2.9%	Nicaragua	76.8%
Chile	34.3%	Guatemala	30.9%	Panama	29.4%
Colombia	32.5%	Japan	10.7%	Peru	41.3%
Costa Rica	27.2%	Mexico	16.6%	United Kingdom	1.6%
Ecuador	51.4%	Netherlands	1.5%	United States	16.8%
				Venezuela	7.4%

4. Public Law 91-469. 91st Congress, 1st Session. 84 Stat 1018.
5. See U.S. Department of Commerce, *Annual Report of Maritime Administration*, 1972, p. iv.
6. See *Ship Transfers to Foreign Flag*. Hearings before Merchant Marine and Fisheries Subcommittee of Committee on Interstate and Foreign Commerce. United States Senate. 85th Congress, 1st Session, on S. 1488 (1957). See also C.J. Colombos, *The International Law of the Sea*. 4th ed., London, 1959; Boleslaw A. Boczek, *Flags of Convenience: An International Legal Study*. Cambridge: Harvard University Press, 1962, especially Chapters 1, 2, 7. Information on intent to register a vessel under a Panlibhon arrangement is often filed with the United States Maritime Administration by the owners of the vessel.
7. A total of 467 vessels held by foreign affiliates of United States incorporated companies were listed as being registered in 19 foreign countries on December 30, 1970. See Department of Commerce, Maritime Administration, *Foreign Flag Ships Owned by United States Parent Companies*. Washington, 1971, No. MAR-560-22.
8. Panama Canal Company, *Annual Reports*, Table 14.
9. "The Maritime Container Industry, 1972-1975." Published by Flexi-Van, Inc., New York. See *Maritime Reports and Engineering News*, May 1, 1973, p. 22.
10. The S.S. *VENPET*, built for the Gulf Oil Corporation's crude oil carrying fleet in 1973, 325,645 dwt tons, is, for example, 1,115 feet long, 175 feet wide, and draws 80 feet 9.5 inches when fully loaded. *The Orange Disk*, Sept.-Oct. 1973, p. 33.
11. 128.7 million dwt tons of tankers, combination carriers, and dry bulk carriers were on order for delivery in 1974. When completed, these will provide a 50 percent increase in the lifting capacity for ocean liquid and dry bulk trades. H.P. Drewry (Shipping Consultants), Ltd., *Shipping Statistics and Economics*, No. 15, January 1972, pp. 18, 26, 44.

12. Communication to author from Acting Chief, Executive Planning Staff, Panama Canal Company.

13. See testimony of Alfred Maskin, American Maritime Association, in Hearing before Subcommittee on Panama Canal of Committee on Merchant Marine and Fisheries, House of Representatives, 93rd Congress, 1st session. *Shipping and Canal Operations*, Serial No. 93-19. Washington, July 17, 1973, pp. 62-63.

14. See also Atlantic-Pacific Interoceanic Canal Study Commission, *Interoceanic Canal Studies, 1970*, Appendix IV, p. IV-55, and studies reported in this section on Interoceanic and Intercoastal Shipping.

Table 1

Cargo Movement On
Principal Panama Canal Trade Routes*
(thousands of long tons)

Current Rank No.	Route	1974	1973	1970	1965	1960	1950
1	E.C. United States - Asia	59,005	51,723	49,663	22,540	14,061	4,209
2	E.C. United States - W.C. South America	8,614	7,877	8,619	7,824	8,147	4,615
3	Europe - Asia	7,801	5,672	8,853	215	245	70
4	W.C. United States - Europe	6,413	6,397	4,899	3,293	3,590	1,021
5	Europe - W.C. Canada	5,225	3,866	4,117	3,589	3,140	1,705
6	Europe - W.C. South America	4,729	4,748	5,943	7,163	4,584	3,545
7	W.C. United States - E.C. South America	4,566	2,742	2,903	2,839	2,624	210
8	W.C. South America - E.C. South America	4,506	3,423	4,223	1,983	1,115	116
9	United States Inter-coastal	4,418	3,942	3,707	5,198	6,782	7,376
10	E.C. United States - W.C. Canada	4,046	2,760	1,882	1,220	747	634
11	Asia - E.C. South America	3,982	2,154	1,950	1,849	549	12
12	E.C. United States - Oceania	3,536	2,943	2,222	2,435	1,057	780
13	Europe - Oceania	3,364	3,226	2,817	2,379	2,082	1,718
14	Caribbean (West Indies)- Asia	3,019	2,882	2,859	1,586	696	85
15	West Indies - W.C. United States	2,766	2,521	2,825	1,910	797	349
16	Asia - E.C. Canada	2,436	2,154	1,680	739	317	28
17	W.C. Central America - E.C. United States	2,181	1,962	1,347	945	549	437
18	E.C. South America - W.C. Central America	1,840	2,225	1,347	1,006	283	--
19	West Indies - W.C. Central America	872	1,257	1,377	303	436	118

*Panama Canal Company, Annual Report, respective years.

74

CARGO AND TRAFFIC TRENDS

Introduction

The cargo transiting the Panama Canal is a cross section of the raw materials, semi-finished products, and manufactures of the modern industrial age. Cargo comes from many points of origin, and is en route to widely scattered destinations. It interlaces the relations of both large and small states, advanced and developing countries.

Among the economies served by the Canal, United States commerce benefits extensively. The United States has much to gain, and to lose, from whatever affects this movement.

General Characteristics of Canal Cargo Movement

Worldwide Nature of Canal Traffic

The trade that passes through the Panama Canal is no localized traffic. Vessels of as many as 60 countries have passed through the Canal in a single year.[1] In a given year cargo has either originated in or been destined to as many as 63 different countries.[2]

Importance of Canal to Commerce of Nations

Among the trade routes passing through the Canal, 19 bore more than a million tons of cargo each in 1973, counting traffic moving in both directions. These are listed in Table 1, with corresponding tonnages for four previous years.

Goods exported from the United States, and destined to it, comprise a large part of the trade moving on 9 of the 19 principal trade routes. The importance of the Canal to this commerce lies in the fact that it otherwise would have to take longer or more expensive routes to reach its destinations.

As a percentage of a nation's overseas trade, Canal cargo composes widely varying proportions. Thus, 41 percent of Peru's overseas commerce passed through the Canal going one way or the other in 1973, while 29 percent of Panama's foreign trade moved through the Canal in the same year. For the United States, 17 percent of its overseas trade passed through the Canal notwithstanding the fact that cargo moving to or from the United States through the Canal amounted to 81,827,603 long tons out of a total commercial cargo movement at the Canal of 118,627,000 long tons in fiscal year 1971.[3] Two points of view emerge on the importance of the Canal to oceanborne commerce. One is the relative size of what goes through the waterway en route to and from a particular country as a percentage of its overall trade with other countries. The second is the gross volume of the cargo going to and coming from individual countries as a portion of the total tonnage that passes through the Canal in a given year.

Countries, such as the United States, Japan, Britain, and Germany, with large national incomes and widely spread foreign trades derive no less benefit from Canal cargo movement than do small countries that have a high percentage of their exports and imports passing through the Canal. Peru and Panama, to mention two instances, would be deprived of material advantages if the Canal were not in existence. Their trades, on the other hand, are a small part of international commerce taken as a whole. The existence of the Canal enables the larger industrialized nations to ship the products of their industries throughout the world, and to engage in trading relationships with a great many countries drawing raw materials, consumer goods, foodstuffs, and machinery into the stream of the world's economy where this otherwise would take place on a much smaller scale.

Through the lower transportation costs made possible by the shorter trade routes of the interoceanic Canal, the latter works to the economic advantage of nations and peoples everywhere. As the overall volume of cargo movement expands, many nations are benefited by the shortcut.

Table 2 shows the distribution, by volume and percentage, of cargo originating in countries of the Atlantic area, amounting to one percent or more of the total, with the principal destination lands on the Pacific. The largest volume of exports have for years originated from the East and Gulf Coasts of the United States, Venezuela, the East Coast of Canada, the Netherlands Antilles (petroleum products), and Cuba (sugar). The largest receivers are normally Japan, the West Coast of the United States, Chile, and Peru.

Table 3 presents comparable data for cargoes originating in the Pacific bound for the Atlantic, with the principal receiving countries shown. In this case, ten lands led by Japan, Ecuador, the West Coast of the United States, the West Coast of Canada, and Peru exported over one million long tons of cargo each in 1973, compared to six countries shipping similar amounts from the Atlantic. It will also be noted that there were 12 countries in the Pacific receiving more than one million tons of cargo each, as well as 12 in the Atlantic.

A remarkable feature of Canal trade is the prominent position of the United States—East and West Coasts—both as shipper and receiver. It is in the first or second position in most instances.

A second feature of note is the decided preponderance of cargo moving from the Atlantic to the Pacific. This has not always been the case. Prior to World War II, the preponderant tonnage moved from the Pacific to the Atlantic with heavy shipments of oil and lumber leading the way. In future decades, products from lands adjoining the Pacific may again become ascendant as the economies of these countries grow.

Predominance of U.S.-Asian Trade

As seen in Table 1, the East Coast United States-Asia trade route carried 40 percent of all commercial cargo moved through the Canal in 1973. The next largest route, East Coast United States-West Coast South America, carried 6 percent of the total cargo tonnage. Space does not permit a detailed examination of all trade routes listed in Table 1, but the preeminent position of the East Coast United States-Asia route merits further attention.

This route has been the leader in terms of cargo tonnage since 1955. Tonnage has multiplied six times during the period to reach a record

Table 2

Leading Countries of Origin and Destination of
Commercial Canal Cargo Fiscal Year 1973*
(one percent or more)
ATLANTIC TO PACIFIC

Countries Originating Cargo	Tonnage	% Total	Countries of Destination	Tonnage	% Total
E. Coast U.S.	48,398,420	66.0	Japan	36,699,315	50.0
Venezuela	6,776,920	9.2	W. Coast U.S.	8,911,781	12.1
E. Coast Canada	2,105,939	2.9	Chile	2,515,574	3.4
Neth. Antilles	1,942,110	2.6	Peru	2,209,576	3.0
Cuba	1,769,551	2.5	South Korea	2,168,564	3.0
Belgium	1,021,736	1.4	China	2,048,734	2.8
Jamaica	948,105	1.3	Taiwan	1,712,104	2.3
Mexico	946,715	1.3	Mexico	1,660,133	2.3
West Germany	832,270	1.1	W. Coast Canada	1,376,679	1.9
Netherlands	826,751	1.1	Ecuador	1,347,183	1.8
United Kingdom	796,651	1.1	Australia	1,068,110	1.5
Panama	752,579	1.0	El Salvador	1,013,081	1.4
			South Vietnam	944,839	1.3
			Colombia	824,940	1.1
			USSR	814,622	1.1
			Nicaragua	776,856	1.1

Summary by Regions

Cargo Originating From	Tonnage	% Total	Cargo Destined To	Tonnage	% Total
E. Coast U.S.	48,398,420	66.0	Asia	47,462,050	64.7
E. Coast So. Am.	7,985,491	10.9	W. Coast U.S.	8,911,781	12.1
Europe	6,539,160	8.9	W. Coast So. Am.	7,147,642	9.7
West Indies	6,022,042	8.2	W. Coast Cent. Am.	6,059,969	8.3
E. Coast Canada	2,105,939	2.9	Oceania	2,436,373	3.3
E. Coast Cent. Am.	1,756,845	2.4	W. Coast Canada	1,376,679	1.9
Africa	544,439	0.7			
Middle East	32,158	–			
Total	73,394,494	100.0		73,394,494	100.0

*Panama Canal Company, Annual Report, 1973, Table 19.

of 59 million long tons in 1974. It is expected to reach further highs in the years to come.

The greater part of the cargo moving on this route has gone to and come from Japan. Coal and coke shipments to Japan alone amounted to nearly 21 million tons in 1971. Due to the opening of alternate supplies in Australia and Canada, and declining orders for steel within Japan, the shipments were down to 13 million long tons in 1973.

Many commodity groupings are represented in the trade on this route. Four-fifths of the total is made up, nevertheless, of bulk commodities including coal, grain, phosphates, and scrap iron. Manufactures of iron and steel, automobiles, electrical goods, canned and frozen foods, and a wide assortment of miscellaneous items are shipped from Japan to the United States. The U.S.-Asia trade as a whole amounted to

Table 3

Leading Countries of Origin and Destination of
Commercial Canal Cargo Fiscal Year 1973*
(one percent or more)
PACIFIC TO ATLANTIC

Countries Originating Cargo	Tonnage	% Total	Countries of Destination	Tonnage	% Total
Japan	12,144,003	23.0	E. Coast U.S.	22,808,656	43.4
W. Coast U.S.	6,944,438	13.2	West Germany	3,236,415	6.1
Ecuador	6,459,124	12.2	United Kingdom	3,200,563	6.1
W. Coast Canada	6,213,087	11.8	Netherlands	2,927,282	5.6
Peru	4,211,222	8.0	Belgium	2,410,123	4.6
Australia	2,785,874	5.3	Trinidad/Tobago	1,923,396	3.6
Colombia	2,208,614	4.2	Italy	1,394,289	2.6
Philippines	2,108,831	4.0	Colombia	1,343,877	2.6
Chile	1,671,608	3.2	Netherlands W. Indies	1,176,961	2.2
New Zealand	1,212,758	2.3	Panama	1,169,472	2.2
South Korea	929,061	1.8	E. Coast Canada	1,130,979	2.1
Taiwan	800,564	1.5	France	1,102,844	2.1
			Puerto Rico	928,071	1.8
			Venezuela	903,719	1.7
			Cuba	756,870	1.4
			Spain and Portugal	713,760	1.4
			Brazil	558,421	1.1
			Greece	518,703	1.0

Summary by Regions

Cargo Originating From	Tonnage	% Total	Cargo Destined To	Tonnage	% Total
Asia	18,116,402	34.4	E. Coast U.S.	22,808,656	43.4
W. Coast So. Am.	14,671,023	27.8	Europe	18,619,891	35.3
W. Coast U.S.	6,944,438	13.2	West Indies	5,170,784	9.8
W. Coast Canada	6,213,087	11.8	E. Coast So. Am.	2,929,790	5.6
Oceania	4,734,940	9.0	E. Coast Cent. Am.	1,537,872	2.9
W. Coast Cent. Am.	2,029,645	3.8	E. Coast Canada	1,130,979	2.1
			Africa	393,102	0.7
			Asia (Middle East)	118,461	0.2
Total	52,709,535	100.0		52,709,535	100.0

*Panama Canal Company, Annual Report, 1973, Table 20.

over 40 percent of the entire cargo movement at the Canal in 1971, 1972, and 1973.

The growth and composition of the East Coast U.S.-Asia trade is shown in Figure 19.

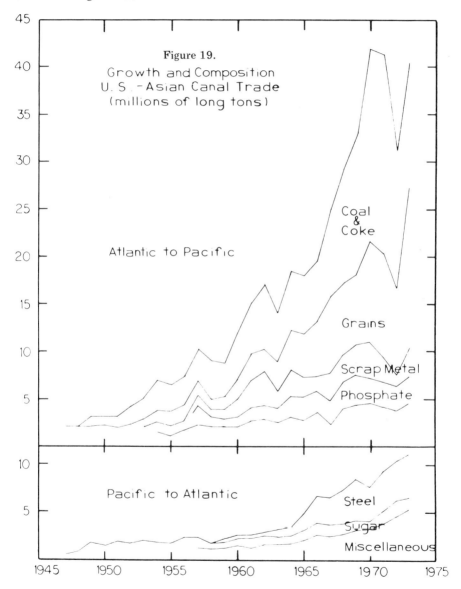

Figure 19.
Growth and Composition
U. S. - Asian Canal Trade
(millions of long tons)

There are elements associated with this trade that make its future uncertain. Orders for vessels built in Japanese shipyards have played a large part in the movement of coal and scrap iron from the United

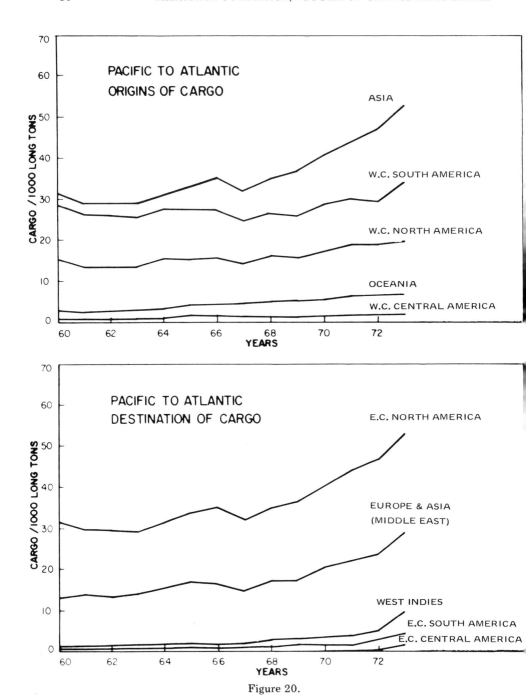

Figure 20.

States. With a glut in world shipping tonnage now, a curtailment of orders for coal and scrap may occur. Other factors may enter the picture, such as increases in Australian supplies of coal, exports of Siberian coal, and the construction of deepwater terminals in or near Chesapeake Bay allowing superships to carry coal to Japan by all-ocean routes around the Cape of Good Hope. Increasing demands for energy in the United States will call for greater use of coal in this country. For the near future, however, coal shipments through the Canal will probably continue within the range of 10-18 million long tons a year.

Other cargoes may eventually supersede the large coal movement. In 1973 grain shipments to Asia, for example, amounted to over 17 million tons. Under agreements concluded by the Nixon administration with China and the Soviet Union, large grain shipments will be made to these countries. Part of this will transit the Canal. Phosphates and chemicals shipments may also increase to the Asian lands. The markets of China, Taiwan, Indonesia, and the Philippines each have potentials for growth that will supply additional opportunities for U.S. trade in the coming decades.

Roles of Different Areas as Origins and Destinations of Cargo

Figures 20 and 21 illustrate the roles various areas of the world have played in generating Canal cargo movement. The top half of Figure 20 shows how much of that Panama Canal cargo moving eastward originated in various geographical areas. The West Coast of Central America, Oceania, the West Coast of North America, and the West Coast of South America have increased their exports through the Canal only slightly over a 23-year period. Asia, on the other hand, has become the predominant exporter and most of the increase in eastward moving trade has originated in Asian countries.

The bottom half of Figure 20 shows that North America and Europe have been the primary recipients of Panama Canal eastbound cargo for the base period, but the West Indies, South America, and Central America are now developing economies capable of absorbing a healthy growth in imported goods. Most of these imports are petroleum and petroleum products from the West Coast of South America.

The top half of Figure 21 shows the volume of Canal cargo imported by various areas bordering the Pacific Basin. The general level of westbound cargo is larger than eastbound, and again Asia stands out. Most of these imports are bulk commodities and they move largely to Japan. The dip in the fiscal year 1972 total is due to a recession in Japan which sharply curtailed imports of bulk commodities from the East Coast of the United States.

The bottom half of Figure 21 shows where the Pacific-bound Canal cargo originated. It is no coincidence that the East Coast North America cargo figure matches that of Asia's as a destination. This match

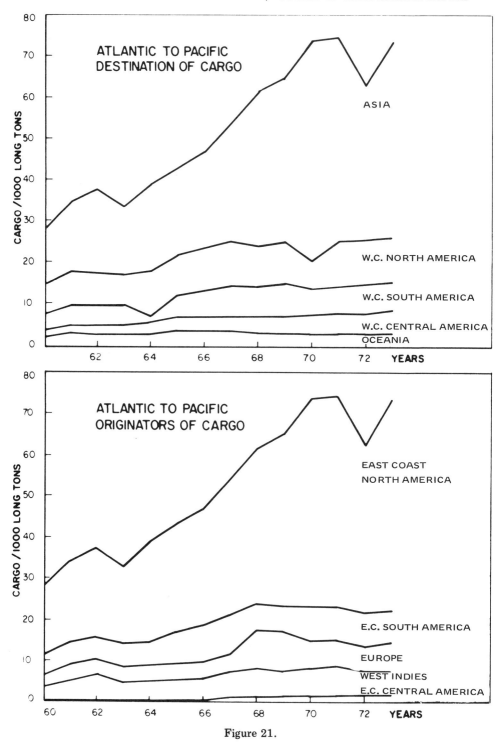

Figure 21.

reflects the dominance of the East Coast United States-Asia trade route and illustrates that United States and Japan trade through the Canal has been closely tied for a number of years. The worldwide scramble for oil and other raw materials is likely to cause an alteration in this pattern in the future as Asia and the United States look for new sources of materials and new markets for their goods. The overall level of Canal cargo movement will be affected by the strength of national economies. Assuming these do not falter, traffic levels should remain high.

Growth Patterns of Cargo Movement

Cargo movement is a sensitive index of commodities in demand. It is also an index of the health of the world economy.

The overall trend of Canal cargo movement was shown in Figure 13. The persistent growth of cargo since 1945 has been particularly notable. Periods of low growth have occurred, as well as some intervals of decline, but these have been temporary. The general trend has been one of strong growth. The 127 million long tons attained in 1973 is a large vault ahead from the 27 million tons that passed in 1945.

Much of the commerce that has moved through the Canal would probably have made its way between the principal trading countries without the Canal. But the existence of the shortcut has facilitated the interchange by providing faster, more economical movement.

The Period 1963-1973

Cargo movement more than doubled between 1963 and 1973, rising from 63.0 million to 127 million long tons. The closure of the Suez Canal, economic prosperity and growth in major countries, heavy demands for coal, scrap iron, and grain in Japan, along with a heavy movement of goods to South and Southeast Asia, contributed to this.

Large shipments of petroleum products from Venezuela and the Netherlands Antilles to Pacific ports, iron ore from Chile to Europe and the United States, coal to Japan, and grain from Gulf Coast ports to Asia contributed to the doubling of Canal cargo, and make up a large proportion of the movement. On the reverse side, there is a substantial flow of manufactures of iron and steel from Japan to the United States and Western Europe.

Table 1 of Chapter Three lists the growth of Canal cargo. The movement of 26 commodities accounted for one million tons or more in 1973, as listed in Table 4.

The total shipments of coal and coke have outrun other trades in recent years, although crude oil and manufactures of iron and steel and grain are catching up.

Most of the large-volume cargoes are raw materials, agricultural items, petroleum products, and semi-manufactures. Manufactured goods, like automobiles and trucks, machinery, electrical apparatus, etc., afford less overall tonnage.

Many of the cargoes moving from the Atlantic to the Pacific are the products of industry, of intensive agriculture, or stem from applications of advanced technology. The flow of many of these items to countries bordering the Pacific is a reflection of the needs and demands of societies located there.

Some economists are suggesting that the Pacific region will become the global center of world trade by the year 2000, as the Atlantic has been in the past. With the industrial growth of Australia, Japan, China, Taiwan, and Indonesia, along with the further development of the West Coast countries of Latin America, the potential exists for large interchanges of goods with other parts of the world in the decades ahead.

Table 4

Principal Items of Canal Cargo*
(thousands of long tons)

Atlantic to Pacific	1974	1973	Pacific to Atlantic	1974	1973
Coal and coke	18,233	13,645	Lumber products	5,586	5,392
Crude oil	6,120	4,548	Mfrs. iron & steel	6,737	7,867
Phosphates	5,195	4,581	Iron ore	2,346	2,100
Corn	10,920	8,436	Sugar	3,229	3,347
Soybeans	4,349	4,498	Crude oil	10,727	7,046
Fuel oil (rsdl)	6,429	2,946	Pulpwood	1,716	1,151
Scrap metal	3,457	3,234	Petroleum coke	1,695	1,897
Sugar, raw	1,861	1,749	Bananas	1,487	1,304
Sorghum	2,872	2,563	Refrig. foods	1,693	1,599
Gasoline	1,367	1,650	Automobiles,	946	1,030
Wheat	4,418	2,785	trucks & access.		
Fertilizers, various	1,349	1,096	Various ores	1,480	1,781
Alumina-bauxite	1,054	1,567			
Mfrs. iron & steel	2,052	1,768			
Chemicals, petroleum	2,679	1,248			

*Panama Canal Company, Annual Report, 1973, Table 25.

Although the tonnages of manufactured goods proceeding from Asian ports to the East Coast of the United States, Canada, South America, and Europe are relatively modest, being in the neighborhood of 9 million long tons a year, they have been increasing steadily.[4]

Cargo Outlook

Coal, petroleum products, grain, lumber and products, ores, phosphates, sugar, and manufactures of iron and steel have been the leading commodities in Canal cargo movement during the past decade, varying in position from one time to another.

In the next decade, coal, coke, and iron ore will probably be supplanted as leading cargo items at the Canal. Japan will be obtaining supplies of coal from sources nearer to her shores. Steel mills near the East Coast of the United States will be drawing rising quantities of iron ore from Venezuela and West Africa.

Crude oil from the North Slope of Alaska, from Indonesia, and from East and West Coast United States oil fields, both on- and offshore, seems likely within a few years to be supplanting quantities of petroleum products that now pass through the Canal en route to the West Coast of North America. Venezuelan- and Aruban-refined oil will continue to move through the Canal, but probably in decreasing quantities as reserves are brought into production in the Pacific area.

Shipments of grain, phosphates, manufactures of iron and steel, raw sugar, tropical fruits, coffee, alumina/bauxite, wool, refrigerated foods, and general cargoes are expected to increase with the passage of time. Shipments of lumber and forest products should remain more or less constant, given world demand, the development of substitutes, and the fact that there are few stands of virgin timber remaining to be cut.

The outlook for Canal trade is for growth in the general cargoes and for large-scale expansion of miscellaneous manufactures shipped in containers. These are not expected to produce sudden, dramatic increases in Canal traffic, as the coal trade did between 1966-71. They will rather contribute to an upward expansion stretched over many years as economic growth and industrialization proceed in many parts of the world.

Projections of Present Trends

In considering the future of the interoceanic canal, it is important to obtain an estimate of the probable measure of cargo tonnage that will be transiting the Canal in the remainder of the century. Although the number of lockages is the measure of Canal capacity, the volume of cargo seeking passage is the primary basis upon which transits occur.

International trade, and the cargo it generates, is an expression of the condition of the world's economy. Relating historical variations in the economic base to Canal cargo movement and assuming that the relationship will continue over time, it is possible to forecast future magnitudes of Canal cargo.

By surveying what has happened over the past 25 years, indications can be gained of what is possible in coming years.

Estimate of Future Traffic Pattern

In estimating possible future traffic, we have made four assumptions. These are that (1) the present locks will be retained at least until the year 2000; (2) tolls will not be increased at a rate faster than the world rate of inflation; (3) international economic and monetary conditions will be generally stable; and (4) no great power war will occur.[5] Changes in these assumptions, as in the development of large new trades, or the disappearance of existing ones, could alter the basis of the estimate, leading to different results.

Analysis Based on World Economic Growth

The following analysis is based upon three additional assumptions: (1) that Gross World Product (GWP), which is the sum of all known gross national products, is an appropriate measure of world economic well-being; (2) that GWP will continue to grow at a percentage growth rate closely approximating the historical trend from 1950 to 1967; and (3) that the historical relationship between total Canal cargo and GWP will not change appreciably in the next two or three decades.

Table 5
Gross World Product Data

Year	1967 U.S. Dollars in Billions	Total Canal Cargo (long tons)
1950	$ 828.7	30,364,982
1951	885.8	31,281,525
1952	961.1	36,902,908
1953	958.5	41,203,401
1954	977.6	41,882,368
1955	1,043.3	41,548,037
1956	1,079.4	46,331,901
1957	1,113.9	50,659,057
1958	1,124.4	48,982,036
1959	1,186.9	52,328,987
1960	1,244.3	60,401,733
1961	1,293.9	65,216,581
1962	1,364.9	69,003,475
1963	1,425.3	63,877,200
1964	1,519.6	72,168,690
1965	1,586.8	78,922,931
1966	1,682.4	85,323,463
1967	1,743.6	92,997,958

The third assumption is critical to the analysis. This assumption rests on the premise that trade carried on in a rational manner permits parties to achieve a higher national income and thus a higher gross national product. A rise in trade should result in a rise in GWP. Some portion of this trade will transit the Panama Canal.

It is possible for an individual country's GNP to rise without a corresponding increase in oceanborne trade. However, in the aggregate these should remain closely related. As production increases, business looks for profitable markets generally. Since the Panama Canal is a focal point for trade in the western world, its traffic levels reflect levels of production and vice versa. For purposes of analysis, we shall assume that the relationship between GWP and Panama Canal cargo movement will be generally consistent with what has prevailed in the past. The fact that GWP and Panama Canal cargo have grown almost precisely in step for the past 17 years partially verifies this assumption.

GWP data for this analysis is taken from the compilation given in the Interoceanic Canal Study Commission Report of 1970 and from a number of other sources.[6] This data is summarized in Table 5.

The average percentage growth rate of GWP from 1950-67 was determined by a Least Squares Curve Fitting computer program. This rate was calculated to be 4.33 percent a year, with a correlation coefficient of 0.99 out of a possible 1.00, indicating that the growth rate of GWP has differed little year to year from its overall average. This supports the premise that 4.33 is a reliable base figure. The actual 1971 GWP was only 4 percent higher than our calculations forecast for that year.[7]

Assuming that no major political crises disturb economic growth in the next thirty years, this program forecasts GWP to be approximately $6.9 trillion in 1967 U.S. dollars by the year 2000.

GWP and Canal Cargo Prediction

A linear least-squares analysis of GWP versus total cargo data produced a straight line approximation with a correlation coefficient of .98. Given a $6.9 trillion GWP forecast, theoretically there should be a cargo movement of approximately 426.4 million long tons passing through the Canal by the year 2000.

This figure represents a projection of present trends, but is only a guideline for thinking. The question associated with extrapolating past growth is to determine to what extent changes in trends will cause actual cargo movements to deviate from the guideline.

Four Additional Approaches

In an effort to gauge the effect of different assumptions on projections of movement, four other analyses were performed. In these, emphasis was placed upon gross national product as a measure of capacity for trade.

The historical role of a small number of principal trading nations, representing a large percentage of Panama Canal traffic, was analyzed in a manner similar to the first case as a means of giving an estimate of future traffic.

The second effort was divided into two parts, and each of these in turn contained two analyses again. Four analyses thus resulted.

The assumptions that have been alternately employed are as follows:

(a) Countries responsible for more than 700,000 long tons of cargo each in 1969 merit particular attention. This index results in a selection of 17 countries for analysis.

(b) Countries responsible for more than 1,000,000 long tons of cargo each in 1969 likewise merit special attention. Employing this screen produces a group of 12 countries.

In each case, "responsible for" was interpreted to mean Panama Canal cargo moving in one direction only, either originating from or else bound to the ports of the selected countries.

For purposes of brevity, only one of the four analyses which resulted from these assumptions will be presented here.[8] The GWP analysis presented earlier resulted in a cargo forecast falling below those of the other four analyses and was retained as a lower bound. The highest forecast of the remaining four analyses will be presented here to illustrate the method and represents an upper bound on forecasted Panama Canal cargo.

Estimate Based on Trade of Principal Cargo-Receiving Nations

Twelve nations each had over one million long tons of Panama Canal cargo destined for their ports in 1969. These were:

Australia	Peru
Canada	United Kingdom
Chile	United States
Ecuador	German Federal Republic
Japan	South Korea
Netherlands	Italy

Cargo data is given in Note 9.[9] Total GNP for these 12 nations is given in Note 10.[10]

Computer analysis shows that the total GNP for these countries has been growing at approximately 4.3 percent a year since 1950, with a correlation coefficient of 0.99. If this growth rate continues, the total GNP of these nations will be approximately $4.6 trillion in 1964 U.S. dollars by the year 2000.

Using a second least-squares analysis on total GNP versus cargo transiting the Canal, it was found that as the 12-nation GNP total rose cargo did also in direct proportion. A $4.6 trillion GNP would therefore infer that in the year 2000 the 12-nation related cargo transiting the Canal should be on the order of approximately 387.2 million long tons.

The value of Canal cargo set out above does not represent the total cargo expected to pass through the Canal in the year 2000, but only that contributed to the total potential cargo by the 12 nations.

Probable Future Relationship of Receiving Cargo to Total Cargo

Some assumption must be made for the remaining volume of traffic. The percentage of total commercial cargo contributed by these 12 nations as destination has been fairly constant with time, averaging 82 percent. Note 9 gives the yearly percentages.

Overall, the 12-nation related cargo may come to represent a slowly declining percentage of the total Canal cargo movement as the economies of other countries contribute more to world trade. Taken altogether, nevertheless, the percentage represented by the base group should remain above 75 percent of the total cargo movement at the Canal for the remainder of the century.

An estimate of total commercial cargo, using the 75 percent valuation for the part contributed by the 12 nations, gives a figure of approximately 515 million long tons of commercial cargo that might transit the Canal by the year 2000. The noncommercial component may be on the order of possibly 15 million tons, which is a generous estimate, giving a grand total of about 530 million long tons.

Summary of Estimated Cargo Traffic

For the preceding analyses, five different assumptions led to five estimates, two of which were presented here, of possible future cargo movement through the Canal by the year 2000. The estimates given for total cargo appear in Table 6.

These estimates can be compared with those arrived at in the Report of the Interoceanic Canal Study Commission. This predicted a total of 485 million long tons of cargo for the year 2000.[11] The Commission figure grew out of the assumption that historical trends would be continued and represented an upper limit. The Commission in the end concluded that actual cargo gains would probably fall lower than this to a value of approximately 357 million long tons due to an expected reduced rate of growth of traffic to and from Japan.[12]

Given the uncertainties built into an extrapolation of past trends, the forecasts contained in Table 6 are not significantly different from other results.

The computations suggest, in short, that cargo movement on the order of something as high as 400 to 500 million long tons is conceivable by the year 2000 if trends continue.

Adjustment for Foreseeable Changes in Trends

The recent dramatic increase in the cost of energy introduces a new factor into the forecasts. Lack of petroleum, reflected in higher prices, is expected to cause an economic slowdown in Japan, Europe, and the United States in the next few years. Shipments of heavy bulk commodities may be affected if shipping has difficulty in obtaining fuel oil.[13]

Table 6

Initial Cargo Projections

Method	Gross Prod. (tril. $US)	R^2_{GNP}	Cargo (mil. tons)	R^2_{CARGO}	% of Commercial Cargo	Total Cargo (mil. long tons)
World Aggregate	6.909 (1967)	.992	426.4	.978	100	426.4
17-Nation Originators	4.435 (1964)	.994	390.5	.989	80	503.0
17-Nation Receivers	5.369 (1964)	.995	372.0	.991	80	480.0
12-Nation Originators	3.549 (1964)	.990	351.1	.987	75	480.0
12-Nation Receivers	4.615 (1964)	.995	387.2	.990	75	530.0

Petroleum shortages can affect both world productivity and transportation modes for international trade. Such an energy shortage did not exist in the 1950-69 base period of this study; hence, some account must be taken of it.

The long-run impact of the Arab oil price increases upon production and commerce is difficult to assess in advance of publication of Gross National or World Product figures assembled subsequent to the arrival of dramatic energy cost increases. President Nixon asserted in 1973 that the United States would be self-sufficient in energy by 1980. Others have expressed doubt that this can be accomplished.[14] Meanwhile, shortages of raw materials resulting from heavy past exploitation, together with transportation difficulties, may curtail industrial production within the century. Predictions in this area often lack precision, but it seems possible that national growth rates in the more industrialized economies may drop to an average of 1.5 to 2.0 percent a year in place of 4 to 6 percent, and that world productivity will not continue to grow as rapidly in the future as it has since 1950. To the extent that this happens, it will affect maritime commerce.

In order to estimate what this may do to Panama Canal cargo, an assumption will be made that the growth in Gross World Product will be reduced to an annual rate of 2.5 percent until 1985, down from the approximate growth rate of 4.3 percent from 1950 to 1967, and then rise to 3.3 percent for the following 15 years. This yields a GWP of $4.9 trillion in 1967 dollars for the year 2000.

Assuming that a linear relation between GWP and Canal cargo movement continues to hold, such a GWP would forecast a level of 296 million long tons of potential cargo in 2000, or down 31 percent from the unadjusted level.

Assuming a similar 31 percent reduction for the forecasts for the 17- and 12-nation analysis results in estimates of the following orders of magnitude for Canal cargo movement:

Gross World Product Analysis	300 million long tons
17-Nation Originating Group	350 million long tons
17-Nation Destination Group	330 million long tons
12-Nation Originating Group	330 million long tons
12-Nation Destination Group	370 million long tons

The percentage growth rates of the Gross Product analysis are a subjective estimate. They will need to be corrected when more definitive studies become available on world economic growth.[15]

Shortages in energy, if widely extended, are bound to force curtailment of transportation on both land and sea, as they did in the United States and Europe in 1973-74. Transportation can be interpreted as part of the overall production process in that, to a certain extent, the estimated reduction of production growth includes a reduction in trans-

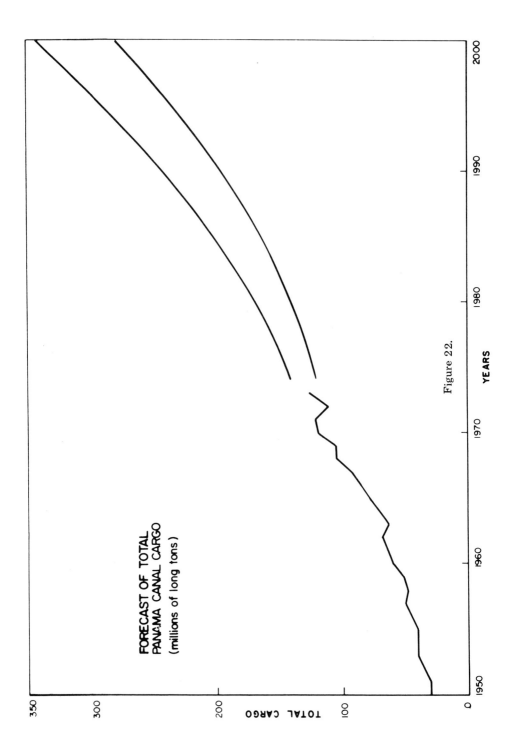

FORECAST OF TOTAL
PANAMA CANAL CARGO
(millions of long tons)

Figure 22.

portation. However, while a slowing in the production and consumption of such manufactured items as automobiles will reduce the quantity of such goods passing through the Canal, a reduction in the availability of ship's fuel, resulting in higher transportation costs or reduction of transport services, will have a more direct impact. The assumption that Gross Production and Panama Canal traffic will vary in direct proportion in the future as it has in the past is unwarranted in light of the direct impact fuel cost increases have on shipping services. The use of nuclear ship power plants, more efficient designs, higher load factors, and better scheduling may tend, alternatively, to reduce the long-run impact of costly, uncertain energy supplies on shipping services.

New technologies cannot be foreseen and should not be counted upon to reduce transport costs significantly. Barring the development of nuclear fusion technology and large new oil discoveries, energy supplies will become progressively scarcer and more expensive than previously. This will offset the long-run cost advantages of some of the new technologies.

As the assumption for future Gross Product growth was a subjective estimate, so also must be the assumption for the future relation of actual Panama Canal cargo to Gross Product levels. Based on the close relationship that has existed in recent peace-time between Panama Canal cargo and national economic growth and the increase in transportation costs, we believe that cargo will continue to grow in step with world productivity, but at a proportionally slower rate than previously. [16]

Assuming that the effect of energy and raw materials scarcity reduces the growth rate relation of cargo to GWP by 5 percent, a GWP of 4.9 trillion dollars in 2000 would then imply that total Canal cargo would be of the order of 280 million long tons that year. Similar 5 percent reductions in the growth rates arising for the four other analyses yield comparable estimates:

Gross World Product Analysis	280 million long tons
17-Nation Originating Group Analysis	325 million long tons
17-Nation Destination Group Analysis	310 million long tons
12-Nation Originating Group Analysis	310 million long tons
12-Nation Destination Group Analysis	345 million long tons

Figure 22 plots the maximum and minimum orders of magnitude forecasts of cargo growth that follow from the preceding analysis. Table 7 lists the maximum and minimum tonnage forecasts in five-year increments.

Other Cargo Forecasts

Two other attempts have been made to estimate future Panama Canal cargo movements. The Interoceanic Canal Study Commission estimate of 357 million long tons for the year 2000, mentioned previously, assumed that some of this cargo would be attracted away from the Canal by other competing modes of transport such as mini-bridge transport and all-ocean carriage in superships around South America and Africa. An Economic Research Associates (ERA) study, based on a detailed examination of economic market factors for 27 commodity classes, applies only up to 1985. Table 8 lists their conclusions. Other ERA results will be discussed in Chapter Five.

These figures are in substantial agreement with the author's, but were arrived at by a different technique.

Table 7

Total Panama Canal Cargo Tonnage Forecast
(millions of long tons)

	1975	1980	1985	1990	1995	2000
Maximum	145	170	200	240	290	345
Minimum	122.6	141.8	163.5	196.4	235.2	280.7

Table 8

Projected Panama Canal Traffic by Economic Research Associates*
(thousands of long tons)

FY 1974	FY 1975	FY 1976	FY 1980	FY 1985
135,418	136,489	141,003	160,300	184,942

*Proposal to Increase Tolls, Panama Canal Company, 1973, p. 72.

Transit Forecast

Given a range of projected potential cargo movement, it is possible to derive an estimate of possible future levels of ship transits through the Canal. In order to forecast future transit levels, it is assumed that:

1) The diversion of projected cargo from the Panama Canal to other transport modes, such as mini-bridge or superships moving on all-sea tracks around Cape Horn or the Cape of Good Hope, will be small and thus that forecasted potential cargo tonnage will closely approximate actual tonnage figures;

2) The average cargo capacity of ships transiting the Canal will continue to grow at a constant rate as it has for the past eight years;

3) The average load ratio of ships will be the same as the average value of the last eight years; and

4) Each lockage will transit only one ship. There will be few tandem lockages.

It was assumed that future bypass traffic would be insignificant for several reasons. First, the present land-bridge and mini-bridge operations in the United States are economically attractive only for high-value, low-density commodities, moving on a limited number of trade routes. Studies indicate that about 15 percent of Panama Canal cargo could eventually be diverted to the mini-bridge operation, although this may change if ship fuel oil prices continue to rise relative to rail costs. There are many institutional problems with the mini-bridge which have yet to be resolved, and these will determine how successful the mini-bridge operation is in attracting cargoes from the Panama Canal.[17] This could change if it became Federal policy to support this operation through subsidy or favorable regulation. Unless a change occurs which is possible and perhaps desirable, but unforeseeable, it does not appear likely that land-bridge or mini-bridge operations will attract significant levels of potential Panama Canal cargo.

Second, pipelines for both petroleum and slurried solids may some day move commodities that would otherwise go via the Canal. Where these pipelines will be located, how big they will be, and what they will carry are questions that cannot be answered in a 30-year time frame. The discovery and development of coal fields, oil fields and various mineral ores will have an effect upon pipeline usage. The use of coal and oil will depend on where the deposits are located, what it costs to extract and transport them, and what other energy sources are available, such as nuclear power plants. The energy policy of governments will also play a role. Given the lack of any pipeline presently in competition with the Canal, and the worldwide distribution and search for raw materials, it seems unlikely that a long-term high-volume transcontinental movement of a single raw material will develop. Since this is the kind of movement needed to justify use of a pipeline, it appears that, while some pipelines may be built, we cannot foresee them having an identifiable effect on Canal cargo movement. Chapter Seven contains more on the economics of pipelines.

Third, the increasing use of superships to carry bulk commodities poses a significant question for Canal planners since the locks are unable to accommodate ships over 80,000 deadweight tons (dwt). Tankers on the order of 350,000 dwt are not uncommon, and a significant proportion of all tonnage afloat is now composed of ships too large to pass the Canal.

At present, the United States has few ports deep enough to handle ships of 100,000 dwt and over, and until deepwater ports become more generally available in the United States, the dimensions of the Canal locks will not be a factor limiting supership use. This follows because 66 percent of Canal traffic passes through U.S. ports. Furthermore, supership need large volumes of cargo to make them profitable. There are few trades moving through the Canal which appear likely to be diverted to superships operating on all-sea routes when deepwater ports become available.

The construction of deepwater ports, permitting ship drafts of up to 100 feet compared to the present average of 40 feet, is awaiting answer to the questions of who will regulate them, and how to lessen their effect on the coastal environment. The cost savings possible through use of supershipships makes it desirable to have deepwater ports. At an estimated cost of $200 million 1970 dollars, a deepened Delaware Bay port could accommodate 250,000 dwt ships and could tranship up to 45 million tons of coal and 12.5 million tons of iron ore annually.[18]

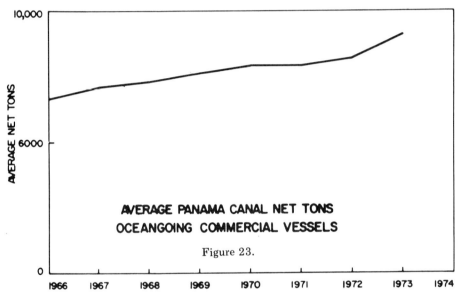

AVERAGE PANAMA CANAL NET TONS
OCEANGOING COMMERCIAL VESSELS

Figure 23.

A primary economy the supershipships achieve is in their crew costs. A modern 300,000 dwt bulk carrier can be operated with no more crew than one of 80,000 tons. On the other hand, considerably more fuel must be expended in taking the all-ocean routes compared with vessels that can operate by way of the Canal shortcut. The penalty the larger ships must pay for their longer trips is increased as the cost of fuel rises. This thus offsets the economies of supership operation as compared to use of traditional size ships.

During the next 10 years the lack of deepwater ports in the United States will discourage the use of supershipships to and from the United States. Over the longer run, the combination of fuel savings plus flexibility for serving smaller shipments of goods will favor use of ships able to transit the Panama Canal versus supershipships. There will doubtless be exceptions to this, but this appears to be the likely trend. We therefore do not expect the superships to draw off significant volumes of Panama Canal cargo in the foreseeable future.

The average cargo capacity of oceangoing commercial vessels transiting the Panama Canal, their Panama Canal net tonnage, is shown in Figure 23 for the past eight years. A least-squares linear computer approximation of this trend forecasts average Panama Canal net tonnage as 14,670 for the year 2000. Since the T.S.S. *Tokyo Bay* is approximately 36,000 Panama Canal net tons and represents an upper limit on ship size capable of transiting the Canal, one-half of its cargo capacity, or 18,000 Panama Canal net tons, is a reasonable estimate of how high the average value of ship cargo capacity may eventually rise. The linear extrapolation of recent growth trends approaches, but does not exceed, this estimated upper limit by the year 2000 and was thus deemed an acceptable representation of future statistics. Table 9 contains the forecast derived from this computer approximation.

Table 9

Forecast of Average Panama Canal Ship Net Tonnage

1975	1980	1985	1990	1995	2000
9,007	10,139	11,272	12,404	13,537	14,670

Table 10 lists the average load ratio for oceangoing commercial ships for the last eight years, i.e., the ratio of average cargo tonnage per ship to average Panama Canal net tonnage per ship.

Table 10

Average Load Ratio

1966	1967	1968	1969	1970	1971	1972	1973
1.03	.973	.996	1.00	1.05	1.06	.963	.996

The average value for the 1966-1973 period was 1.00. This is to say that, on the average, for each Panama Canal net ton of ship cargo capacity that transited the Canal one long ton of cargo transited. This has been the case despite the wide variability in the density of cargo and the fact that ships have transited with varying degrees of loading ranging from fully laden to entirely empty.

As a test for long-term changes in trends, a similar analysis was performed on Panama Canal data from 1937 to 1940, a period subsequent to the last change in rules defining Panama Canal net cargo tonnage spaces, and prior to significant wartime activity. The average

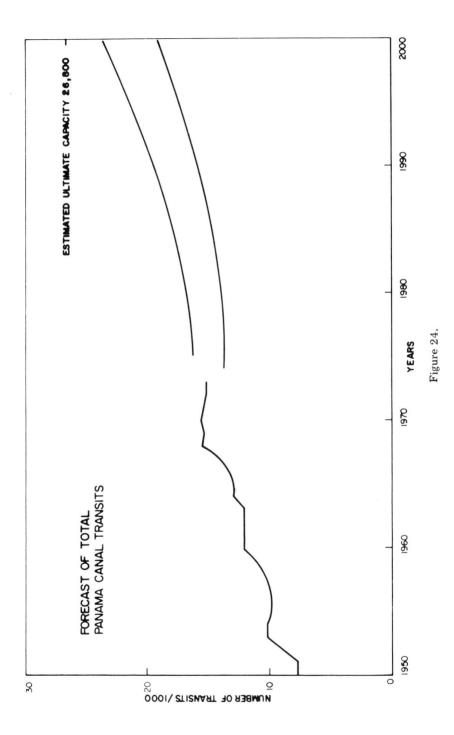

Figure 24.

ratio for this period was 1.07 or only seven percent different from the average 30 years later. This implies that the ratio of transited cargo to Panama Canal net tonnage is reasonably constant with time.

It was assumed that there would be no tandem lockages. This assumption permits equating lockages to transits. Lockages are the limiting factor for Canal capacity, but it is less confusing to discuss capacity in terms of transits. Tandem lockages of oceangoing commercial vessels were fairly common early in Canal history when freighters were no more than five or six thousand gross registered tons. Such lockages are much rarer at this time, being less than one in ten. They will decrease further as the average size of ships increases.

Forecast of Canal Traffic Levels

With the forecasts of average cargo capacity of transiting vessels, of total Canal cargo movement and using a load ratio of unity, it is possible to calculate the number of oceangoing commercial transits likely to occur in particular years. No effort is made to distinguish the types of cargo, types of transiting vessels, or even to separate cargo carried in oceangoing commercial ships from other types of Panama Canal traffic.[19] These refinements would contribute little to the accuracy of the transit forecast, given the uncertainty in actual cargo movements and the many economic and political variables that affect international trade which cannot be quantified.

The equation used to compute possible future Canal transits is as follows:

Number of transits = tons of cargo transiting divided by (load ratio x average Panama Canal net tons)

Working this out with the data contained in Tables 7 and 8 yields a forecast range of transits by five-year periods as shown in Table 11.

Table 11

Forecast of Canal Transits

	1975	1980	1985	1990	1995	2000
Maximum	16,100	16,770	17,740	19,350	21,420	23,517
Minimum	13,610	13,980	14,500	15,830	17,370	19,130

This is plotted in Figure 24.

We view these forecasts as suggesting a range of possibilities within which traffic is reasonably likely to fall. The farther into the future the forecasts extend the more indefinite they must be, for future cargo movements become less a function of present circumstances and more a reflection of intervening events.

In industry, forecasts are usually made for a period of no more than ten years. This is done because (1) industry is sufficiently flexible that it can respond to foreseen developments in a period of ten years or less; (2) forecasts beyond ten years are of questionable value due to the reasons mentioned above.

So long as traffic remains below approximately 26,800 transits per year, additional capacity can be attained by following the phased program of improvements adopted in 1970 which are discussed in Chapter Five. Beyond this point, a third system of locks or a new sea-level canal must be constructed if capacity is to be increased. This requires securing additional international agreements, obtaining congressional approval and appropriation of funds in the United States, actions which are beyond the control of Canal officials. Furthermore, the new facility must be planned and built. All of this can consume years. This is the primary justification for our extending estimates as far as 26 years in advance.

No attempt is made here to identify individual commodity contributions to the traffic level. Individual movements can fluctuate significantly over short periods due to local, national, or international influences. We have tried to identify trends likely to continue over fairly long periods of time that are not likely to be greatly disrupted by temporary circumstances.

Other Transit Forecasts

Both the Interoceanic Canal Study Commission (IOCSC) and ERA have forecast Panama Canal transit levels. The IOCSC made two projections based on assumptions on the percentage levels of cargo carried in general cargo vessels as opposed to bulk carriers such as tankers. These forecasts are displayed in Figure 28. Actual Canal experience has been that roughly 30 percent of cargo is moved in freighters so that the "IOCSC 25%" in this figure appears to be the more accurate of these two analyses. Table 12 lists the ERA forecast.

Table 12

Panama Canal Transit

Projection of Economic Research Associates*

FY 1974	FY 1975	FY 1976	FY 1980	FY 1985
14,300	14,337	14,619	15,960	18,091

*Proposal to Increase Tolls, Panama Canal Company, 1973, p.73.

Effect of Suez Reopening on Panama Canal Forecasts

None of the preceding forecasts allow for the reopening of the Suez Canal. After the 1967 closure of the Suez Canal, the Panama Canal experienced an increase in traffic associated with Middle East trade routes. In 1973 approximately $9.5 million in tolls were recovered from this traffic that otherwise might not have transited.

Due to continued strife in the region and the as-yet-unknown level of Suez tolls, it is problematical how much of the traffic diverted from Suez will return once that waterway is reopened. Since this traffic represents about 7 to 8 percent of total Panama Canal business, forecasting the effect of reopening the Suez Canal would require a finer line of precision than has been attempted.

Allowing for Unforeseen Elements

The foregoing calculations have rested upon trade figures, national income, and mathematical computations. They have not attempted to equate the possible effects of political, social, or psychological forces that may arise to modify or spur cargo shipments. They likewise do not reflect the consequences of decisions to devalue currencies, raise protectionist barriers, or stimulate trade through new international agreements.

Many elements will come into play over the next 30 years affecting overseas commerce in one way or another. The bearing of these upon Canal cargo movement is difficult to foresee. Nor can their course be mapped with accuracy.

To make allowance for the intervention of such forces and actions, the data base used in this study was purposely broadened to take account of a variety of historical circumstances.

The time and experience covered by the years 1950 to 1969 encompass a number of favorable and adverse circumstances. It is hoped that these will make sufficient allowance for the appearance of other variable elements in the future.

Conclusion

With overall transits for the year 2000 forecast at a level of no more than 23,500 where capacity of the existing canal is figured at something less than 26,800 transits, depending on the size and mix of ships at that time, it appears that the interoceanic canal will not be taxed beyond reasonable service limits within this century. This is not likely to hold true beyond about 2010. While the annual number of ships transiting the Panama Canal has been constant for the last four years, the increasing size of the vessels has continued the upward pressure on Canal capacity. The gap between the ultimate capacity of the Canal and the level of transits is still closing because the estimated ultimate capacity in numbers of transits is coming down as ship sizes increase. The Canal

Company is reviewing its estimate of ultimate capacity in light of recent ship size trends. This review is expected to result in a figure considerably below the 26,800 transit estimate. Exactly when the capacity of the Canal will be exceeded cannot be clearly foreseen. For this reason, we recommend that a close watch be kept on traffic conditions during the next ten years in order to project possible lines of development to the 2000 to 2010 period.

CHAPTER FOUR FOOTNOTES

1. Panama Canal Company, *Annual Report*, 1973, Table 13.
2. *Ibid.*, 1973. Tables 19-20.
3. Statistics on overseas trade are derived from *Shipping and Canal Operations.* Hearings before the Subcommittee on Panama Canal of the Committee on Merchant Marine and Fisheries, House of Representatives, Washington, 1973, p. 12.
4. Table 24 in the *Annual Reports* summarizes the shipments from Asia to the various regional areas.
5. The Panama Canal Company has recently proposed a 20 percent increase in tolls. See *New York Times*, December 22, 1973. Should the increase take effect, it would be the first change since 1936 and thus would not violate our assumption.
6. Sources of GWP data:

   Gross National Product: Growth Rates and Trend Data by Nation and Country, April 1969. Washington: AID, Department of State; *Finance and Development Quarterly*, No. 1, 1969. International Monetary Fund and World Bank Group; *Statistical Yearbook of the United Nations*, 1967; *Yearbook of National Accounts*, 1967. The United Nations.
7. *Statistical Yearbook of the United Nations*, 1972, p. 50.
8. The analyses as a whole are presented in *Projections of Possible Future Cargo Movement at the Panama Canal*, M.I.T. Sea Grant Program, Interoceanic Canal Project, Draft Report No. 7, Cambridge, Mass., January 1973.
9. Principal Countries Receiving More Than One Million Tons Cargo 1969* (in long tons)

	Australia	Canada	Chile	Ecuador
1950	558,843	370,068	987,472	91,731
1958	667,203	482,870	1,678,778	236,005
1960	820,998	1,340,126	2,032,803	300,693
1963	1,069,862	1,156,487	2,420,061	446,211
1965	1,761,279	1,342,227	2,582,181	667,864
1968	1,556,003	1,482,397	3,237,276	1,137,599
1969	1,367,957	2,335,207	4,063,013	1,215,417
	Italy	Japan	Netherlands	Peru
1950	130,296	1,993,363	122,203	302,370
1958	344,502	7,831,164	1,487,364	974,965
1960	309,724	10,990,869	2,101,103	1,166,213
1963	1,318,880	13,697,778	2,175,861	1,559,606
1965	946,028	17,905,485	2,089,097	1,718,617
1968	1,425,120	32,163,941	2,421,949	2,261,217
1969	1,032,002	33,558,400	2,737,546	1,768,126

*Panama Canal Company, Annual Reports, respective years.

(continued)

	S. Korea	U.K.	U.S.	German Fed. Rep.
1950	150,000	2,905,798	15,425,150	148,527
1958	678,282	3,944,667	18,872,799	1,633,050
1960	574,062	3,913,982	24,465,969	1,941,272
1963	546,885	3,917,521	21,171,794	1,989,979
1965	807,377	4,199,502	25,229,655	2,477,374
1968	1,150,503	3,782,512	26,446,294	2,009,792
1969	1,672,353	3,362,642	27,618,128	2,085,378
	Total	% Total	Total Canal Traffic	
1950	23,185,821	80.3	28,872,293	
1958	39,191,649	81.4	48,124,809	
1960	49,957,814	84.3	59,258,219	
1963	51,470,925	82.7	62,247,094	
1965	62,527,641	81.7	76,573,071	
1968	79,074,603	81.9	96,550,165	
1969	82,816;169	81.7	101,391,132	

Note: Data for years 1958 and 1963 are included for calculating
       the percentage of total Canal cargo versus time.
       These data could not be used for relating GNP to cargo,
       however, because GNP data for 1958 and 1963 are not
       available.

10. GNP of 12 Principal Cargo Destination Countries*
              (millions 1964 U.S. dollars)

	Australia	Canada	Chile	Ecuador
1950	$ 11,360	$ 21,535	$ 2,109	$ 490
1955	12,663	26,776	2,371	628
1960	15,664	31,422	2,848	791
1965	20,227	40,320	3,646	982
1968	22,181	45,511	3,990	1,188
1969	24,137	47,554	4,147	1,188
	Italy	Japan	Netherlands	Peru
1950	20,822	20,786	8,094	1,548
1955	28,849	30,083	10,637	2,435
1960	37,754	47,995	13,011	2,479
1965	48,718	76,443	16,414	3,376
1968	58,001	110,813	18,306	3,841
1969	60,976	124,664	19,247	3,916
	S. Korea	U.K.	U.S.	German Fed. Rep.
1950	1,474	55,089	359,000	35,152
1955	2,092	62,631	444,800	54,169
1960	2,567	71,615	491,300	74,286
1965	3,502	83,410	621,700	95,275
1968	4,847	88,384	712,400	105,309
1969	5,612	89,383	732,276	113,554

Note: Six data points were used for computing the 20-year
       growth of the 12-nation GNPs, but year 1955 could
       not be used when relating GNP to cargo as 1955 cargo
       data were not available for some of the nations.

*Gross National Product: Growth Rates and Trend Data by
Nation and Country, April 1969. Washington: AID, Department
of State.

(continued)

	12 Nation Total
1950	$ 537,459
1955	678,134
1960	791,732
1965	1,015,013
1968	1,174,720
1969	1,226,654

11. *Interoceanic Canal Studies, 1970,* p. IV-A-62.

12. *Ibid.,* page IV-54.

13. *The Wall Street Journal,* November 30, 1973.

14. "Energy Self-Sufficiency: An Economic Evaluation," *Technology Review,* May 1974.

15. Studies such as those by D.L. Meadows, *The Limits of Growth* (Cambridge, M.I.T. Press, 1972), suggest that world resource situations are already beginning to place obstacles to unlimited world economic growth.

16. The relation between GWP and Panama Canal cargo for the 1950-1967 data base can be described mathematically as

$$\text{Cargo} = -23403.3 + 65.1 \text{ multiplied by GWP}$$

where GWP is in billions of 1967 U.S. dollars and cargo is in thousands of long tons. This equation was determined by a least-squares analysis applied to the data of Table 5. The coefficient of 65.1 is the growth rate of total Panama Canal cargo relative to GWP.

17. Lim H. Tan, "The Mini-Bridge and Panama Canal Traffic," Draft Report No. 12, M.I.T. Sea Grant Program, Cambridge, Mass., 1974.

18. *U.S. Deepwater Port Study,* Institute for Water Resources, Department of the Army Corps of Engineers, 1972, Vol. 1, p. 45. See also Henry S. Marcus, "The U.S. Superport Controversy," *Technology Review,* March/April, 1973.

19. Vessels over 300 net tons, Panama Canal measurement, are considered to be oceangoing.

CHAPTER FIVE

THE LIMITS OF CAPACITY

A lock canal has limits to its capacity. These are fixed by the dimensions of its locks, by the water supplies that are available for navigation and for lockage purposes, and by the constraints that lockage operations place upon the numbers of ships that can be passed through the waterway within a given time frame.

For several decades after the opening of the Panama Canal it seldom occurred to mariners that its lock structures would impose limits to its capacity. The builders had worked on a large scale, and the vessels of those days were dwarfed by the lock chambers.

As time has passed, the situation has changed. The lengths, breadths, and drafts of many bulk carriers, passenger vessels, and containerships are now pressing the dimensions of what can be accommodated at the Canal, so large have shipbuilders stretched the sizes of vessels.

The increase in the sizes of liquid and dry bulk carriers and of specialized vessels such as containerships pose a new range of problems for the Panama Canal as ships have been outgrowing the dimensions of the locks.[1] These problems are likely to become costly as the demand for bulk raw materials increases and deepwater ports are developed in the United States and elsewhere.

Although traffic growth has flattened in late years, the growth in ship sizes has continued the pressure on Canal capacity. Thus, it is important to gauge the limits of capacity in order to be prepared to meet the future needs of international commerce.

Limitations in the Present Lock Canal

Lock Dimensions Restrict Ship Sizes

The dimensions of the lock chambers impose physical limits upon the sizes of vessels that can transit the interoceanic canal as noted in Chapter Two. No ship having a length of more than 975 feet, or a beam of more than 106.9 feet, or a draft of more than 39.5 feet can pass through the Canal locks on a regular basis (fig. 25). The 106.9-foot beam lighter-aboard-ships (LASH) *Acadia Forest* and a sistership are the widest commercial ships that have transited the Canal. Draft is set by the lock sills and the safe depth of water available in Gatun Lake.

These dimensions establish limits upon the sizes and cargo-carrying capacity of ships that can transit the Canal. With certain configurations of hulls, it is possible for a vessel of 100,000 deadweight to pass through the Canal in ballast.

The most powerful commercial vessels to transit have been the British-registered containerships *Tokyo Bay* and her sisterships, *Liverpool Bay* and *Kowloon Bay*, three of a group of 17 giant container carriers owned by a consortium of British, Japanese and German shipowners, some of which are in service on the Europe-Asia run. These ships of 950-foot length, with beams of 105.8 feet, transit the Canal on an average of once a month (fig. 26).

The largest passenger vessel to pass through the Canal was the pre-war S.S. *Bremen* of 936 feet. The post-war express liner S.S. *United States* was designed to fit within the locks, but never made a transit. The giant Cunard liners, H.M.S. *Queen Mary* and *Queen Elizabeth*, and the French liner, S.S. *France*, each over 1,000 feet long, were too large for the Canal locks and had to "go around" when they wished to pass from the Atlantic to the Pacific and vice versa.

MAXIMUM SHIP SIZE

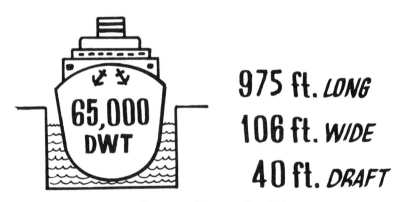

975 ft. *LONG*

106 ft. *WIDE*

40 ft. *DRAFT*

Fig. 25 Courtesy of Panama Canal Company

The average-size cargo liners, tankers, dry bulkers, refrigerator ships, passenger vessels, and containerships on the seas today have no difficulty using the Canal. The lock dimensions do, nevertheless, impose limits on an increasing number of very large vessels. Ships that are 110,000 deadweight or more, whose configurations exceed the lock dimensions, are precluded from traversing the Canal.

With the growth in contemporary ship sizes, the margin of capacity that was originally incorporated into the Canal has shrunk to the point that the locks are becoming restrictive.

Water Supplies Curb Drafts

A second form of limitation that is cropping up in some dry seasons at the Canal is a shortage of fresh water for lockage and navigation

Fig. 26. One of the largest ships to transit the Panama Canal is the T.S.S. *Tokyo Bay*, seen here picking up her locomotive wires from the center wall. She is 950 feet long, 105 feet 10 inches wide, and pays a toll of over $40,000. The T.S.S. *Tokyo Bay* was on her way from England to Japan. Panama Canal Company

purposes. This has not been a problem until recent times. Now it is occurring almost yearly.

Water from tropical rains produces approximately 130 inches of rainfall a year at the Isthmus. This flows into the streams and lakes that are a part of the Gatun and Madden Lake watersheds.

The main collecting basins are Madden Lake, formed by Madden Dam which was constructed just before World War II to increase water supplies and provide hydroelectric power, and Gatun Lake. Due to the prolific rainfall, the Chagres River can rise a foot an hour in the rainy season. The enormous quantity of water which this pours into Gatun Lake at Gamboa is the principal source of replenishment of fresh water for the Canal operation. Gatun Lake is restrained by the one-mile-wide Gatun Dam, one of the largest earthen fill dams in the world, which holds the level of the Lake and the Canal at 85 feet above sea level. Near the end of the rainy season, surplus water is allowed to pass through the spillway gates at the Dam.

In some unusually long dry seasons draft levels within the Canal have had to be restricted to 35 feet in place of the normal 39.5 feet due to the shallowness of the lake level until the rains begin again. The longer the dry season and the greater the water usage to meet traffic demand, the lower the lake level falls.

Water supplies thus place limits on the capacity of the Canal in both numbers of transits and ship draft in dry seasons. Steps are being taken to increase reserves, but in the meantime the situation has to be tolerated.

Time Constraints of Lock Operations

Lockage operations consume time. In so doing, these add to the limitations on the overall capacity of the Canal. With each average-sized vessel taking approximately 65 minutes to clear the three-tiered Gatun Locks, and about the same time at the Pacific locks, assuming no delays or tie-ups, there are limits to the numbers of vessels that can transit the Canal in a day or year. Thus far traffic demand has not reached the limit that can be handled in a year, but with each increment of vessels the point comes closer.

It is the function of the Marine Traffic Control Office to schedule shipping so that it gets through the waterway with the least possible delay and to monitor and control the operation so accidents are avoided. This entails organizing transits so that insofar as possible large ships such as tankers, containerships, passenger liners, bulk or ore-carrying vessels that must go through the Cut in one-way traffic—"clear Cut"— arrive there early in the day in order that traffic bound in the opposite direction not be held up. This means starting very large vessels, such as big containerships and bulkers, from the Pacific anchorage or terminal as early as 4:30 a.m. in order to get to Gamboa Reach at the south end of Gatun Lake by the time southbound large vessels are approaching the same point.

Finely-adjusted scheduling is required when there are long lines of vessels waiting to get through the Canal. Smaller craft are scheduled around the larger vessels since these smaller craft are permitted two-way movement within the Cut and in Miraflores Lake. The Traffic Controllers get all large ships through the Canal in daylight, as well as ships with dangerous cargo or unusual configurations. Vessels that can go through the lock chambers with ample room to spare are moved around the clock.

Under normal conditions, one ship is moved into a lock chamber as soon as another has been locked through, cleared the locks, and the towing locomotives have returned. On days when traffic loads are heavy, vessels can be seen moving into both flights of locks almost continually in the same or opposite directions.

Small vessels can occasionally be locked through in tandem with another ship. This saves lockage water. The extent to which this is done depends upon the priorities that have to be given to some vessels, and the room there is to fit more than one ship into a lock chamber at a time. The latter is determined by the Traffic Control Office upon the basis of the records it keeps of the specifications and handling characteristics of each ship calling at the Canal.

Where the beams of ships are in excess of 80 feet, as increasing numbers of them are among containerships, tankers, OBO-vessels, passenger liners, and others, more time has to be taken getting a vessel through the lock chambers. As much as 80 minutes to an hour and 40 minutes is needed to get a very large vessel through the Gatun Locks, and half an hour or more at each of the chambers at Pedro Miguel and Miraflores. Long lockage times reduce the number of lockages possible in 24 hours.

An element that complicates the life of the Marine Traffic Control Office is the varying mixture of vessels—large and small, difficult or easy to handle—that turn up for transit. For vessels that are regular customers, preparations can be made in advance. But for many others there is often little knowledge ahead of the 48-hour notice that is required of arrival for transit. Some vessels arrive with no advance notice or are off schedule. Consequently, there has to be some juggling of schedules, although the Traffic Controllers endeavor to make up lists a day ahead of time.

Irregularity makes business more crowded on some days than others, and sometimes requires considerable waiting time for transit. It is the goal of the Canal to get ships through within about 17 hours following arrival at a terminal. On the whole, it succeeds in doing this. But there are times when ships have had to wait 24 hours and more because of the numbers and complications of vessels to be transited. These situations jam up schedules, creating temporary undercapacity.

Outages for Overhaul and Repairs

Locks require periodic overhauls of machinery, checking of corrosion, and repairing operating parts in order to maintain them in good working order.

For many years lanes of locks were taken out of service and drained every fourth year, each lane for a three to four weeks' overhaul period. During this time, the lock gates were scraped and painted, checks were made on the gate bearings and hinges, culverts, valves and sills. Motors and reduction gears for moving the gates and barrier chains were carefully inspected for wear and cracks. By this method the Canal was able to keep the mechanisms in excellent operating condition. While this was going on, all traffic had to be run through the other lane of lock chambers. Important as this maintenance work was, a point was reached where the six to eight weeks' outage began to impose unacceptable delays upon shipping.

With the substantial increase in yearly ship transits following 1958, it became necessary to find ways of reducing the outage times. Experimentation showed that the time could be compressed by making certain alterations in overhaul techniques. This is possible by virtue of chambers being provided with two pairs of gates at each end. By lifting one pair of gates off their hinges by means of the floating cranes kept at the Canal, these can then be floated and towed to the Company shops at Balboa where the bearing replacement, cleaning and repainting is performed. A spare pair of gates are then floated in to replace the first pair.

By concentrating work forces, it is possible to make the necessary checks and repairs as need be on other parts of the lock systems within a five-day period when a given lane is taken out of service. In this way delays to shipping are minimized and traffic is kept moving. Techniques have been developed and facilities provided to permit dewatering any one culvert and overhaul of the associated valves without taking a lane out of service (fig. 27).

Once in a while, strut arms have broken or teeth have been stripped on the reduction gears for working the gates. The Canal is able to repair or replace the damaged parts. If necessary, the lock gates can be worked by hand while these are being fixed, so perfectly balanced are the huge gates. The motors that operate the gears can also be repaired at the Canal shops if they become burned out. Replacement parts are kept accessible at the Canal for practically every movable piece of equipment, including lock gates.

There is an element of risk in taking out a pair of gates for overhaul. But safeguards are built into the system and have functioned satisfactorily thus far. Given the care that is taken in handling ships at the Canal, the element of chance is reduced to a minimum.

CROSS SECTION OF PANAMA CANAL LOCK CHAMBER

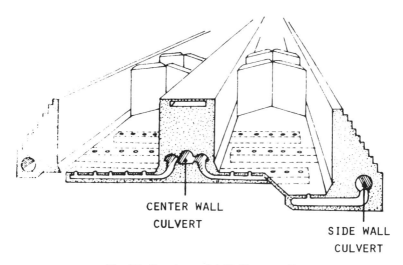

CENTER WALL
CULVERT

SIDE WALL
CULVERT

Fig. 27. Courtesy of A.T. Kearney, Inc.

The Human Element

Discussion has focused upon physical and mechanical impediments to traffic at the Canal. These are real. They impose limits upon the numbers, sizes and drafts of vessels that can transit the interoceanic highway.

There are also human elements relating to the endurance and efficiency of pilots, lockmasters, work crews, schedulers, control house operators, and others that bear upon the functioning of the Canal. Tension is present when traffic is heavy, when there are large ships in the Canal that are difficult to handle, or when vessels stray off course, run into the banks or accidents occur.

The Canal Company seeks to avoid human errors and breakdowns. Each person has limits to endurance; each has a certain amount of tolerance. There are bounds beyond which men become prone to accidents, judgments weaken. These can affect the capacity of the Canal. Slowdowns can occur, as in the 1973 pilots' strike, which related to work conditions as well as to pay. Such events can cause traffic to back up. Attention to interpersonal relationships is a part of the job of running the lock canal. Smooth operations require many people working together, practicing restraint, and exercising considerable judgment.

Estimated Capacity of Canal

Varying combinations of physical and human factors described above fashion limitations on the amount and kind of shipping that can pass through the Panama Canal, and on the times required to reach the high sea lanes on the far side of the Canal.

When business is slack, when shipowners know for a fact that certain vessels have difficulty getting through the waterway because of their size or draft, adjustments can be made. But when traffic is heavy, when shipping space is at a premium, each hour of unanticipated delay is a serious matter. Inability to transit the waterway in average time can produce increased costs. It can lead to losses of profits or of business. It consequently is important to know what the general limits of capacity are, what is being done to alleviate bottlenecks, and to plan ahead.

With traffic levels approaching 15,000 ship transits a year, and now averaging 40 a day, questions of ultimate capacity are germane.

Capacity Studies

Studies made by independent experts have estimated that the ultimate overall number of transits the Canal can effect in a year are likely to be something less than 26,800 after completion of all scheduled improvements done in phase with growing traffic demands.[2]

The critical elements in handling traffic are (1) the number of lockages that can be performed in a 24-hour day; (2) the mixture of vessels that turn up for transit and the number that can be put through in each lockage operation; and (3) the adequacy of the water supply for lockages.

The Canal Company, looking at the problem in 1960 with the preponderance of relatively small, general purpose freighters that were then transiting the Canal, took the view that it could eventually handle up to 76 lockages and a total of 87 ships a day.[3]

To attain 26,800 transits a year will require completion of each lockage in an average of 23 minutes including approach, taking aboard line handlers, lining up the vessel, making fast to the towing locomotives, pulling into the chamber, closing the gates, filling or emptying the chamber, moving out of one chamber into the next, repeating the process, and clearing the lock walls at the end. The total that can be put through will be governed by the mixture of vessels that seek transit and the complications the larger vessels produce.

The Interoceanic Canal Study Commission (IOCSC) in its 1970 Report to the President of the United States predicted that ultimate capacity would be reached by 1988 on the basis that 46 percent of the cargo passing through the Canal would still be carried in general cargo freighters (fig. 28).[4] By readjusting the estimate to 25 percent of the cargo in general freighters the predicted capacity date would be reached in the year 2010. Governor Parker, testifying before the Congress in 1973, stated that freighters were at that time carrying approximately 30 percent of the cargo tonnage.[5]

Forecasting from the current ship mixture, Canal consultants estimate that by 1985 there will be between 16-17,000 transits a year, and that if the present mixture continues to prevail 26,800 transits a year will not be reached until approximately the year 2020 or later. However, 26,800 large ship transits are likely to exceed the capacity of the Canal. The original figure was based on an assumption that ship size would not grow significantly.

FORECAST TOTAL OCEANGOING COMMERCIAL TRANSITS

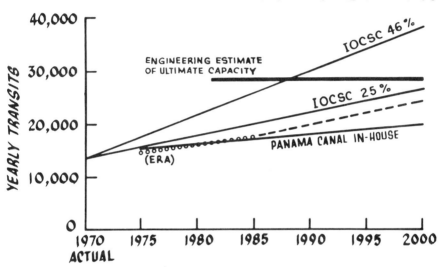

Fig. 28. Courtesy of Panama Canal Company

Studies by the Canal Company, extrapolating from the present mixture of containerships, bulk carriers, tankers, and break-bulk freighters, point to no more than 20,000 transits in the year 2000.

Bearing of Ship Mixture on Capacity

With the larger size ships that are coming to the Canal today, as contrasted with the years before 1968, the mixture of shipping to be transited is quite different from what it was previously when estimates were made of the numbers of vessels that could be transited in a year at capacity operation.

From shipbuilding information, and the types of vessels now plying world trade routes, it seems likely that the trend toward use of larger vessels and more specialized shipping, such as automobile carriers, refrigerator ships, containerships, OBO-vessels, and the like, will continue.

Efforts are being made to forecast the mixtures of ships that will be seeking transit 20 years hence. With the advances taking place in engineering and ship technology, it is difficult to make accurate forecasts this far ahead. With the worldwide need to make optimal use of existing energy supplies, the signs point to construction of more ships near the maximum dimensions that can transit the Canal locks.

The principal commodity groups that pass through the Canal provide some index of the types of shipping that can be expected in the years ahead. The percentages of commercial cargo transiting the Canal in 1973 and forecast for 1985 are listed in Table 1.

Table 1

Principal Commodity Groups*

Percent of Total Canal Commercial Cargo

Commodity	1973	1985
Petroleum and Products	18%	18%
Coal and Coke	10	8
Grain and Soybeans	15	21
Mfgrs. Iron and Steel	8	6
Lumber	4	4
Sugar	4	3
Phosphate	4	3
Scrap Metal	3	2
Autos and Trucks	1	1
All Others	33	37

*Proposal to Increase Tolls, Panama Canal Company, December 15, 1973, p. 72.

This suggests that the percentages of dry and liquid bulk carriers will be somewhat lower in number of total transits. But, given the trends in world shipbuilding existing today, the vessels will be close to the maximum sizes the locks can take. Containerships, which primarily transport items that fall in the category of "All Others," will be carrying the higher percentage of Canal traffic. They will therefore be both more numerous customers and approximate "Panamax" specifications like the big containerships of Sea-Land Lines.

Predicted Capacity

These considerations reinforce the belief that the numbers which the Canal can transit in a year will be below the 1969 estimate of 26,800 transits. If circumstances continue as they have, the limit may be more nearly in the range of 23,000 to 24,000 transits a year as the saturation point.

Standard of Service Afforded by Canal

Over the years the Panama Canal has afforded a standard of service to world shipping. This is measured in the length of time a ship spends within Canal waters. It is the aim of the Company to see that the average time a ship is in Canal Zone waters, waiting its turn and transiting the Canal, does not exceed 17 hours, except in periods of lock overhaul. Of this time, eight to ten hours must be spent in the actual transit.

This objective cannot always be realized. Delays do occur now and then, as for ships getting away from bunkering docks on time, tie-ups occurring at a lock, fog occurring in the Cut requiring vessels to lie by for some time, accidents, and other circumstances. But 16 or 17 hours is the model on which operations are conducted. It is a standard that is achieved most of the time.[6]

This standard has grown out of experience in operating the Canal: finding out what can be done, refining procedures so they take the least amount of time, while constantly holding in view that the reason ships come to the Canal is to save time, distance, and expense.

The Canal Company has from the beginning sought to get ships through the Canal and on their way in the shortest possible time consonant with protecting the lock mechanisms and safe-guarding the ships themselves from harm. Its goal is service to shipping.

Holding to a 17-hour standard has been possible as the yearly number of ship transits has risen because of the carefully trained, competent personnel employed by the Company, the high esprit de corps maintained within the organization, and the finely attuned procedures applied in operations.

Maintaining the same standard as the number of transits rises by another quarter or third will require comparable excellence of personnel, efficiency of operations, meticulous attention to detail, and careful upkeep of equipment. In addition to this, there must be added supplies of water and further improvements in navigation conditions. This will necessitate ongoing financial support, freedom from political interference, and a stable international environment. The uncertain outlook in the political and legal sphere is cause for some concern.

Improvements to Extend Capacity

Through the years the Canal has attempted, as Governor David S. Parker has stated, to anticipate the needs of shipping "before the traffic presents itself so it does not find itself in a bind when that time arrives." [7]

Improvements that have been made in the past with this in mind have included obtaining storage water and flood control before World War II by constructing Madden Dam; widening Gaillard Cut from a 300-foot channel to 500 feet during the 1960s; shortening lock outage times by improving overhaul techniques so that two-way traffic can be assured for most of the year; purchasing new towing locomotives to move ships more quickly in the locks; adding larger, more powerful tugs to help guide the larger ships now coming to the Canal; installing modern lighting on the locks and through the Cut to aid nighttime navigation.

Traffic demands at the times these improvements were inaugurated did not necessitate such action. Each step, nevertheless, improved an aspect of the overall operation by adding to safety, shortening lockage time, providing a more regularized supply of water, facilitating around-the-clock operations, cutting lock outage time, and so forth. In the process it extended the assured capacity of the Canal, making it easier to handle increased traffic loads as these arose.

AVERAGE TIME IN CANAL ZONE WATERS COMPARED TO GROWTH IN TONNAGE

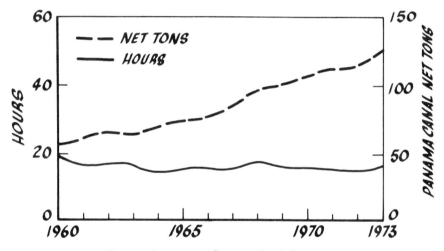

Fig. 29. Courtesy of Panama Canal Company

Going to 24-hour operations in 1963 gained added capacity.[8] And, by the combination of widening Gaillard Cut and cutting the lock outage time, the capacity of the Canal was increased by almost 50 percent. The effect of the improvements is borne out by the constancy of the average time spent by vessels in Canal Zone waters, while transits have risen sharply and vessel tonnage has virtually doubled (fig. 29).

In the long run, the Canal must achieve full capacity. This means that eventually it must be able to handle all ships that can fit within the lock chambers up to the maximum number that can be transited within the time frame of a year.

To achieve "full capacity," coupled with holding to the goal of service, certain further specific improvements must be completed. These can be grouped under three heads: (1) gaining additional water supplies; (2) further improving navigation conditions; and (3) shortening transit times to the minimum.

Gaining Added Water Supplies

Obtaining additional water for lock operations and for maintaining suitable draft limitations throughout the year is a cardinal requisite for reaching sustained capacity.

Each vessel locked through the Canal requires an expenditure of 52 million gallons of fresh water. Once used, this passes out to sea and is lost. Thus the expenditure amounts to a net drawdown of that much fresh water for each lockage from the reserves stored in Gatun and Madden Lakes. These reserves hold five million acre-feet of fresh water of which one million acre-feet is usable for lockages. This is ample to sustain navigation, plus the lockages, during the rainy season when torrential downpours add tons of water to the reserves. The problem arises during the four-month dry season when lack of daily rain, continued lockage operations, municipal use, and evaporation due to the high temperatures cause the water levels to drop so that the Canal may have to restrict ship drafts to less than 38 feet. Each additional lockage then places added strain upon the reserves. If the levels are drawn down beyond a given point, the draft restrictions become onerous to shipping. Furthermore, in some years it is not possible to restore the lakes to their full levels in the following rainy season. The Canal cannot afford to let the lakes become so depleted that they will not return to normal. Otherwise, its standard of service will be compromised through forced restrictions on ship drafts over longer periods of the year.

When it becomes necessary to restrict ship drafts, the Canal Company publishes a warning three weeks prior to the imposition of the restriction. This procedure has helped minimize the costly effects of lockage water shortages by giving shippers time to arrange their schedules and properly load their vessels. The problem can be seen if a bulk carrier loaded with coal for Japan arrives loaded to 39-foot draft when only 37 feet of water is available for navigation because of water shortages. In such a case, the vessel would have to go into port and unload sufficient coal to bring its draft to 37 feet, or it would have to jettison cargo at sea, or take the long, expensive voyage around the Horn, thereby risking its profit. The present objective is to be able to guarantee a 38-foot depth at all times.

There are several alternative methods for procuring added water. One that is currently being employed is to deepen the navigation channel through Gatun Lake and the Cut. This is being done in units of three feet. This will permit storing more water in the Canal itself. Although

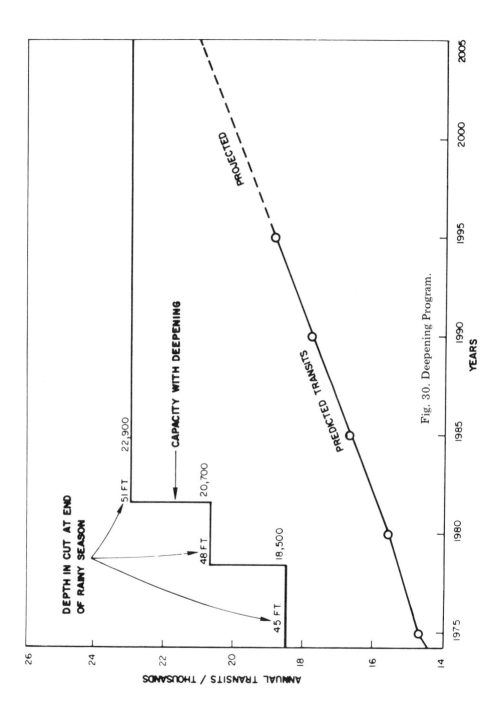

Fig. 30. Deepening Program.

118

the Cut may be 50 feet deep at times, the 40-foot-deep locks at Gatun and Miraflores limit maximum ship drafts to 39.5 feet (fig. 30).

Construction of an additional dam has been considered. This will require a separate agreement with the Republic of Panama.

A further alternative, but one of poor economic prospect, is to raise the level of Gatun Lake by five feet. This would give a substantial addition of reserve water. But it would cause flooding along the edges of the Lake, requiring agreement with Panama, and would affect recreational use of the Lake.

Thought has been turned to cloud seeding to gain more water. A five-year program of experiments is about to be conducted to determine the feasibility of this in the Isthmian environment.

A last resort is the possibility of pumping sea water into Gatun Lake in some dry seasons to supplement the fresh water. This idea, while feasible, is resisted because of the change this would cause in the ecology of Gatun Lake through making the water brackish and possibly harming plant and wildlife. Should a third locks system be embarked upon, use of supplemental salt water would almost surely have to be adopted in order to provide adequate quantities of lockage water and to hold sufficient draft levels in dry seasons.[9]

Beyond these alternatives, there is little the Canal can do to increase lockage water supplies other than reconstructing the chambers and lowering the sills on the upper lock floors. It would be better, in our opinion, to construct a new sea-level waterway rather than laying out the money required to do this, for the locks would still have the physical limitations on the lengths and beams of ships that could be transited.

Improving Navigation Conditions

Capital improvements to assist navigation include widening and straightening channels, especially where pilots cannot see far enough ahead, deepening channels to guarantee 38-foot draft at all times, finding ways of enabling ships to navigate safely through the Cut in fog, and going to a semiautomated traffic control and schedule system.

Fog and heavy rain squalls pose unresolved hazards to navigation. Fog restrictions may last six to eight hours in a night when it settles in the Cut during the rainy season, necessitating anchorage until visibility is considered adequate. Efforts so far to find ways of dispelling the fog have proved fruitless. Attempts are now being made to develop radar assists, as well as other techniques, that will permit at least one-way traffic movement during the fog spells. This will become imperative as traffic builds up toward full capacity. 1980 is the target date by which the Company expects to have this problem solved.

A new computer-assisted data handling and display system is due to be in operation in a new Marine Traffic Control Center in late 1975. The new system will permit the recording of essential data on each ship's record and retrieving this quickly when a ship arrives for transit. The system will automatically check to insure that data are complete, and will analyze reports from pilots, control towers, and other stations, and signal deviations from schedules. Marine Traffic Controllers will thus obtain an improved flow of information on the location of ships. Status of the waterway will be displayed on a large ship position display board and data will appear on individual consoles. Controllers will be able to disseminate information and directions to tug operators, lock control towers, and other important users. Pilots will receive individually tailored directions at the launch landings.

The Operations Room, to be located in the new Center, will provide more ample space for activities. Sound deadening and controlled access is planned for the operations area. An information clerk/receptionist will receive ships' agents and other visitors, answer inquiries, and handle public telephone calls. Figure 31 shows the present Operations Room. Figure 32 is an artist's rendering of the new arrangement.

Even with all scheduled improvements completed, there will still be a question whether the Canal will be fully able to handle 26,800 transits a year without further improvements.

Scheduling

Scheduling is a particular problem for Canal operations. Ship captains are sometimes unpredictable and do not always up-anchor to start their transits when expected. Heavy rain squalls can slow movements and mechanical breakdowns aboard poorly maintained ships are common. Canal pilots may report in sick and, despite efforts on the part of the Canal Company, instructions for personnel are not always clear or interpreted correctly. When ships are moving in close sequence and a sudden problem develops, 20 or more ships and the actions of hundreds of people can be affected. With commercial ship costs running $8,000 per day (depending on ship size, age and type), lost time is costly. This puts pressure on Marine Traffic Control to orchestrate a smooth, rapid solution.

Canal schedules are updated as needed, and this may be as many as several times an hour for a 12-hour horizon. This involves manipulating work gang schedules, many of which are subject to complicated labor rules. Finding even a feasible schedule of pilots, tug boats, locomotive crews, line handlers, lock personnel and transit capacity taxes experienced schedulers.

In the future, when the Canal is handling 60 or more ships a day, it is doubtful that the manual method now employed will be able to generate even a single feasible schedule due to the limits of human ability.

The new data flow system employing computer technology should help traffic controllers with this problem.

Shortening Lockage Times

To reach full capacity, the Canal must compress lockage times to the absolute minimum for all ships. Large vessels must be locked through in less than 35 minutes per chamber.

There are various things that can be done to reduce lockage times. Among the principal steps are adding more new, powerful locomotives on the lock walls, relocating the tracks to speed up return of locomotives to pickup stations, instituting improved locomotive movement procedures, modernizing the lock control systems which include faster switching and more reliable safety features, and adding more tugs for vessel assistance in maneuvering into and out of the locks.

By adding more locomotives and instituting new movement procedures, vessels can be passed through a flight of locks faster than at present. This can be done by shifting tows to a second team of locomotives when a vessel is secured within a chamber and returning the first team to the approach wall to pick up a following vessel. By adding an additional lane of tracks on the lock walls, a "merry-go-round" procedure could be instituted that would allow somewhat more ships to transit the Canal within a 24-hour period.

The last order for locomotives was completed in 1966. At that time, the locomotives cost $110,000 apiece. These have functioned well after initial adjustments. Despite their excellent characteristics, heavy usage is shortening their lifetime. More will be sought as replacement for older locomotives or as net additions as increasing traffic demands suggest. New locomotives will cost in excess of half a million dollars each. Similarly, the improvements program calls for adding more tugs for vessel assistance in phase with growing numbers of ship transits. Five of these at $2 million apiece are needed in the immediate future. These will probably have special equipment that will increase their maneuverability in confined spaces.

Completion of these improvements, which are scheduled for more than a decade ahead, will speed up lockage times, smooth out the flow of traffic around the clock, help eliminate causes of accidents, and enable the Company to handle a larger body of shipping. The improvements mentioned have been estimated to cost in the range of $100-120 million, or roughly $12-20 million a year, although inflation will increase this.[10] This is a modest cost program. It will extend the useful life of the Canal by many years.

The program for expanding Canal capacity calls for undertaking a project only when it will do the most good. If the Congress decides to construct a sea-level canal, unnecessary expenditures will not have been made.

Fig. 31. Present Marine Traffic Control Center. Panama Canal Company

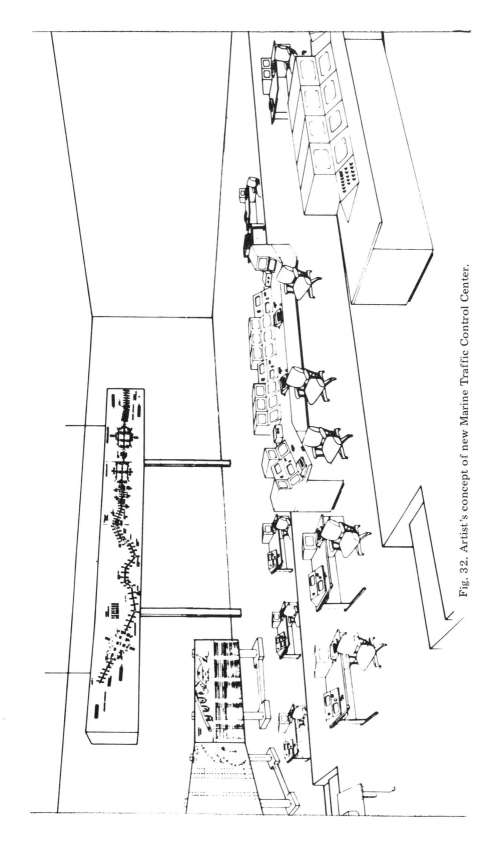

Fig. 32. Artist's concept of new Marine Traffic Control Center.

Conclusion

It is the considered judgment of the Panama Canal Company, and of our study as well, that the current improvements program will get the Canal up to the range of something over 23,000 transits a year.

Each of the steps outlined is an essential ingredient to achieving this level of activity. Obtaining adequate water is a key to realizing the whole, unless one is willing to settle for lower drafts in some years. This would mean, however, compromising an element of the standard of service the marine community has come to expect for over five decades.

If there is average rainfall, it is reasonable to believe that combinations of deepening the channels, and possible impoundment of one more stream will provide adequate lockage water. As a final resort, pumping of salt water into Gatun Lake in some exceptionally dry years is possible. It is hoped that this can be avoided for the life of the present canal. If a larger lock system is ordered, pumping appears unavoidable, however.

The improvement program will keep the capacity of the lock canal ahead of shipping demand for at least twenty years as estimated by the presidential study commission, by Panama Canal Company consultants, and by our independent projections discussed in Chapter Four. These steps should extend the useful life of the Canal into the 21st century.

The prepared statement submitted by Governor David S. Parker to the House of Representatives Subcommittee on the Panama Canal in July 1973 admirably summarizes the conclusions of our study on the capacity of the Canal.

We are confident that by implementing many or all of the various Canal improvements projects, and in the absence of a decision to build a sea-level canal or new locks for the present Canal, we can keep the present Canal as a viable and useful adjunct to world trade. All indications are that the Canal's usefulness should extend beyond the end of the century but obviously predictions that far in advance are subject to rather wide variation.

The Canal will do, the Governor concluded, the things it can do so that it will be able to "continue to serve to the advantage of world commerce in the future as it has in the past." [11]

A combination of the diversion of much of the Europe-Asia-Oceania trade to the Suez Canal when that is reopened, a growth in bypass dry bulk trade moving around the Cape of Good Hope between the East Coast of the United States and Japan, and expansion of the land-bridge operation across the United States by the rail lines, will withdraw some of the business that has been going through the Canal since 1967 and is currently patronizing it.

Some of this cannot be prevented by anything the Canal can do to improve the standard of service which it offers to oceanborne commerce. There is no solid evidence that all of the cargo or yearly ship transits which the Canal picked up after 1967 will disappear. Shipping interests have been able thus far to meet transcontinental rail transport competition leagued with one-ocean ship carriage by building and putting into operation high-speed containerships that have reduced passage times by all-water transport to equivalent times advertised by land- and mini-bridge promoters. In addition, they are able to offer shippers of cargo the advantage of nontransfer of cargo from ship to shore to rail to consumer with the inherent danger of damage en route.

The land-bridge schemes offer the United States an opportunity to strengthen its transcontinental rail system, to modernize and improve its port facilities, and to strengthen the merchant marine serving its ports. This can benefit the national economy.

The attractiveness of alternatives such as mini-bridge and superships with their potential for quality service may be a signal that the role the Panama Canal has historically played in maritime commerce is changing. It is conceivable that the improvements in maritime commerce may make use of modest size ships less advantageous for some trades than heretofore. This was alluded to in Chapter One and will be further addressed in Chapter Seven.

Taken on balance, the outlook for the Canal for the near future is for an ongoing growth of business, preserving, but not necessarily duplicating, the profile of growth that has characterized cargo and transit movement since 1950.

CHAPTER FIVE FOOTNOTES

1. *The Prospects for Bulk Carriers of "Panamax" Size Plus*, H.P. Drewry (Shipping Consultants) Limited, 1972, p. 17.

2. A summary of the report by the A.T. Kearney & Co., Consultants, will be found in *Panama Canal Traffic, Capacity and Tolls*. Hearing before Subcommittee on Panama Canal, Committee on Merchant Marine and Fisheries. U.S. House of Representatives. Washington, April 22, 1970, pp. 20-29.

3. *Isthmian Canal Plans, 1960*. Panama Canal Company, February 11, 1960, p. 14.

4. *Interoceanic Canal Studies, 1970*, Washington, The White House, 1970, Annex IV, p. 82.

5. *Shipping and Canal Operations*. Hearing before Subcommittee on Panama Canal, Committee on Merchant Marine and Fisheries. U.S. House of Representatives. 93rd Congress, 1st Session, Washington, July 17, 1973. Serial No. 93-19, pp. 16-17.

6. 2,353 vessels were in Canal Zone waters over 24 hours in 1973. Panama Canal Company, *Annual Report*, 1973, p. 13.

7. *Shipping and Canal Operations*. Hearing cited above, p. 24.

8. *Ibid.*, pp. 23-29.

9. See testimony of Governor Parker. Hearing, *op. cit.*, pp. 40, 70-71.

10. *Ibid.*, p. 72.

11. Hearing, *op. cit.*, p. 7.

CHAPTER SIX

TOLLS: THE COST OF TRANSITING THE WATERWAY

The Panama Canal is an international utility serving oceanborne commerce. The costs of operating and maintaining the Canal are recovered by assessing tolls on transiting vessels. The level of the toll and the manner in which it is assessed affects the trade of maritime nations which depend on the Canal for service.

Short History of the Panama Canal Toll System

The Panama Canal Act of 1912 delegated the exercise of rights acquired by the United States through the 1903 Treaty with Panama,[1] and the Hay-Pauncefote Treaty with Great Britain,[2] to the appropriate branches of the United States Government.[3] This Act, among other things, empowered the President to fix toll charges which were not to exceed $1.25 per registered ton.

The Act stipulated that a change in tolls should be proclaimed by the President six months in advance of application and that tolls should recover basically the cost of operation and maintenance of the Canal.

Dr. Emory R. Johnson, Special Commissioner to the President on Panama Traffic and Tolls, recommended in his initial report that Panama Canal tolls be set at $1.20 per net ton for merchant vessels carrying cargo or passengers; $0.72 per net ton for merchant vessels in ballast, and $0.50 per displacement ton for non-mercantile vessels.[4] Net tonnage was recommended as the standard for assessing tolls because shippers paid tolls from their earnings, and the space set aside for carrying cargo and passengers gave a crude, but straightforward, measure of a vessel's earning capacity.

The rates were determined so that the benefit derived from using the Canal would be greater than the toll. At that time, the benefit was figured as the saving in costs of sailing around Cape Horn. Basically, the policy of the Panama Canal system is that charges to shippers be set to recover only the actual cost of providing the service. The charges are made proportional insofar as possible to the earnings shippers realize from using the waterway.

A second report recommended rules to be used in calculating net and displacement vessel tonnage.[5] The Panama Canal toll system, as recommended by the Special Commissioner, was established by Executive Orders of President Taft in 1912-1913.[6]

A special set of rules was recommended for use in measuring the tonnage of ships because:

(1) Each maritime country had a differing set of rules for deter-

mining the net tonnage of its commercial vessels. Sisterships under different flags would have had a different net tonnage on their national registry certificates and therefore would have been assessed different tolls. Assessing different tolls to identical ships was considered unfair to shippers and might have caused the United States to violate its treaty obligation that there should be no discrimination among nations or their citizens.

(2) None of the major maritime powers of the day used measurement rules which made net tonnage a close equivalent to earning capacity. Suez Canal rules were rejected. At that time, the policy of the Suez Canal Company was to levy tolls solely for the purpose of maximizing profits from the waterway. This led to a definition of net tonnage space, the basis of the Suez toll system, which Dr. Johnson felt would be inappropriate for a United States-owned canal operated for the purpose of promoting maritime commerce.

The wording employed in the Panama Canal Act created a long and troublesome problem. The Act set a tolls ceiling interpreted by the Attorney General as to be determined using the measurement rules specified in the general maritime laws of the United States. These measurement rules exempted more space from assessment than the Panama Canal rules and were subject to change with time. As a result, Canal tolls had to be computed under both United States maritime and Panama Canal rules. The lesser of two calculations, United States registered tons times $1.25 or Panama Canal net tons times $1.20, established the toll. As the years passed, and the United States rules were revised, the discrepancy between the two measurement formulas increased and the Panama Canal rules seldom determined the toll for laden vessels.

In April 1936, Congress authorized President Franklin D. Roosevelt to appoint a committee to reexamine the toll problem. This committee recommended adoption of the Panama Canal Measurement Rules with some minor modifications as the sole standard. It also recommended that lower rates be applied in order that the toll on most ships not increase with the adoption of a single measurement system. President Roosevelt urged the Congress in 1937 to adopt the modified Panama Canal rules. A few days after the Congress passed the appropriate legislation, the President proclaimed that the new rate for laden commercial vessels would be $0.90 per net ton measured according to the special Panama Canal rules.[7] The rates for commercial ships transiting in ballast and for noncommercial ships remained unchanged. The rates have not been altered since then, but the interpretations of the rules for computing the net measurement tonnage change occasionally.

The Legal Framework of Panama Tolls

Numerous treaties and laws establish a framework for Canal operations.

The 1901 Treaty with Great Britain provided that:

The canal shall be free and open to the vessels of commerce and of war of all nations . . . on terms of entire equality, so that there shall be no discrimination against any such nation, or its citizens or subjects, in respect of the conditions or charges of traffic, or otherwise. Such conditions and charges of traffic shall be just and equitable.

A 1903 treaty with the Republic of Panama provided that:

The Government of the Republic of Panama shall have the right to transport over the Canal its vessels and its troops and munitions of war in such vessels at all times without paying charges of any kind.

This treaty also established the level of annuity payments to the Republic at $250,000 per year. In 1936 the United States agreed to increase the annuity payment to Panama to 430,000 balboas per year,[8] the balboa and the dollar having been fixed at parity.[9] By a later treaty of 1955, the annuity was again increased to 1,930,000 balboas, the increment being paid by the State Department.[10]

By a treaty signed with the Republic of Colombia in 1914, but not ratified until 1922, it was provided that Colombian government vessels should also have free transit through the Canal.[11]

The Panama Canal Act of 1912 provided for the opening, operation, maintenance, and protection of the Panama Canal, and the sanitation and government of the Canal Zone. This Act authorized the President of the United States to set the toll rate for, and operate the Panama Canal through a Governor of the Panama Canal.

Legislation, effective July 1, 1951, changed the organizational structure of the Canal enterprise.[12] Business operations were separated from civil government functions and established in the Panama Canal Company. Civil government, police, fire, health, and sanitation functions were grouped in the Canal Zone Government. The Company was given authority to prescribe toll rates with the approval of the President of the United States.

The Company is required by law to operate on a self-sustaining basis, the law reading in part:

Tolls shall be prescribed at rates calculated to cover, as nearly as practicable, all costs of maintaining and operating the Panama Canal, together with the facilities and appurtenances related thereto, including interest and depreciation, and an appropriate share of the net costs of operation of the agency known as the Canal Zone Government.[13]

The Company is permitted to make use of funds appropriated from the Federal Treasury for capital improvements and operating losses so long as these are repaid. The Treasury is reimbursed by the·Company for interest on the investment of the United States in the corporation.

The Panama Canal Toll System in Operation

Toll charges are assessed against ship spaces which can be used to carry cargo and passengers. This is determined by calculating the total internal volume of the vessel and subtracting therefrom the volume of machinery rooms, crew quarters, navigation house, and other areas used in working the ship which cannot be used to carry cargo. The rules for calculating this are contained in Title 35 of the *Code of Federal Regulations.* The volume remaining after subtracting exempt and excluded spaces is the Panama Canal net vessel tonnage where each 100 cubic feet is defined as being equivalent to one net ton.

Cost of Tolls: Sample Instances

The toll paid by most ships is in the thousands of dollars. The *San Juan Ore,* an ore carrier capable of lifting 40,000 long tons, pays $9,000 to transit. The *Liberia,* a general bulk carrier, which also lifts 40,000 long tons, pays $18,000 because its cubic capacity is larger. The *Japan Maru,* operating on the East Coast-Japan trade route carrying 9,000 long tons of phosphate rock, rosin and cotton on a westbound transit in 1966, paid $7,200 in tolls. Eastbound, it carries general cargo. The Lighter Aboard Ship (LASH) *Acadia Forest,* one of the more advanced ships from a technical aspect, can carry 26,000 long tons of general cargo and pays $18,570 to transit. Large containerships such as the *Tokyo Bay* pay about $40,000 to transit. One transit of this ship replaces the lifting capacity of five smaller general cargo ships. The largest ship to transit the Canal is the *San Juan Prospector* which is 972 feet long, with a potential draft of 50 feet. This transited in ballast and paid a toll of over $41,000. The average toll paid by transiting ships has been increasing, being $6,946 in 1971; $7,175 in 1972; and $7,960 in 1973. This reflects the trend toward use of larger ships.

Receipts from Tolls

Table 4 of Chapter Three lists Canal toll statistics by flag of vessel. United States flag transits accounted for 8.8 percent of the 1973 total.

Canal Finances and the Need for a New Toll System

Sources and Levels of Panama Canal Company Income

In 1973, the income of the Panama Canal Company was $199,848,000. These monies were derived from two sources, supportive services, and tolls.

Supportive services receipts were $86,467,000.[14] These services included navigation assistance at the Canal terminals and through the Canal, general ship repair and maintenance carried out at the Company

Table 1*

Statement of Toll Revenue Deficiency for Fiscal Years 1973 and 1975
(in thousands of dollars)

	FY 1973 Actual	FY 1975 Projected	Increase (decrease)
Operating expenses:			
Maintenance of channels and harbors	$ 10,426	$ 21,553	$11,127
Navigation service and control	24,229	30,683	6,454
Locks	17,129	21,667	4,538
General repair, storehouse, engineering and maintenance services	6,455	6,125	(330)
Marine terminals	13,941	15,776	1,835
Transportation and utilities	14,336	15,917	1,581
Retail and housing	37,886	42,670	4,784
Other	7,214	9,588	2,374
General and administrative	32,195	39,783	7,588
Interest	12,569	14,595	2,026
Net cost of Canal Zone Government	24,795	25,540	745
Total operating expenses	$201,175	$243,897	$42,722
Revenues other than tolls:			
Navigation service and control	$ 14,650	$ 18,205	$ 3,555
General repair, storehouse, engineering and maintenance services	4,251	3,596	(655)
Marine terminals	15,634	18,154	2,520
Transportation and utilities	14,277	16,648	2,371
Retail and housing	35,832	40,725	4,893
Other	1,823	1,567	(256)
Total revenues other than tolls	$ 86,467	$ 98,895	$12,428
Net operating expenses to be recovered from tolls	$114,708	$145,002	$30,294
Toll revenues at existing rates	113,381	121,150	7,769
Toll revenue deficiency	$ 1,327	$ 23,852	$22,525

$$\frac{1975 \text{ toll revenue deficiency} \quad \$ 23,852}{1975 \text{ toll revenues at existing rates} \quad \$121,150} = 19.7\%$$

*Proposal, p. 13.

drydocks, sales of fuel oils, cargo handling, transportation and utility services to United States Government agencies and to the Republic of Panama, and sales of commodities and services to employees such as food, clothing, and housing rental.

The revenues derived from these services generally offset the costs of providing such services. Much of the income comes from the Panama Canal Company and Canal Zone Government personnel, so that recovering more than costs would constitute a reverse subsidy. These services are not deemed appropriate for consideration as sources of additional receipts.

Toll revenues in 1973 were $113,381,000 [15] which was an all-time record and was not quite twice the amount received in 1963. Toll receipts have grown recently at approximately 7 percent annually due to the political effects of Suez closure, the Vietnam war, and the economic development of many countries.

Since its formation in 1950, the Panama Canal Company has paid the United States Treasury $40 million from funds excess to working capital and reasonable foreseeable requirements for authorized plant replacement and expansion. However, in 1973, despite record income, revenue fell $1.3 million short of covering costs. This was the first time revenues did not exceed costs in the period since 1950.

Rising Costs

The cost of operating the Canal has risen steadily over its 60-year life. Only the phenomenal growth in traffic, together with significant managerial improvements, has permitted maintenance of a constant toll rate. Costs of operating the Canal are now rising faster than the growth of traffic. Wage increases in 1973 accounted for much of the $19-million rise in operating expenses over 1972 costs. [16]

The Panama Canal Company estimates that operating and maintenance costs for fiscal year 1975 will rise by $42.7 million over the 1973 level, resulting in a need for income from tolls of $145 million, and that there will be a shortfall of $24 million if tolls are not raised.

Table 1 lists Canal cost categories and shows how these figures were obtained. Table 2 gives a breakdown of the anticipated cost increases. A $13.8-million projected wage increase makes no provision for a change in the minimum wage which will be raised as a result of a revision of the Fair Labor Standards Act, effective May 1, 1974. Governor David S. Parker estimated that this might add from $5 to $9 million to Company costs. [17] Beginning in 1974, the Company is figuring on a depreciation of $10.1 million on the costs of lands, titles, treaty rights, canal excavations, fills, and embankments, as well as on recently acquired physical plant.

Lands, titles, treaty rights, canal excavations and the like were not depreciated previously because the United States has held rights to these "in perpetuity." It now appears possible that a date may be set for eventual transfer of the Canal and Zone to the Republic of Panama unless the United States Congress refuses to agree to this. These accounting changes reflect the changing realities of diplomacy.

Table 2*

Anticipated Changes In Panama Canal Company
Costs for F.Y. 1975*

	Increase (in millions)
Wage increases (does not provide for increase in minimum wage level)	$13.8
Increase in total number of work hours	6.0
Increase in Company contribution to the premium for employees' health benefits	2.1
Depreciation	10.1
Cost of commodities sold	3.2
Interest expense	2.0
Net cost of Canal Zone Government and related services furnished the Company	2.5
Materials consumed in operations	4.3
Rentals, transportation and other miscellaneous	1.4
	$45.4
Less--	
Increase in costs of materials and services charged to construction and to the Canal Zone Government	2.7
	$42.7

*Proposal, p. 11.

Treaty Negotiations with the Republic of Panama

At the present time, the United States Treasury pays the Republic of Panama an annuity of $2,328,200, of which $518,718 is reimbursed to the Treasury by the Panama Canal Company. The Statement of Principles agreement between Secretary of State Henry Kissinger and Panamanian Foreign Minister Juan Tack in February 1974 promised in effect that the United States will increase its payments to Panama.[18]

A draft treaty package developed by United States and Panamanian negotiators in 1967, which was not ratified, included provision for royalty payments to Panama rising from 17 to 22 cents per long ton of cargo transited through the Canal.[19] A 17-cent royalty on cargo transiting the Canal in 1973 would have amounted to a payment of $21,685,495. This figure may be taken as an indication of the level of payments Panama would like to receive.

The preceding figures suggest that the Panama Canal Company is in no position to reimburse the United States Treasury for increased payments to Panama without incurring deficits. This assumes that Congress chooses to consider additional annuity payments to Panama as part of Panama Canal operating costs.

The rising costs of operating the Canal, and the desire to recover investments in the waterway make it necessary to consider a rise in the toll rate, or possibly a change in the toll system.

Views of American Merchant Marine

Albert E. May, Vice President of the American Institute of Merchant Shipping (AIMS), a national trade association of the U.S.-flag steamship industry, appeared before the Subcommittee on Panama Canal in July of 1973. AIMS comprises 34 member companies who own and operate oceangoing vessels. During his presentation, Mr. May made several remarks in regard to the Panama Canal toll system and its relation to American shipping and the economy of the United States. In regard to the value of the Panama Canal:

Other [AIMS] companies transit the canal . . . on virtually every voyage. If the canal were no longer available, the effect on these latter carriers and on the U.S. and world commerce would be disastrous. [20]

In regard to the effect of a toll increase of 50 percent, AIMS took the position that:

(1) The ability of intercoastal shipping to compete with the railroads would be reduced, thereby displacing intercoastal shipping operations, particularly shipments of chemicals;

(2) Toll increases would be passed on in the form of higher freight rates, raising the price of products shipped through the Canal;

(3) Substantial reductions in the number of vessels and cargo tonnage transiting the Canal would occur, resulting in considerable reduction in toll revenue which would probably offset any anticipated revenue increase;

(4) The economics of pumping petroleum across the Isthmus through a pipeline would be enhanced to the disadvantage of moving tankers through the Canal. [21]

The impact of a toll increase on general cargo would be moderate, but, according to Mr. May,

However, on bulk commodities where you have a very low value per ton and where the cost of transportation in bulk carriers is a more vital element in movement—then—if you increase cost $1 per ton (100 percent), you would begin to price certain bulk commodities out of the market that takes them through the canal. [22]

Finally, Mr. May voiced the opinion that a distinction should be made between the economic costs of the Canal operation and political costs that might arise in the course of meeting Panama's legitimate aspirations.

Fundamentals of Toll Policy

The toll system of the Canal is primarily an economic matter. To appreciate toll problems, some economic principles must be developed. Understanding these may prove somewhat taxing for the non-expert, but will provide greater insight into the factors which make the Panama Canal a valuable resource.

Definitions

Toll Policy. The policy establishing the level of Panama Canal tolls is determined by the United States Congress. The present policy objective is that operating costs should be recovered from toll receipts.

Toll System. The toll system encompasses the method used to determine the toll. This typically has two parts: the toll rates, and a second part which varies with the system, but for the present system it is the net tonnage.

Benefits. Benefits and profits are usually synonymous and are measured in dollars. Benefits may also be of a political nature such as those the United States obtained by putting men on the moon. Political or foreign policy considerations must be weighed subjectively.

Table 3

Average Effective Toll for Selected Commodities
Transiting the Panama Canal*

Commodity	Effective Toll per Weight Ton
Manufactured steel	$ .46
Coal	.55
Rice	.65
Soybeans	1.09
Paper	1.53
Bananas	2.76
Automobiles	7.23

*IOCSC, p. IV-137.

Effective Toll Rate. The cargoes that transit the Canal are the carriers' source of income. The carrier pays the toll, but cargo bears the toll burden. The effective toll rate is the incidence of tolls against the cargo calculated in dollars per long ton of 2,240 pounds.

The density of the cargo is significant when computing the effective toll rate. A Japanese auto carrier may be able to carry 1,000 long tons of cars on its eastbound transit, but, after discharging its cargo, it may pick up 12,000 long tons of Florida phosphate rock for its return trip.

The toll for either transit would be approximately $7,300. The effective toll for the autos would be $7.30 per long ton and only $0.60 for the phosphate rock.

The effective toll rate is unique to each shipment, depending on the density of the cargoes aboard and how fully laden the ship is. Table 3 gives some sample average values.

Value of Service. Each transiting commodity derives some ultimate benefit from employing the Canal shortcut. The value of service is the savings which use of the Canal permits. For example, lumber costs $40.37 per long ton not counting Panama Canal tolls to move from Seattle to New York going by the Canal. The next cheapest alternative to use of the Canal is railroad shipment at $49.30 per long ton. The value of service is the difference between these two rates, $8.93, which is also called the willingness to pay since the lumber would bear an effective toll up to $8.93 before being diverted to rail shipment.

Consumer Surplus. The consumer surplus is the net benefit of obtaining transit services. It is the difference between the value of service and what shippers must pay to use the Canal shortcut. The Canal was constructed for the purpose of creating these benefits. In the example of lumber moving from Seattle to New York, the consumer surplus is $8.93 minus the effective toll of approximately $1.00 equaling $7.93 per long ton. In 1973, 376,000 long tons of lumber moved through the Canal between the West and East Coasts of the United States. Thus, consumers saved approximately $3 million in their lumber bills as a consequence of the provision of Canal transit services.

Sensitivity. The smaller the consumer surplus for a commodity, the more sensitive it is to increases in its effective toll rate. A small rate increase could cause it to be diverted to the nearest price competitive mode of transport.

Major General Walter P. Leber, Governor of the Panama Canal Zone and President of the Panama Canal Company, made some insightful remarks relating to the above definitions in a presentation to the House of Representatives Subcommittee on Panama Canal.

> One major objective [of a new toll study] was to determine what will happen to canal traffic and revenues if tolls are adjusted upward. Is traffic sensitive to change? We know that shippers will complain, but will they go elsewhere? If we were to believe a common misconception about the canal, customers have no choice—there is no serious competition to the canal and we could just raise tolls as we please. This is not the case—the canal must compete.[23]

He went on to say that there were three concepts which must be borne in mind when studying the role of competition.

(a) Shippers have many alternatives for moving their products.

These alternatives are carefully evaluated long before a decision is made to ship a commodity through the Canal.

(b) Despite the fact that toll rates have not risen over the years, they are still a significant factor in figuring shipping costs. This is because technological improvements have reduced the costs of other forms of transportation so that the competitive position of the Canal has actually decreased over the years.

(c) The value of the cargo transiting the Canal is not a good basis for assessing tolls. This is because both high and low value cargoes have similar opportunities for diversion to other transport modes. So, although a high-value commodity may be capable of paying a higher toll, it does not follow that it will be willing to do so.

Governor Leber further pointed out that the maximum toll is one which makes the total cost of using the Canal equal to the cost of the cheapest alternative. If tolls greater than the value of service are charged, which is the monopoly profit maximizing toll, business will be lost.

There are a variety of objectives related to a toll system which the Congress and the Panama Canal Company may wish to consider over and above recovering costs. These may be achieved by a variety of systems.

Objectives

The policy objectives of a new toll system could be to:
1. Minimize change from the present system
2. Maximize use of the Canal by shippers
3. Promote a fair system
4. Maximize economic benefits accruing to the world
5. Maximize economic benefits accruing to the United States

1. *Minimize Change from the Present System*

The present toll system was formulated in 1912-1913 and remains largely unchanged. The United States derives prestige benefits from having maintained an acceptable system over the years.

Changes in the rules for computing the toll, other than a simple change in rates might lead to financial as well as diplomatic benefits. Ultimately, these must be weighed with the costs of implementing new rules. For example, eliminating tolls altogether and having a free passage, such as that at the Cape Cod Canal, would cost the United States $150 million a year, but this might be offset by the improved international relations such a move would promote. This would amount to subsidizing shipping using the Canal, but would possibly cause many countries that are now critical of United States Canal policy to shift their positions. At the same time, this would make it difficult to reimpose tolls without incurring general protest.

The Congress may wish to implement desired changes in the system over a number of years. Extensive changes in the toll system now, however, may make future changes less disruptive or necessary. Alternatively, future costs and benefits may be discounted in present decisions. These factors are related to the permanence and durability considerations of the toll system.

Depending on the nature of the changes involved the economic costs and benefits of change could be large or small and would ultimately be borne by shippers and consumers of commodities passing through the Panama Canal.

2. *Maximize Use of the Canal by Shippers*

The Congress could seek to recover operating and maintenance costs from toll revenue while simultaneously encouraging the maximum number of shippers to use the Canal who could do so profitably. This is essentially the present policy.

Some shippers may benefit more from use of the waterway than others. These have a high consumer surplus. Such shippers would absorb a larger toll increase without diverting their cargoes from the Canal. It might be possible by some manipulation of rates for the Canal to price its services to yield a given level of toll revenue collected from all users, paying equally, or from a few users, willing to pay considerably more, letting others pay token charges. The latter might be desirable from a global economic viewpoint, but it is likely that those paying the most would object that they were subsidizing others. Such differential pricing would be necessary to completely achieve the present policy.

3. *Promote a Fair System*

The manner in which the Panama Canal is operated reflects upon the United States. It could be an objective of the government to employ tolls to advance some foreign policy purpose. Tolls might be structured, for instance, so that the incidence of toll charges on the economies of developing countries would be lighter and more advantageous than on those of more advanced states. This might be considered fair and equitable by all, or it might not. What constitutes a fair system depends largely on the point of view.

The treaty with Great Britain, however, forbids the United States using tolls to discriminate against any nation or its citizens. To change the toll system to benefit the economies of a certain class of states would require a revision of the basic treaty structure. This may be possible, but there would be political questions that would require careful analysis. If the altered toll system were to work to the disadvantage of the economy of the United States, for example, there would be sure to be obstacles raised in the Congress.

4. *Maximize World Economic Benefit*

The objective of Canal toll policy might be to assess tolls so as to maximize economic benefits without specifying to whom the benefits would accrue. Since the Panama Canal facilitates world trade, benefits of this policy would be distributed world-wide, although the United States economy would benefit the most since a large percentage of Canal trade originates from or is destined to United States ports. This policy weighs income to both rich and poor on an equal basis, ignoring the equity aspect of toll policy.

Such an objective is achieved in a price and service competitive situation. Pure competition depresses the prices charged down to a level which just recovers costs and maximizes the consumer surplus. The Canal Company holds a monopoly on Isthmian ship transit services, but the present policy results in prices which approximate those of a competitive situation.[24]

The objective of maximizing world benefits conflicts with a policy of maximizing use of the Canal by shippers only in that the latter objective might result in the transiting of cargoes whose benefit from the transit is less than the cost of providing the service. A small amount of such transits may be taking place under the present system since it has been found that approximately $1.2 million in 1967 costs, which were incurred from transiting small ships, were not recovered from the tolls these ships paid.[25]

5. *Maximize United States Economic Benefit*

A fifth objective might be to attempt to maximize United States economic benefits, using tolls as an instrument. This could be accomplished by charging Canal cargoes effective toll rates equal to their value of service. The benefits of Canal usage in the form of toll receipts would be captured by the Canal Company acting as a monopolist. The portion taken from U.S. citizens could in theory be returned in the form of tax cuts. That which remained could be used as foreign exchange or to retire Government debts.

Alternatively, traffic originating in or destined to the United States might possibly be charged lower tolls. This would be an inefficient method of achieving the stated objective, however, as part of the toll cut would be passed on to foreign interests, except for United States intercoastal trade. Furthermore, United States-related transits would have to be subsidized by foreign-to-foreign transits which would doubtless be objected to.

The objective of maximizing United States economic benefits is precluded by the terms of the 1901 treaty. A revenue maximizing toll system and rates may come about, however, if the United States agrees to pay Panama a large annuity to be recovered from tolls. In terms of toll charges, this would be little different than turning the Canal over to the Republic of Panama, since in either case maximum tolls would be charged and Panama would profit.

Since objectives may be partially in conflict, some compromise must be reached in efforts to achieve them. Methods have been developed in the last fifteen years in the academic community to deal with multi-objective investment problems, chiefly in the field of United States Government-sponsored water-resource planning.[26]

The Marginal Toll Policy: A Synthesis of Objectives

Having noted how the value of service rendered by the Canal relates to net economic benefits, it is interesting to consider a pricing policy which would set the effective toll rates so as to equalize the consumer surplus of each Panama Canal user. This pricing policy was proposed by the Atlantic-Pacific Interoceanic Canal Study Commission for application to a sea-level canal.[27]

Because each Canal user would obtain the same consumer surplus per ton of commodity transited, this might be considered equitable by many. It would also encourage maximum use of the Canal while remaining economically efficient.

To implement this policy would require that the Company exercise control over the effective toll rates of commodities transiting the Canal. This would entail charging different cargoes different rates which might be interpreted by some as discriminating among nations or their citizens, and would be complicated and costly to administer.

Administrative Costs

A toll system capable of recognizing the individual Canal user's value of service would be difficult to administer. Given the right of the Canal Company to require submission of various ship data and documents, there are few conceivable toll systems that would not be feasible. As the complexity of a system dependent on such documents increases, so do administrative costs. One cannot maximize the gross benefits of a toll system while minimizing its costs. Rather, one must maximize the benefits minus the costs or the net benefit.

The costs of administration will rise with increased levels of traffic. It would, thus, become more difficult for the Canal Company to process and transit commercial vessels promptly as the volume of traffic employing the Canal increases.

Should a toll assessment system be instituted that required several hours per ship to administer, it would erode the Company's ability to provide rapid service. It would be costly to commercial shipping to delay or inhibit its free movement. The provision of rapid service is a matter of considerable prestige to the United States Government.

It is also desirable that the toll system discourage shippers from fraudulently representing ship tonnage or cargo volume. The detection of misrepresentations would place an added burden on Canal Company personnel and the prosecution of offenders would be costly for the Company as well as embarrassing for the Government.

Possible Toll Systems

Just as different designs are more or less successful in achieving the objectives of a project, so toll systems may be more or less successful in achieving the objectives of Panama Canal toll policy.

The Present System

The Panama Canal net tonnage toll system is widely accepted and has proved to be satisfactory to both the Panama Canal Company and ocean shippers.

The present system does not directly recognize the value of service rendered to shippers, nor is it economically efficient in terms of competitive cost pricing, so it can be neither equitable according to our definition, nor economically optimal. These deficiencies cause no problems at low toll rates.

Studies based on 1967 traffic data showed that moderately higher revenue needs could not be achieved with the present system without charging excessive amounts of Canal cargo effective toll rates above willingness to pay.[28] This would be inefficient economically since much of the traffic lost to the Canal would employ the next most costly alternative such as the land-bridge, superships on all-sea trade routes, or air freight. These alternatives use more resources than ships to accomplish the same result. Furthermore, traffic continuing to use the waterway would have to bear a higher toll burden than if no traffic were lost.[29]

The primary advantages of the present toll system are that it is simple, predictable and minimizes paperwork. Only one document, the certificate of Panama Canal tonnage, is needed to assess tolls, together with a determination of whether the vessel is in ballast or is laden. Toll charges can usually be determined in one hour or less by the Company admeasurer.[30]

An entirely new toll system can probably be reconciled with the requirements of the Hay-Pauncefote Treaty so long as the new system is based solely on economic factors.

Other Toll Systems Now in Use

The three other major canals, the St. Lawrence Seaway, the Kiel, and the Suez Canal, all have some variations and differences in toll systems. The toll systems of the Suez Canal and Kiel Canal are similar in principle to the Panama Canal in that the basic fees are related to cargo-carrying capacity of the ship rather than to type or value of cargo carried.[31]

1. *The St. Lawrence Seaway*

The system used by the Seaway differs considerably from that used by the Panama Canal. The Seaway assesses a toll against the tonnage of the ship somewhat like the Panama Canal, but gross tonnage, as computed according to the rules of the nation of registry of the vessel, is the standard. Furthermore, there is a charge per short ton of cargo carried, using either a bulk rate and/or a general cargo rate depending on the type of cargo. There is also a charge per passenger, a charge for each lock transited, and a minimum charge for pleasure craft and for other vessels.

2. *Suez Canal*

Tolls at the Suez Canal are assessed on a Suez measurement tonnage basis with a laden and ballast rate. The Suez Canal Tonnage Certificate is the primary document for assessing Suez Canal tolls. The Suez Canal also applies a surcharge for vessels whose draft or beam exceeds specified measurements, in contrast to the Panama Canal system. In 1967, before closure, laden vessels were charged 34 Egyptian piastres—$0.87—per net ton. Ballast vessels paid 15.5 piastres—$0.40—per net ton.

3. *Kiel Canal*

The toll system for the Kiel Canal is based on gross tonnage as computed according to the rules of the national registry of the vessel. There is a basic charge for transiting and additional charges for the Kiel Canal Agency and for pilotage, all payable in Deutsche marks. The rate per gross ton is steadily reduced as the tonnage of the vessel increases, like an inverted graduated tax. The rates are reduced for vessels in ballast. There are extra charges for vessels exceeding a specified draft as well as a rebate to regular users.

In a study prepared for the Panama Canal Company, five ingenious toll assessment systems were analyzed. [32] A computer program was written, which approximately described how each of the proposed systems would have distributed the toll burden according to ship size, vessel type, and cargo type at moderately and substantially higher toll levels. Space permits only abbreviated discussion of the proposed systems here.

Toll Systems Based on Charges Against Cargo

A Commodity Surcharge and a Commodity Rate system have been suggested. These attempt to price Panama Canal services according to the value of service rendered by the Canal. These systems were found to be capable of extracting the maximum amount of toll revenue while overpricing a minimum amount of traffic which could profitably employ the Canal.

While these systems would achieve revenue objectives, their administrative costs would be significantly greater than the present system's. High costs would result from the necessity of determining the types and volumes of the various commodities carried by the transiting vessels.

Common carriers usually carry a variety of commodities for different shippers and consignees. If available, the cargo manifest may be 500 pages in length. There may be no information available regarding the contents of containers because container and general cargo ships are usually dispatched before a complete manifest is prepared. The complete manifest is airmailed to the port of destination while the ship is en route. To require detailed commodity information prior to transit would be a burdensome change for shippers, and would lower the value of service they receive from transiting the Canal.

Commodities would be charged under these proposed systems as either individual commodities or in classes. Classification and rates would be subject to controversy and lobbying by shippers to establish favorable tolls for their shipments. The rates would be at least partially a matter of subjective judgment, possibly leaving the Company open to criticism in regard to equity considerations.

Canal personnel would have to verify the declarations submitted by transiting ships. For general cargo vessels, inspections of the cargo holds might be necessary. A certain amount of undetectable fraud would be likely. Also, disputes between the Canal Company and shippers might become more common.

As the value of service for individual commodity flows changes due to improving technology and local market fluctuations, it is likely that rates would have to be altered if the objectives of the system were to be met. Necessary rate adjustments are likely to be frequent due to the systems' complex rate structure.

In order to ascertain changes in value of service, the Company would have to make regular surveys of international shipping markets. There would be little incentive on the part of shippers to be candid concerning the value of service they receive from Canal use since evasions could result in a low value of service rating and lower toll assessments.

These two systems would achieve the objectives of the marginal pricing toll policy.

A third proposed system would base toll charges on the market value of the cargo carried by transiting vessels. This toll system was found to possess all of the administrative costs of the other cargo-related systems without possessing any of their advantages. The primary shortcoming of a Cargo Value system would be its limited recognition of the value of service rendered by the Canal. It is not the value of the cargo so much as the cost of alternative means of transport that sets the maximum amount shippers will pay to transport their goods.

Toll Systems Based on Earning Capacity

Two other systems would assess tolls against the cargo-carrying capacity of transiting vessels. A Variable Ship Charge system would employ the present Panama Canal rules for calculating the tonnage part of the toll system. The other half of the system, the toll rate charge per net ton, would depend upon the value of service of the predominant cargo commodity carried by the vessel, the idea being to vary the tonnage charge so as to bring the effective toll rate up to some desired level.

Since a ship may carry a variety of cargoes of mixed value of service, this would not be a perfect value of service pricing system. Also, it would require fairly complete documentation of the cargo carried by transiting vessels and these documents would have to be verified by the Canal Company boarding party.

A Ship Size system would be based on the existing Panama Canal tonnage measurement rules, but the rates would depend on the tonnage of the ship. The tonnage rate would decrease as the tonnage of the ship increased, like an inverted graduated tax. The reduction in rate per net ton as total tonnage increases has the effect of reducing the average toll per net ton paid by the larger vessels.

The rates would be constructed so as to recognize, insofar as possible, the relative value of service of the transiting commodities. The recognition would be only indirect, however, since this system would assess tolls without regard for the volume or type of cargo carried. The basis for recognition is that bulk commodities, having a generally lower value of service than general cargo, tend to be transported in larger vessels. There are many exceptions to this, however, such as the Panamax-sized containerships now plying trade routes passing through the Panama Canal.

Administratively, this would be little different from the present system. Assuming a reasonable rate structure, shippers are likely to accept this system because it is similar to the present one. The Ship Size system would discriminate only in respect to ship size, granting large ships quantity discounts which is a common business practice. Furthermore, rates would be structured to recover more from the smaller ships of less than 1,500 net tons.[33]

A poor ability to recognize value of service, an ability which will be eroded further as the average size of vessels transiting the Canal grows, is the Ship Size system's primary shortcoming.

Proposal to Increase Toll Rate

Projection of 1975 Revenues and Costs

The Panama Canal Company has projected that toll income will fall $24 million short of the $145 million required of toll revenue in 1975. This projection assumed that the Suez Canal would remain closed. The Company has estimated that in 1973 $9.5 million in toll revenues were realized from traffic previously associated with the Suez Canal trade routes.[34] When the Suez Canal reopens, it is likely that some Suez-related Panama Canal traffic will be lost. The 1975 shortfall of toll revenue may be larger than anticipated.

Studies for the Panama Canal Company forecast toll revenues if no change is made in toll rates. See Table 4.

Table 4

Toll Revenues*
(in millions)

| | Fiscal Year | | |
	1973 Actual	1975 Projected	Increase (Decrease)
Commercial vessels	$111.1	$119.6	$8.5
United States Government vessels	2.3	1.6	(.7)
Total	$113.4	$121.2	$7.8

*Proposal, p. 9.

Table 5

Proposed Toll Rates for the Panama Canal
(per net ton)

| | Toll Rates | | Amount of |
	Present	Recommended	increase
Laden condition	$0.90	$1.08	$0.18
Ballast condition	0.72	0.86	0.14
Per displacement ton	0.50	0.60	0.10

In addition to revenues from tolls, the Company derives revenues from supportive operations. These are estimated to grow by $12.4 million over 1973 figures to $98.9 million in 1975, but will be approximately offset by rising costs of these same services.[35]

In order to comply with the requirements of law, the Board of Directors of the Panama Canal Company has proposed a 20 percent increase in the rate on laden vessels and proportionate increases in the ballast and displacement rates.[36] This increase is expected to generate additional revenues just sufficient to cover the $24 million shortfall. The Fair Labor Standards Act revision and the reopening of Suez, means that even with the toll increase, the Company will probably experience a deficit of $10 million or more in 1975. Table 5 lists the proposed rates. The only previous proposal to raise rates was turned down in 1949.

Effect on Canal Traffic of Proposed Rate Increase

Beginning in 1963, the Board of Directors authorized the Comptroller of the Panama Canal Company to initiate studies of the adequacy of the toll rates. These included studies of the sensitivity of Panama Canal traffic to toll rate increases, and inquiry into the consumer surplus shippers were receiving from Canal use. The latest of these continuing studies was completed in late 1973.[37]

The study concluded that toll increases of 15 percent or greater would cause some containerships moving on the Europe-Asia trade route to move onto tracks avoiding the Canal. Table 6 lists the estimated percentage loss of Panama Canal cargo tonnage for various toll rate increases.

Evidently, the proposed 20 percent toll rate increase will have a negligible effect on Panama Canal traffic patterns, although all shippers will have to transfer some of the benefits they derive from Canal use to the Panama Canal Company. Insofar as these benefits were accruing to consumers of Panama Canal-transited commodities, the market price of these commodities will rise.[38]

Table 6

Estimated Percentage Loss of Forecast Panama Canal Cargo Tonnage*

Toll Rate Increase	1975	1980	1985
15%	0	0.1	0.3
25%	0.4	2.1	2.7
50%	1.5	5.6	6.2

*Proposal, pp. 80-81.

Future Toll Strategies

Aside from the factors mentioned above with which the Panama Canal Company must deal, three other questions merit attention. These are:

1. Should the Universal Measurement System be used by the Canal in the event that it is adopted internationally?
2. What should be done in the years ahead when the Panama Canal begins to attract more traffic than it can serve?
3. What should be the toll policy and system for a sea-level canal?

International Convention on Tonnage Measurement

The Inter-Governmental Maritime Consultative Organization (IMCO), a specialized agency of the United Nations, has under it a Subcommittee on Tonnage Measurement whose purpose is to develop a universal tonnage measurement system. There is at present no single set of rules for establishing all national ship registry tonnage.

Under the sponsorship of IMCO, an International Conference on Tonnage Measurement of Ships, held in June 1969 in London, proposed a Convention to establish a universal measurement system (UMS).[39] This Convention will come into force two years after the date on which not fewer than 25 States, the combined merchant fleets of which constitute not less than 65 percent of the gross tonnage of the world's merchant shipping, have signed without reservation as to acceptance, or deposited instruments of acceptance or accession with IMCO.

The United States is signatory to this Convention and 15 Governments have ratified it, representing 46 percent of the tonnage of the world's merchant shipping.[40] There is a general consensus that the system will come into force by the end of 1977.

The Convention applies to international voyages of ships registered in countries whose governments are contracting parties. The President's submission of the Convention to the Senate for ratification recommended exempting the Panama Canal from use of the system for the time being.[41]

The existence of a universal measurement system could eliminate the need for the Canal Company to maintain its own rules. It is in the interest of the United States to conform to commonly accepted practices, and if UMS comes into wide use, the possibility of applying these rules to the assessment of Canal tolls should be carefully analyzed. Furthermore, Panama Canal certificates of tonnage are presently derived from the calculation of national gross tonnages. Under UMS, national tonnages might no longer be calculated. This could possibly mean that the Panama Canal Company would have to measure each ship from scratch which would be a tremendous task.

A possible drawback of UMS is that it is designed to approximate as nearly as possible existing rules for determining national tonnages. These rules are not formulated to measure the cargo-carrying capacity of ships as emphasized by the Panama Canal rules. As a result, there appears to be no way to set the ballast and laden rates of a two-rate system using UMS so as to approximate the present distribution of tolls burden among various shippers.[42]

It is unknown at present whether the inevitable redistribution of tolls burden would result in a better or worse agreement with the distribution of value of service. It is conceivable that the distribution under UMS could be quite inequitable in this sense. The Canal Company is continuing its study of UMS directed toward recommending a course of action in the event the new system comes into force.

Toll Policy for the Panama Canal When It Is Saturated with Traffic

If toll rates are kept low, it is probable that the Panama Canal will eventually attract more traffic than it has capacity to handle. We forecast this to occur about 2010 as stated in Chapter 4. A saturated Panama Canal would be undesirable for a number of reasons, but the primary one is economic.

When the Canal nears full utilization, the following will occur:

1. The Company's marginal cost of transiting vessels will rise due to an inability to provide transit service to all vessels in an efficient manner.

2. Some vessels, whose cargo has a high value of service, will not be able to transit because other vessels arrive at the Canal first whose cargo has a low value of service.

   The Canal's limited transiting resources will be allocated randomly among ships, some of them benefiting from using the Canal less than the cost incurred in providing them transit.

Cargoes having a high value of service should have priority to transit when the Canal is saturated. This segregation can be accomplished by:

1. Rationing Canal services;
2. Setting tolls sufficiently high to insure that the marginal cost of providing service is recovered. The number of ships seeking transit then would equal the number that the Canal could accommodate.

Either of these techniques would insure that economic loss due to ships lying idle at anchor while waiting to transit would be kept to a minimum. The formation of a queue of waiting ships would be an indication that resources were being wasted.

The Governor of the Panama Canal agrees with the above conclusion. Quoting Governor David S. Parker:

Although priority for use of a limited capacity canal ought to go to those willing to pay the higher tolls, the basis on which the tolls are paid . . . determines who can get the most economic benefit from the canal and be willing to pay higher tolls. [43]

Incidentally, if tolls are raised as a method to deal with saturation of capacity, the Canal will begin to recover revenues in excess of operating costs. These profits would be a measure of the resources that otherwise would have been wasted. Presumably, the profits could be set aside to finance larger facilities, such as a sea-level canal [44] or they could be given away as a form of foreign aid. Since raising tolls would discourage transits, in a sense the Canal need never be saturated.

Toll Policy for a Sea-Level Canal

The objectives of tolls policy for a sea-level canal would be the same as for the lock canal. Many of the operational constraints which hold in the 1970s for the Panama Canal may not be binding for a sea-level canal, however, because of continuing technological progress. The advancement of computer science may eventually reduce the administrative costs of the more complicated proposed toll systems.

Conclusion

The Panama Canal toll system was formulated 62 years ago. In light of the many factors involved in selecting a policy and designing a system, the original achievement of Dr. Johnson and the others who played a part must be admired. Despite the many changes that have taken place in maritime commerce over the years, and the considerable body of economic knowledge accumulated since Dr. Johnson's day, the present toll system cannot be faulted. It makes concessions to economic efficiency, but these are probably more than compensated for by its ease of application.

The Panama Canal toll system does have weaknesses, however, and if the level of receipts is to be significantly increased, a new system may prove necessary. The Panama Canal Company is continuing to explore possible new systems while policies are debated at the highest levels.

The Panama Canal Company has decided its course of action with respect to the present dilemma of rising costs and diplomatic maneuverings. The next opportunity for change in the toll system will probably not come for several years,[45] the Government being reluctant to make frequent changes.

In this chapter no simple recipe for solving toll problems has been proposed. Rather, possible objectives have been formulated, and consequences of achieving them examined. When questions arise as to the adequacy of the present toll system, the merits of possible changes in the system or rates should be examined with regard to the achievement of desired objectives.

Our treatment of toll problems did not address operational methods because:

1. Objectives and consequences must be known before rational decisions can be made;
2. The feasibility and effectiveness of operational techniques will change with time.

We recommend that more detailed studies be made of the total economic benefits the Canal provides. When this is determined, it will provide both United States and Panamanian negotiators with a tangible measure of the worth of the Canal, and facilitate negotiations and decisions.

CHAPTER SIX FOOTNOTES

1. 33 *United States Statutes at Large* (hereafter cited as Stat.) 2234.

2. 32 Stat. 1903.

3. 37 Stat. 560.

4. Emory R. Johnson, *Report on Canal Traffic and Tolls*, Washington, 1912.

5. Emory R. Johnson, *Measurement of Vessels for the Panama Canal*, Washington, 1913.

6. Executive Order, November 13, 1912, pp. 131-132. Executive Order, November 21, 1913, p. 154.

7. Proclamation 2247, August 25, 1937, amended by Proclamation 2249, August 31, 1937. 35 *Code of Federal Regulations* 133.1.

8. 53 Stat. 1807.

9. Exchange of Notes dated June 20, 1904, S. Doc. 401, 59th Congress, as modified by exchanges of notes dated March 26 and April 2, 1930, and May 28 and June 6, 1931.

10. Treaties and International Agreements Series (U.S.) 3297. The two recent devaluations of the U.S. dollar, having reduced the real purchasing power of U.S. currency, has resulted in establishment of the annuity at $2,328,000.

11. 42 Stat. 2122. This treaty settled differences arising out of events which took place on the Isthmus of Panama in 1903 when Panama declared independence from Colombia with United States backing.

12. 64 Stat. 1038.

13. 2 Canal Zone Code 412.

14. *Proposal to Increase Tolls* (hereafter cited as *Proposal*), Panama Canal Company, 1973, p. 13.

15. *Proposal*, p. 9.

16. *Proposal*, p. 10.

17. *Panama Canal Briefing*, Hearing before the Committee on Merchant Marine and Fisheries, House of Representatives, No. 93-8, April 13, 1973, p. 19.

18. *Department of State Bulletin*, Vol. LXX, No. 1809, February 25, 1974, pp. 184-185.

19. *Interoceanic Canal Studies, 1970* (hereafter cited as IOCSC), p. 11.

20. *Shipping and Canal Operations*, Hearing before the Subcommittee on Panama Canal of the Committee on Merchant Marine and Fisheries, House of Representatives, July 17, 1973, No. 93-19, p. 45.

21. *Shipping and Canal Operations*, p. 48.

22. *Ibid.*, p. 49.

23. *Panama Canal Traffic, Capacity, and Tolls*, Hearing before the Subcommittee on Panama Canal of the Committee on Merchant Marine and Fisheries, House of Representatives, No. 91-25, April 22, 1970, p. 30.

24. A discriminating monopolist, operating the Canal to his own advantage, would charge each user his willingness to pay and capture all the benefits. The disadvantage of monopolists charging rates greater than the costs of providing service is that there is no incentive to minimize operating costs and too little service is usually offered at too high a price. The United States and other

nations may or may not prefer that the total benefits of providing transit services accrue to the nation operating the Panama Canal. These considerations must be borne in mind when evaluating the Republic of Panama's claim that its geographical location is a natural resource which the United States has prevented it from exploiting fully.

25. *Report on Development and Evaluation of Tolls Policies and Alternative Systems* (hereafter cited as Andersen), a contract study prepared for the Panama Canal Company, 1970, p. VII-17.

26. David C. Major, *Multiobjective Water Resource Planning*, American Geophysical Union Water Resources Monograph 4, draft, 1973, and United Nations Industrial Development Organization, *Guidelines for Project Evaluation*, United Nations, 1972.

27. IOCSC, p. IV-139.

28. Andersen, p. II-41. The data on which this study was based are now out of date. Significantly higher levels of revenue can now be achieved with the present system, but this is due to the devaluation of the dollar, not to any intrinsic merit in the present system.

29. This point is expanded upon in IOCSC, pp. 139-141.

30. If it is necessary to measure the ship, this takes several hours.

31. For a description of the systems, see *Shipping and Canal Operation*, pp. 74-82.

32. The complete report is Andersen.

33. Small ships do not contribute toward the fixed costs of the Canal operation and many of them are not even assessed the Company's marginal cost of providing the service under the present system and rates.

34. *Proposal*, p. 9.

35. *Proposal*, p. 9.

36. *Federal Register*, Vol. 38, No. 247, December 27, 1973, Part 1, p. 7.

37. *The Sensitivity of Canal Traffic to Toll Increases*, December 1973. The results of this study are summarized in *Proposal*, pp. 74-81.

38. A study of the probable distribution of the burden of a Panama Canal toll rate increase among countries is found in *Economic Impact of Panama Canal Toll Increases*, 1968, which was a contract study of the Panama Canal Company.

39. *The International Convention on Tonnage Measurement of Ships, 1969*, Intergovernmental Maritime Consultative Organization, London, 1969.

40. Personal communication, Philip L. Steers, Jr., Comptroller, Panama Canal Company, May 8, 1974.

41. *Convention on Tonnage Measurement of Ships*, Message from the President of the United States, Senate, 92nd Congress, 2nd session, Executive N, June 15, 1972.

42. *Panama Canal Briefings*, p. 61.

43. *Panama Canal Briefings*, p. 54.

44. See G.S. Lingley, *Analysis of Interoceanic Canal Alternatives*, Master of Science thesis, Department of Ocean Engineering, M.I.T., 1973.

45. In testimony before the Subcommittee on Panama Canal, Governor David Parker, President of the Panama Canal Company, indicated that the need for added revenues and the desirability of changing the toll system were being treated by the Company as separate questions and that a proposal to change the system, possibly to UMS, would be addressed after a toll rate increase was settled. *Shipping and Canal Operations*, pp. 74 and 82.

CHAPTER SEVEN

ALTERNATIVES FOR THE FUTURE OF THE CANAL

With the improvements now planned, the Panama Canal will be able to serve the needs of shipping for at least another twenty-five years.

A decision will have to be made sometime within this period, whether to keep the existing lock canal more or less as it is, or to add a larger set of locks to accommodate larger vessels, or to build a sea-level waterway, or alternatively to sell the Canal to Panama and to promote commerce by other means. New developments in technology and engineering give the United States a wide range of options.

The Revolution in Modes of Shipping

Marine transportation will remain a principal means of carrying bulk cargoes overseas for the foreseeable future. A large merchant marine will be maintained by many nations, including the United States. It is necessary to think of the implications of some of the newer trends taking place in the world of business and to free the mind from the limitations imposed by the traditional ways of carrying on trade.

A revolution is taking place in the modes of transporting goods. This is evidenced by the growth of air freight, the turn to container traffic, the development of the land- and mini-bridge systems of fast rail transport across the United States, the carrying of truck trailer rigs loaded with cargo on roll-on roll-off ships directly to overseas destinations via single ocean hauls, and the increasing processing of raw materials near their sources of origin. The general cargo freighter, while still the most numerous user of the Panama Canal, is being superseded by new specialized shipping.

Trends such as these raise questions whether racing technological change may not already be outpacing the usefulness of the older interoceanic shortcuts. These had their day when nations were dependent upon the plodding freighters and passenger vessels to carry goods and passengers overseas. Shippers were only momentarily upset, however, by the closure of the Suez Canal in 1967. Very large crude oil carriers circumnavigating Africa soon were moved into the breach. Fast containerships took the place of older general cargo carriers for much of the freight moving between Europe and the Far East and Oceania.

This historical record, to be sure, shows that ship traffic and cargo movement at the Panama Canal more than doubled between 1947 and 1974. World shipbuilding orders, on the other hand, show a mounting trend toward vessels that are at the maximum size that can be accommodated at the Canal, and larger. And business looks restlessly to markets and conditions of trade that break with older traditions and limitations.

World economic conditions suggest that foreign and domestic trade will continue to grow. Business news, nevertheless, points to rapid growth of channels of trade that are not hemmed in by older bounds of investment or limitations of trade routes.

Changing Importance of Interoceanic Canal

The construction of deepwater terminals, new loading facilities, and new port layouts are paralleling the appearance of larger carriers and specialized shipping. The vast new container ports in cities such as Halifax, Newark, Long Beach, Oakland and Seattle are instances of trends that are becoming increasingly well established. The rapid emergence of express freight carriers across the North Atlantic and the North Pacific, combined with the growth of synchronized and unitized rail service across the United States for high priority modular containers, is cutting into traditional Panama Canal trades to link markets in Asia and North America. And, not to be outdone, the Soviet Union is promoting the trans-Siberian rail system as a land-bridge route to link Europe and East Asian markets and suppliers.

The Panama Canal continues to function smoothly notwithstanding sixty years of service. This has been made possible by the meticulous care devoted to maintaining and improving the Canal and all its installations. There are limits, nevertheless, to the number of vessels that can be transited, and to the size and draft of ships that can be accepted at the locks, as we have discussed in Chapter Five. Furthermore, the Panamax ships are more costly to handle. They require more pilots to guide them through, more tugs to insure their safety, more lock personnel, and they consume more time in getting through confined spaces.

This is reflected in the rising costs of operation, resulting in a need for higher revenues. So steeply, in fact, are costs of operation rising, the initial 20 percent increase in tolls sought for early application will probably have to be followed by applications for additional increases in subsequent years. At some point, if this process is repeated, it may become counterproductive, inducing shippers to look to alternate routings and means of getting their cargoes to market.

Political Uncertainties

For most of the course of this book, attention has been focused upon the nonpolitical aspects of Canal commerce. It cannot be overlooked, however, that differences exist between the Republic of Panama and the United States over control of the Canal and over benefits to be derived from its use that cloud the outlook for the future.

Panamanian nationalism is restive to change the old order of relationships. Leaders seek to end the 1903 treaty, to gain sovereignty over the Canal, by agreement if possible, if not, by other means. They look to the establishment of a different order. This situation is closely related to any expansion of the waterway, even to continuance of United States possession.

The United States has invested a large amount of money and manpower in the Canal enterprise since 1903. The Canal has played a vital role in expanding United States oceanborne commerce. The United States position at the Isthmus has contributed to the influence of the country in Latin American affairs. The presence of United States defense forces has strengthened political and military stability in mid-America and been an important element in extending power throughout the Atlantic and the Pacific Ocean theaters. The Canal has been of major and continuing importance to the national security of this country.

Will the Canal be as indispensable throughout the next twenty-five years as it has been in the past? This cannot be answered with certainty.

The country should ask itself to what extent it may be worth holding onto the Canal if traffic does not continue to grow. It may be worth considering, for example, whether there are other means of transportation from which the United States would obtain greater benefit over the next 50 years if a comparable amount of money were expended upon these as it will require to keep the Canal operating, to defend it, and to enlarge its capacity if the United States deems this necessary. Would it be desirable to spur further new technologies of transport within and outside of the United States that will give the nation a larger edge over others because of its two-ocean position and its comparative advantage in modern technology and engineering?

The United States should also be asking itself what its long-range policy interests are in the hemisphere as a whole, and whether these will be advanced or retarded by holding onto the waterway, particularly if the country is to be made the butt of charges of aggression and colonialism because of the Canal Zone. There are no simple answers to these issues.

Cost of Enlarging the Waterway

Enlarging the Canal waterway beyond present limits will be a costly undertaking, even if collaboration can be obtained from the Republic of Panama and if the Canal Company is permitted to earn a reasonable return on the investment by means of higher tolls.

It is estimated that installing a third system of locks will cost $950 million; that constructing a sea-level canal will run into a minimum of $4 billion, excluding in both instances defense costs, payments to the Republic of Panama, and land procurement if this is needed.

Should the United States try to shoulder costs of this magnitude alone? Or should it endeavor to put together a consortium of investors including other powers and the World Bank, for example? If others are brought into the financing of a larger canal, should the supervision, administration, and operation of the waterway be made a joint responsibility in some way rather than being assumed, as up to now, by the United States alone? Arguments can be made on both sides of these issues.

Or, again, should the United States continue to shoulder the expense of operating, maintaining, defending, and keeping up the standard of operation it has held up at the Panama Canal? Or should it sell the aging Canal to the Republic of Panama and get out of the business of running an interoceanic waterway? A case could be made for doing this, but there are no simple answers as to whether it should be done or not.

The question arises in what direction the national policy should be moving over the next 30 to 40 years with respect to the Canal. Should it be holding onto a strip of land and a waterway that were purchased in good faith and made the marvel of engineering genius in the first decade of the century? Or should it be hastening new forms of transportation, new port systems, new methods in ship design and construction that it alone has the knowledge and the means of attaining? Should the Government not be supporting innovative studies of construction techniques, and new means of moving both large and small quantities of bulk cargo, and of separate varieties, to and from overseas destinations at less cost?

First, let us consider alternatives for handling the Canal itself. There are a half dozen different courses that might be taken with respect to the Canal.

Alternatives for Handling the Canal

1. *Keep Existing Canal Functioning*

One course of action is to keep the existing Canal functioning. Governor David S. Parker, addressing a Committee of the United States Congress in 1973, testified that he felt there is "a future for the current Panama Canal." By pursuing the capital improvement program to completion the Canal can be kept useful to world trade "beyond the end of the century." [1]

The program of improvements, as we have pointed out in Chapter Five, is designed to enable the Canal to reach the limits of its capacity.[2] If ships continue to increase in size beyond what the locks can physically accommodate, it may eventually be desirable to do more. Until such a decision is taken, however, the Canal can function with the present locks.

For the next fifteen years at least, a majority of ships in the world fleet will probably be able to fit within the locks, although the number of ships that are too large to do so will continue increasing unless an unexpected reversal takes place.

Forecasts suggest that more than 90 percent of the world merchant fleet will still be in sizes small enough to transit the existing Panama Canal by the year 2000. The Canal will be valuable to world shipping even if it is not enlarged. The average ship size at the Canal in 1973 was 9,124 tons. This is a long way from reaching the limits of capacity. The 10 percent of ships too large to transit may, however, represent 20 or more percent of the total lifting capacity of the world fleet.

A majority of the 34 member companies associated with the American Institute of Merchant Shipping have indicated that the Canal locks are adequate. Increasing the lock sizes will not materially affect their use of the Canal. Cargoes to be obtained, route designations, marketing arrangements, and port restrictions are the primary governing considerations that determine the sizes of vessels used on particular trade routes. While larger locks or a sea-level canal would permit shipowners to build and employ larger vessels on Canal routes, these would not necessarily follow on all routes. A major increase in tolls, if this should follow construction, would, on the other hand, cause serious concern if this were not matched by higher earnings at the same time.[3]

Keeping the present lock canal functioning until it is clear that a larger facility is needed is the only appropriate course to take. The margin for growth that is built into the system should suffice through the year 2000 unless there is a decided change in the mixture of ships carrying commerce via the Canal.[4]

Approximately 10 years are available for a decision on new construction in order to have it completed between the years 2000 and 2010. It may even be desirable to wait somewhat beyond this to allow traffic demand to build up further to assure commercial success of a new facility.

Postponing a decision beyond the optimum action point may discourage business from making long-term contracts for the development of raw materials that could profitably be exploited and shipped. But this is a risk that may have to be taken. We believe the United States should obtain the maximum usefulness out of its investment in the existing canal before undertaking construction of additional facilities.

Keeping the present canal operative has the advantage of tying up the least additional capital investment at this time. It will leave the United States free to decide what to do 10 or 20 years hence after there has been an opportunity to appraise cargo and transit movements further.

2. *Construct a Third Locks System*

An alternative for expanding the capacity of the Canal when this is

Fig. 33. The alignment of the 1941 Third Locks excavation is visible here to the right of Miraflores Locks. Panama Canal Company

156

desired, and for transiting larger vessels is to construct a third set of locks.

Experts have advocated such a step since 1937. A third locks program was authorized by the Congress in 1939.[5] Excavation for such locks was begun in 1941, but was abandoned the following year because of manpower and materials needs elsewhere. See Figure 33.

This plan was reviewed after the war, but rejected at that time in favor of a sea-level canal. A 1947 engineering study proposed a third locks system in combination with a high summit lake and elimination of the Pedro Miguel Lock.[6] No action was taken on this by the Congress, however. A 1960 study conducted for the House of Representatives recommended a sea-level construction in preference to a third locks system, as did a technical study done for the Secretary of the Army in 1964.

When the President's Interoceanic Canal Study Commission reviewed plans for its 1970 report, it mentioned the third locks plan, but definitely favored a sea-level canal instead. See Figure 34.

A bill introduced into the Congress by Representative Daniel J. Flood (Democrat, Pennsylvania), long-time supporter of the Panama Canal, calls for modernization and expansion of the existing canal by constructing Third Locks at Gatun; eliminating the Pedro Miguel Locks; creating a summit lake at that location; and consolidating the Miraflores and Third Locks in new three-step lock structures corresponding to those at Gatun where the excavation was done west of Miraflores in 1941-42. The lock chambers under this plan would have usable dimensions of 1,200 feet long, by 140 feet wide, and not less than 45 feet deep. A similar bill was introduced into the Senate by Senator Strom Thurmond (Republican, South Carolina).[7]

The object of these proposals is to permit the Canal to handle larger vessels, to speed up transit procedures, and to gain the advantages of a terminal lake anchorage at the Pacific end of the Canal. At the same time, the authors seek to commit the United States to making some progress on enlarging the Canal and to remaining at the Zone.

These proposals would enable the Canal to transit vessels up to 105,000 deadweight tons. They would extend the overall capacity to 35,000 transits a year or up to 87 lockages per day, depending upon the mixture of vessels that arrive for transit.

A variant put forward by the Interoceanic Canal Study Commission in 1970 suggested a Deep Draft Lock Canal with larger chambers that would be 150 feet wide by 65 feet over the sills. Although this would have the same overall capacity, it would take vessels up to 150,000 tons loaded. The initial cost of this was estimated to be $1.5 billion.[8]

None of these plans would take the very large bulk carriers. They would accommodate "intermediate size" tankers with a beam of 136.8

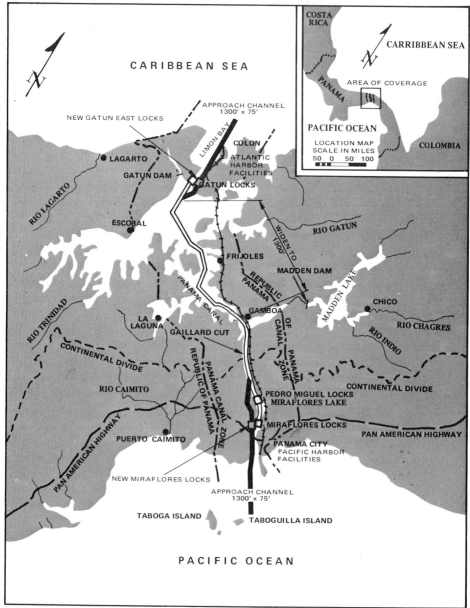

The map is adapted from Interoceanic Canal Studies 1970, Report of the President's Interoceanic Canal Study Commission, Chapter VII.

THIRD LOCKS SYSTEM

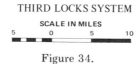

SCALE IN MILES

Figure 34.

feet. By lightening the ships somewhat, these could be brought down to around 100,000 tons with a draft of under 45 feet, and be able to use the Third Locks.[9]

Advantages of Third Locks

In addition to allowing both larger vessels and more ships to pass through the Canal, the Third Locks would facilitate traffic when one lane of the original locks is taken out of service for overhaul. The design would also provide a straighter navigable channel to and from the Pacific terminal, and would have the advantage of adding a high-level lake above Miraflores where vessels could anchor in time of fog or low visibility before proceeding into the Cut. This would allow more vessels to be moved north of the Miraflores Locks when visibility lowers, and thus be on their way sooner when conditions improve.

These locks could be built for less than half the cost of a sea-level canal. Toll increases to recover the cost might be less than what would be needed to recoup the costs of a sea-level canal. Tankers transporting Alaskan crude could probably afford to go through the Canal to East Coast ports or Caribbean refineries with oil not needed on the West Coast, where they could not do so if tolls had to be put up to a point needed to cover the cost of building a sea-level canal. This would depend upon the toll system and policy.

No private land would be needed for construction of the Third Locks and traffic could be kept moving through the existing locks for most of the time while building is going on. The Third Locks would also possibly do more to retain a fresh water barrier and thus avoid disturbing the ecology.

Disadvantages of Third Locks

Additional water supplies would be needed for the functioning of Third Locks, however. Lockage operations would require up to 50 percent more water than the existing locks take, depending on the size of the chambers. This could be secured by impounding additional streams tributary to Gatun Lake, or by pumping seawater into the lake, thus adding to the overall cost of the program. Since the Third Locks could not accommodate the very large bulk carriers, they would not satisfy the long-term interests of shipping.[10]

Furthermore, the Third Locks could not transit the largest aircraft carriers of the Navy. Hence, they would not contribute significantly to national defense. They thus appear to be an inadequate measure.

Acquiring the necessary additional water would be a serious problem. There are no large streams in the vicinity of the Canal that are not now harnessed. Water brought from a distance would be very expensive. Pumping salt water into Gatun and Miraflores Lakes could be done if enough energy can be purchased. This would significantly raise operating costs. These would have to be passed along in the form of higher tolls, thereby undermining the economies of scale larger locks would provide. Pumping salt water into the lakes, even on a part-time basis, would make the lakes brackish. This would impair their recreational use. It would damage the water supply of Panama City which draws upon Gatun Lake. Pumped water would also have deleterious effects upon equipment made to operate in fresh water. What is needed if the Third Locks are to be installed is another large Madden Dam to store more fresh water, but this is unavailable. If salt water pumping is undertaken the possibility exists that biota would be admitted to the Canal in larger quantities than at present with possibly harmful effects. Such problems would need to be examined thoroughly before a commitment is made to construct a larger lock system. [11]

A statement supplied by Governor David S. Parker for the 1973 Hearings summarizes the official position on the water requirements:

> Assuming a third locks was constructed by 1985, with a plan area approximately double that of the present locks, and assuming that they were used for twenty percent of the lockages, the additional water required would be of the same general magnitude as the entire additional capacity obtained through the [channel] deepening project. It would be necessary to immediately obtain additional water which would require a treaty change with Panama for impoundment, or sea water pumping or raising the [Gatun] lake level. . . . Raising the lake is a costly project in terms of the additional water supply created as compared to deepening or to other forms of impoundment. [12]

More skilled technicians would be needed to operate the locks and supervise their upkeep than for the existing canal or a sea-level waterway. This may be seen as an advantage or a disadvantage, depending upon the point of view.

We do not disparage the added capacity the Third Locks could give to the Canal. They would cost less than a sea-level waterway. At the same time, they would not satisfy the needs of the larger carriers, and are not economically viable today. From a defense point of view the lock canal would suffer seriously if Gatun Lake were to be drained by military action blowing out the locks.

Most of the Governors since 1947 have taken the view that the third locks idea is not the answer to the need for larger capacity. [13]

The situation with respect to lockage water is more serious today than it was in 1939 when the third locks project was first studied because the number of transits has already built up to nearly what was then expected in the year 2000.

We see the limited capacity the Third Locks would add, and the vulnerability of the Canal as drawbacks to expending large additional sums upon the Canal, particularly in view of the clouded political out-look at the Isthmus at this time.

3. *A Sea-Level Canal from Logarto to Puerto Caimito in Panama*

Five sites have been thought preferable among the routes possible for a sea-level canal through Central America. First, along the border of Nicaragua and Costa Rica, designated Route 8 by the 1970 Commission. Second, a site just west of the Canal Zone in the Republic of Panama, designated Route 10. Third, Route 14 which generally follows the Panama Canal itself within the Canal Zone. Fourth, Route 17 across eastern Panama at the Darien Peninsula. And, fifth, a line across northern Colombia from the Gulf of Uraba to Humboldt Bay, designated Route 25. See Figure 35.

Of the various possibilities, a route just west of the Canal Zone on a line from the town of Logarto, five miles from the Canal Zone on the Caribbean side, across a section of Gatun Lake, through the Chorrera Gap in the Continental Divide, and out to the Pacific Ocean at the mouth of the Caimito River, approximately 10 miles west of Panama City and Balboa, has been generally considered an optimal location from an engineering viewpoint for a sea-level waterway. Barrier dams would be erected to prevent draining Gatun Lake. See Figure 36.

A canal constructed along this route could be built in stages. A single-lane channel could be dug first and left at that until traffic demand warrants more. Or it could have a 14-mile passing lane excavated midway along the route. Or, alternatively, the canal could have two parallel channels for the entire distance to allow unimpeded two-way traffic. Tidal gates could restrict current flow within the canal to two knots.

Most of this route lies through undeveloped country, largely farming and grazing land. There are no heavily-populated areas along the way. The highest elevation is 400 feet. Nearness to Panama City, Colón and the Canal Zone provides access to a large supply of labor. Engineering personnel and equipment are situated at the Canal Zone for work on construction and maintenance.

The President's Commission was of the opinion in 1970 that "past negotiations indicate that a sea-level canal" on this route "should be acceptable to Panama under reasonable treaty conditions." [14] Subsequent events raise some questions on this score.

A 36-mile, single-lane, sea-level canal with 17 miles of two-lane approach channels was believed to have a capacity of 35,000 transits a year. A 14-mile passing lane added to the waterway could handle 56,000 transits. A full two-lane canal could transit up to 100,000 vessels a year, although the studies on which these figures were based are now considered to be incomplete. The cost of construction of a mini-

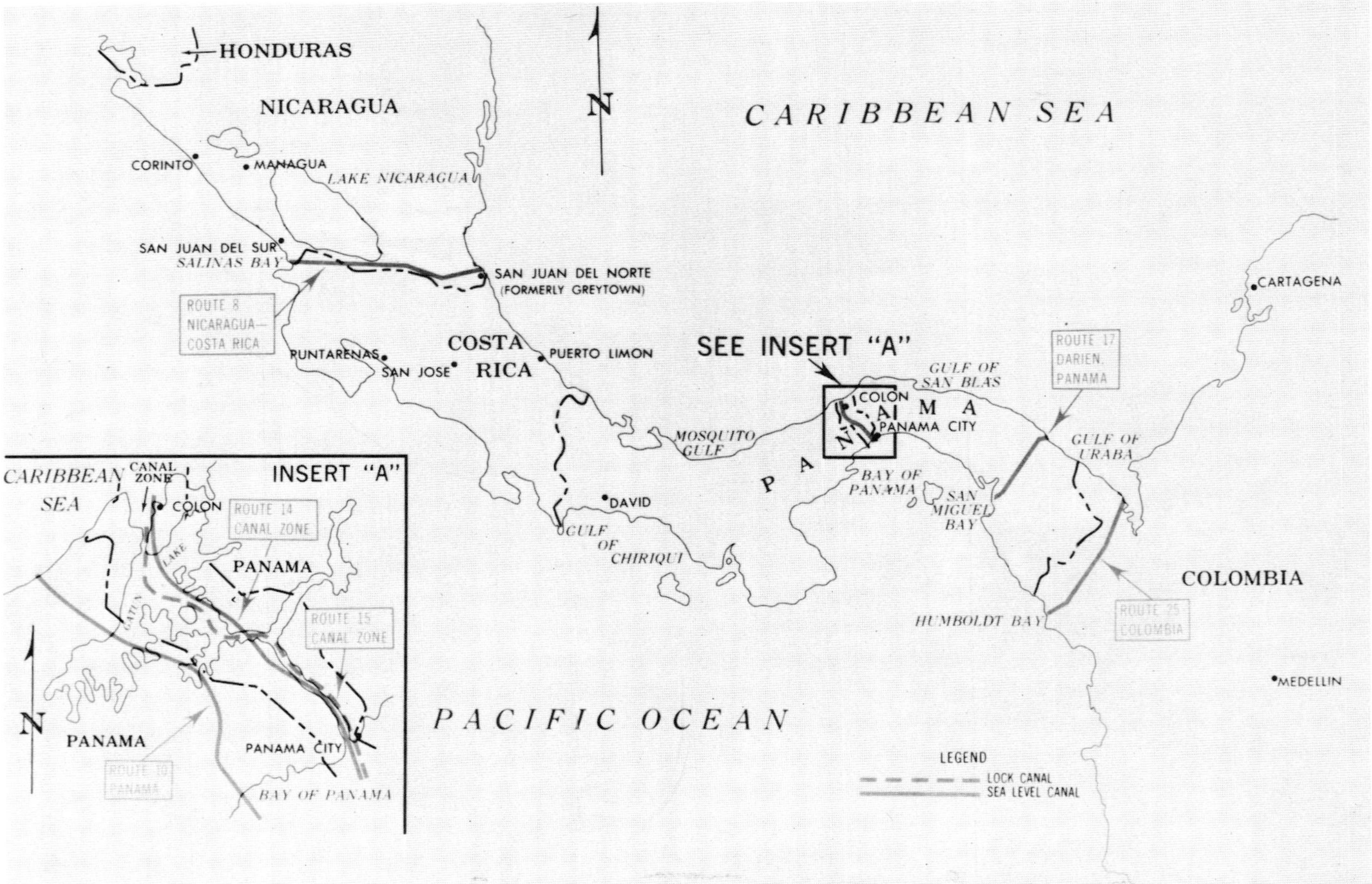

Fig. 35. Possible Sites for Sea Level Canal. Interoceanic Canal Studies, 1970

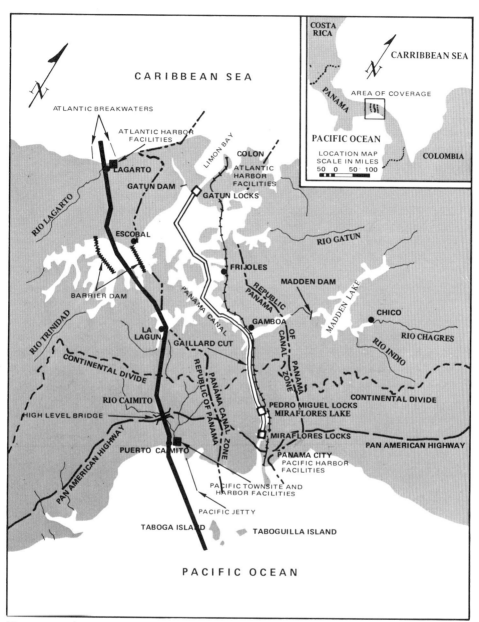

CARIBBEAN SEA

ATLANTIC BREAKWATERS

ATLANTIC HARBOR FACILITIES

LIMON BAY

COLON

ATLANTIC HARBOR FACILITIES

LAGARTO

GATUN DAM

GATUN LOCKS

RIO LAGARTO

ESCOBAL

RIO GATUN

FRIJOLES

MADDEN DAM

REPUBLIC PANAMA

GAMBOA

MADDEN LAKE

CHICO

RIO CHAGRES

BARRIER DAM

RIO TRINIDAD

LA LAGUNA

GAILLARD CUT

PANAMA CANAL

OF CANAL ZONE

OF PANAMA

RIO INDIO

CONTINENTAL DIVIDE

REPUBLIC OF PANAMA

CONTINENTAL DIVIDE

RIO CAIMITO

PANAMA CANAL ZONE

PEDRO MIGUEL LOCKS

MIRAFLORES LAKE

HIGH LEVEL BRIDGE

MIRAFLORES LOCKS

PAN AMERICAN HIGHWAY

PUERTO CAIMITO

PANAMA CITY

PACIFIC HARBOR FACILITIES

PAN AMERICAN HIGHWAY

PACIFIC TOWNSITE AND HARBOR FACILITIES

PACIFIC JETTY

TABOGA ISLAND

TABOGUILLA ISLAND

PACIFIC OCEAN

Location map inset:
COSTA RICA
CARRIBBEAN SEA
PANAMA
AREA OF COVERAGE
PACIFIC OCEAN
COLOMBIA
LOCATION MAP
SCALE IN MILES
50 0 50 100

The map is adapted from Interoceanic Canal Studies 1970, Report of the President's Interoceanic Canal Study Commission, Chapter VII.

ROUTE 10 NORTH OF CANAL

SCALE IN MILES

5   0   5   10

mal canal is estimated to be around $3.7 billion in 1974 dollars, not counting acquisition of land or payments to the Republic for rights-of-way and use, but this may be understated. Operating costs are estimated to be approximately one-half those of the lock canal.

One advantage of the Route 10 proposal is that by pushing the Zone northwestward all installations could be located between the two canals. The east bank could then be freed for return to the Republic of Panama. The engineering tasks associated with a canal along this route were thought by the IOCSC to pose fewer difficulties than along any other route. The elevation of the Chorrera Gap is somewhat less than at Gold Hill in the Canal Zone. The geological structure of the mountain mass is probably similar to that at Gaillard Cut, but it is thought by those who have examined it tentatively to pose fewer problems than were encountered at Gaillard Cut.

A sea-level canal could be built along the Logarto-Caimito axis without disrupting shipping at the present lock canal. This would be an important advantage to ocean commerce, and make the work of the builders much easier.

It would be necessary to acquire privately-held lands along such a route, but this is not thought to be an insuperable problem inasmuch as most of the land is used for farming or grazing, and is not heavily populated. The costs of acquiring the land and of payments to the Republic for constructing an additional waterway were not built into the estimates when submitted in 1970. Use of these could probably be obtained if other issues are resolved.

A sea-level canal along this route would bring added stimulus to the economy of Panama. It would afford local employment and business to merchants. No canal site away from the Isthmus has a comparable reservoir of labor, or equal facilities in housing, stores, medical facilities, or as good a network of highways near at hand.

A sea-level canal could be operated by the staff now employed by the Panama Canal Company. The armed forces located at the Canal Zone are available to defend it.

To obtain the site from the Republic of Panama will require negotiating a separate treaty and concessions. This may now be difficult, but the possibility of returning the east side of the Zone to the Republic, save for a corridor from Madden Lake to Gamboa, would provide compensatory land and a shorter, more direct connection between Panama City and Colon.

A sea-level waterway along the Logarto-Caimito route would make a valuable contribution to commerce and to the Panamanian economy. It would allow vessels to transit in less time than through the lock canal. It would allow larger vessels to pass than can possibly be admitted to a lock canal. It would not become outmoded as a lock canal will. Operation, upkeep and maintenance would be less than the cost of running the present canal. Existing defenses could be used for protecting both watercourses. By relocating personnel between the two waterways, the likelihood of incidents along the border will be minimized.

4. *A Sea-Level Canal in the Canal Zone*

Alternate Routes

Two routes are possible through the Canal Zone. One would run through a straightened Gaillard Cut which would be deepened to 85 feet below sea level. This was termed Route 14C in the Report of the Interoceanic Canal Study Commission. See Figure 37.

An alternate route would depart from the present track near where the Chagres River joins the Canal and proceed to the southwest around Gaillard Cut by a new excavation about a mile to the westward. This is designated Route 14S in Figure 37.

On either route, one-way traffic would operate for 24 miles through the Cut area. If the Atlantic approach were lengthened to include a part of Gatun Lake, the effective capacity could be 55,000 transits a year. Otherwise, the ceiling would be 35,000. Ships up to 150,000 dead-weight could be transited at all times, and larger vessels with appropriate configurations. Tidal gates could hold currents to two knots. These estimates and conclusions should be considered tentative.

If a sea-level canal is built having difficult navigation problems, ships might incorporate bow thrusters to improve maneuverability. This would be undesirable from a shipper's point of view, however.

The estimated cost of the separate Cut plan, which was very much preferred, was set at $3.40 billion in 1970. This would cost $4 billion or more at this time. Operational and maintenance costs were estimated to be roughly half of those for the existing lock canal. Construction time was set at 16 years.

The President's Commission felt that using Gaillard Cut for a sea-level canal was less desirable than making a separate cut along Routes 10 or 14S. The danger of slides being touched off, as well as the interference there would be with traffic while the new work was being done, poses serious questions for both 14C and 14S. Furthermore, the topography of the Continental Divide does not lend itself to widening this portion of the Canal very much beyond the present channel.

It would be necessary using either 14C or 14S to shore off portions of Gatun Lake. Switching over to the sea-level canal would require cutting off all traffic for at least three months with the inconvenience this would cause to shipping. There is some concern whether shipping that is once diverted to other routings will return to the Isthmus after the Canal is reopened. For this reason, the President's Commission very much preferred a sea-level canal constructed outside the present Canal

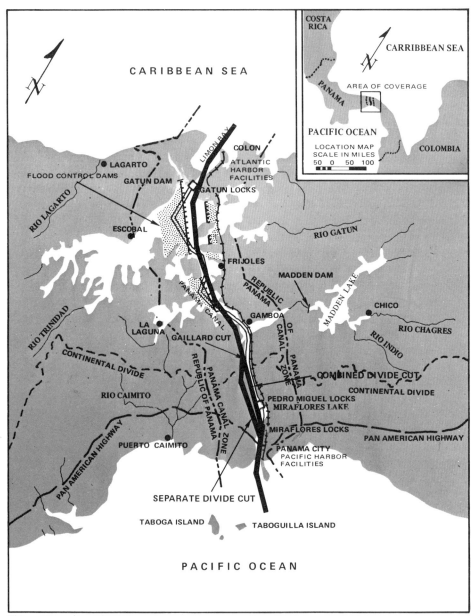

The map is adapted from Interoceanic Canal Studies 1970, Report of the President's Interoceanic Canal Study Commission, Chapter VII.

Route Nos. 14 Combined and 14 Separate

SCALE IN MILES

Figure 37.

Zone so that traffic in the existing lock canal would not have to be interrupted.

Several companies operating U.S.-flag vessels through the Canal reported in 1972 that they preferred a sea-level canal to the Third Locks and that, if such a canal were available, they would use it. These were companies operating tankers and dry bulk cargo vessels. Points stressed were that a waterway able to take vessels up to 150,000 tons would save costs in the use of tugs and line handlers.

Considerations Regarding a Sea-Level Canal

From an engineering point of view, there is considerable to be said in favor of constructing a sea-level canal along Route 10 if agreement can be reached on this. There would be no interference with ship movement while construction is going on. The route runs largely through relatively unsettled countryside. The elevations are quite modest. [15]

A sea-level canal built along any of Routes 10, 14S or 14C would be able to make use of equipment already located at the Zone. This would save duplicating equipment and housing. Harbor facilities are handily present. The Panama Railroad supplies trans-Isthmian transportation. Fuel supplies are located at the Canal terminals. Hotels are situated nearby.

An angle that has not been sufficiently examined as yet is the ecological one of the effects of building a sea-level canal across the Isthmus. More studies will be needed before assurances can be given that opening a sea-level waterway will not afford a serious opportunity for transfer of biota from one ocean to the other, or allow sea life from the Pacific to move into the Caribbean with its many resort areas. Given sufficient time, and effort, these problems should be solvable.

Taken on balance, we feel that, when the time comes to enlarge the interoceanic connection, a sea-level canal is a practical solution for the long-run needs of oceanborne commerce. The insistence, however, of Panamanian leaders on acquiring political control of the Canal routes at the Isthmus and of limiting United States rights and jurisdiction there raises profound questions about the entire enlargement plans. Until these are clarified, there is doubt that the United States Government should proceed further toward a sea-level waterway.

If a sea-level canal is to pay for itself, it would be necessary to maximize toll revenues. This would necessitate a toll system that assessed more nearly what the traffic will bear. [16]

The Canal Company has supported a sea-level project informally. The Governor in 1973 questioned whether the expenditure of funds for Third Locks would be warranted on economic grounds. He conceded that, if a sea-level canal were impossible, he would favor the Third Locks.

A sea-level canal would be able to transit the large naval aircraft

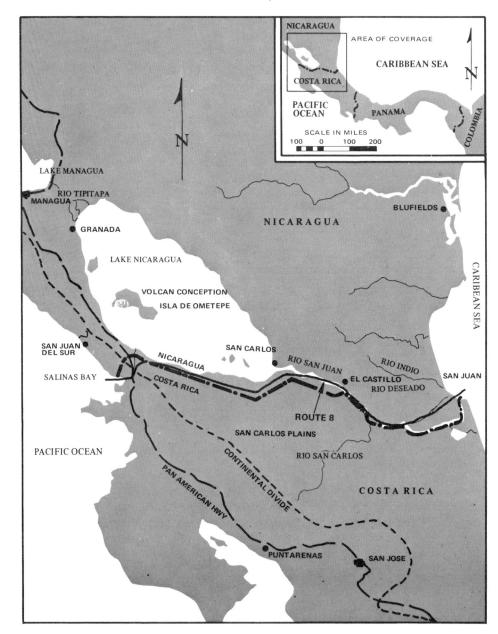

NICARAGUA COSTA RICA BOUNDARY CANAL ROUTE 8

The map is adapted from Interoceanic Canal Studies 1970, Report of the President's Interoceanic Canal Study Commission, Chapter VII.

Figure 38.

carriers. It would be less vulnerable than a lock canal. And it could operate with a lower United States profile inasmuch as fewer personnel would be needed to operate and maintain such a waterway. [17]

Some years can still elapse before a decision must be made on an addition to the Canal. Traffic does not require such an addition at this time. With developments in ocean transportation taking place as rapidly as they have in the past decade, however, it is advisable to remain watchful for trends emerging in the next few years. Larger vessels could come to the Canal, in greater numbers and sooner than now expected. A sea-level waterway could become desirable within the lifetime of shipping now on the seas. The recent dramatic increases in the cost of energy, due largely to political rather than to natural factors, improve the economic justification for a sea-level canal somewhat. We urge that high-level reviews be conducted periodically to spot developments that may further change the picture, and indicate that the net benefits of larger facilities undertaken before the 1990s or the end of the century would be positive.

5. *Other Possible Canal Routes*

Difficulties of one kind or another confront thought of a canal elsewhere. Routes through Nicaragua, Costa Rica, eastern Panama, and northern Colombia have problems of terrain, remoteness from railways, roads, and lack of nearby labor supplies which are reflected in higher construction costs. To overcome physical obstacles along these routes, nuclear engineering has been suggested as a way of bringing costs down. All of these countries are participants in an Inter-American Convention barring nuclear explosions, however. It is not feasible to contemplate building a canal by this method, at least in time of peace or until greater progress has been made with the technique and dangers to local inhabitants are removed. The Plowshare nuclear program was not sufficiently complete to serve as a definitive study of the feasibility of nuclear excavation. The possibility of nuclear excavation should not be ruled out.

A conventionally constructed canal through Nicaragua along Route 8 would be nearer to the United States. It would save 540 miles for vessels going between New York and San Francisco compared with the Panama Canal. This route follows the San Juan River valley. It would turn westward from just below the foot of Lake Nicaragua, proceed close to the Costa Rica border, and exit into Salinas Bay. A 50-mile retaining wall would probably have to be built south of Lake Nicaragua due to the alluvial nature of the terrain there, and expensive excavation would be required near the western terminus. It would be 150 miles long compared to 50 at the Isthmus of Panama and would take vessels more than 40 hours to transit. Costs were estimated in 1970 to be on

Table 1

Summary of Route Characteristics*
(1970 Dollars)

Route	Deep Draft Third Lock	8	10	14S	14C	17	25
Design Maximum Ship (dwt)	150,000	250,000	250,000	250,000	250,000	250,000	250,000
Locks and Size	Single-Lane; 3-Lift 1,450x160x65 ft	—	—	—	—	—	—
Capacity/transits per year	35,000	35,000	38,000	39,000	39,000	42,000	65,000
Construction Cost (billions)	$ 1.53	11.0	2.88	3.04	2.93	3.06	2.1
Annual Operation & Maint. (millions)	$ 71	93	56	55	55	57	84
Constr. Time (years)	10	18	14	16	13	16	13
Construction Type	Conventional	Conven'l	Conven'l	Conven'l	Conven'l	Nuclear	Nuclear

*Interoceanic Canal Studies, 1970, pp. V-215-V-220.

the order of $5.2 billion if nuclear engineering could be used; $11 billion if conventional engineering were employed. This is a seismically active area. Figure 38 shows the conventionally constructed alignment.

A route 100 miles east of the Panama Canal, Route 17, extending from Caledonia Bay on the Caribbean to the Gulf of San Miguel on the Pacific stretching across the Darien Peninsula, holds possibilities. But high mountains in this area would require nuclear blasting and the site is remote from roads, railways, labor, deep ports, and other needs. See Figure 35.

Somewhat easier for much of the distance is a possible route stretching from the Gulf of Uraba in northern Colombia to Humboldt Bay on the Pacific. This is Route 25 in the IOCSC Report. This would proceed up the low-lying Atrato River valley to the village of Rio Souci, then follow the Truando River valley to the Continental Divide before crossing to the Pacific. Construction in this latter section would be difficult for there are high mountain ridges and deep valleys that would have to be cut through for a distance of 14 miles. These are thought to be surmountable only with nuclear blasting.

The disadvantages of a Colombian route are its remoteness from sizable habitations, the absence of communications, the greater distance from New York and San Francisco, the lack of facilities of any kind in the neighborhood, and its length of 100 miles. Furthermore, the Government of Colombia made it clear to the President's Commission that it was not prepared to give the United States unfettered rights and jurisdiction. Table 1 summarizes the characteristics of the various routes.

A canal constructed outside of Panama could provide an alternative should the Panama Canal become blocked for any reason. This would help assure freedom of passage for shipping. It would also provide a competitive situation. This could be advantageous to commerce.

A disadvantage of building a canal in another country would be the need for duplicating construction equipment, operating personnel, communications, and defenses. Although this might be a reasonable price to pay for freedom of movement, it would add measurably to the cost. Political and financial problems would be multiplied.

We think the added costs, political problems, and other difficulties that would be involved in procuring land, housing, caring for labor, developing supply bases, roads, and other essential installations, plus the remoteness of locations outweigh the advantages that are to be gained.

The Isthmus at Panama commands the narrowest passage between the oceans. Its resources have been well developed. It is known to shipping interests. The Republic of Panama offers valuable adjuncts in banking and shipping services, a competent work force, and the best hotel and residential areas near any of the routes.

We think the national interests of the United States point in the direction of staying with Panama and working with the situation there, if this is possible. Not the least important are the extensive facilities the United States has developed over the years at the Canal Zone for administering the Canal, servicing it, and defending it. If Panamanian and United States interests prove to be irreconcilable, it will become necessary to rethink the bases of Canal policy and even of the United States' position in the hemisphere as a whole.

6. *Sell Canal to Panama: Get Out of Canal Business*

An alternative that may strike some as being an unacceptable option is for the United States to sell the Panama Canal lock, stock and barrel to the Republic of Panama, and to get out of the Canal business altogether.

The United States has invested over $2.5 billion in the Canal enterprise up to this time. Panama is getting restive to acquire control of the waterway, much as other developing countries have been seeking to gain possession of resources controlled by foreign interests. The United States has become the object of attack by Panamanian nationalists. Why not, therefore, sell the enterprise to Panama and let it suffer the headaches of trying to keep up the Canal? The United States has probably over-maintained the Canal in the sense of doing more than is absolutely necessary to keep the waterway in operation. Panama could run the Canal at somewhat less cost than the United States has been putting into it.

Panamanians could probably move into many Canal positions fairly quickly. Numbers of them have received extensive training for jobs at the Canal, both in United States technical universities, and through practical training on the job at the Canal Zone itself. The Canal Company has since 1955 been pursuing a program of bringing Panamanians into the business on an increasing scale. Approximately 74 percent of the total main force is now made up of non-U.S. citizens.

Positions could also be contracted out to United States nationals or to Europeans on a similar basis as the United Arab Republic has hired Europeans and others to serve as pilots, dredgers, and other technicians at the Suez Canal since 1956.

It may be argued that Panama would turn the Canal against the United States; that discrimination would be practiced against United States shipping; that U.S. Government vessels would be forbidden transit. These things could conceivably happen. On the other hand, with United States shipping one of the largest users, there is no demonstrated proof that Panama would turn against its customers or exclude them from the Canal. Furthermore, the U.S. rail system has the potential of substituting for the Canal although at greater cost.

It may also be argued that Panama would put the tolls up so that it would cost shipping much more to use the Canal than it has been doing in the past. This could happen. On the other hand, Panamanians are aware that, if tolls are put up too high, cargo will find other ways of moving to destinations. Traffic will shrink. Tolls revenues will decline. The Canal, as we have remarked before, is in the international market-place. Its administrators have to keep tolls at a point where they will attract, not repel, shipping.

It is often argued that some foreign power inimicable to United States interests would grab this strategic crossroads if the United States moved out. This again is conceivable. On the other hand, United States armed forces are not far away from the Canal at any time. It is hardly likely that nationalist forces within Panama would look with favor upon foreign elements seizing what they would have gained.

Selling the Canal to Panama is a possibility. We do not recommend this as a first choice, but it may be worth considering. This would get the United States out of an increasingly uncomfortable position. We do not believe the waterway would be turned against United States shipping, that the toll rates would go far out of line with what the market will stand, or that the operators would tolerate a hostile foreign power moving into the Zone.

Should the United States decide to sell the Canal to Panama it is conceivable that the resources of the World Bank could be called upon to assist in the operation and improvement of present or foreseeable facilities.

With the importance of other modes of transport increasing, this may be an alternative worth considering.

7. Other Transfer Possibilities

Trans-Isthmian Pipeline

It has been suggested that, rather than laying out money for a larger canal, business should be encouraged to construct a commercial pipe-line across the Isthmus with tank farms and suitable deepwater termi-nals located at each end. This would then permit supertankers to bring oil to the Isthmus, have it pumped to the other side, and be loaded there for carriage to refineries in the Caribbean or be tankered to East Coast ports.

Twelve million tons of petroleum went through the Canal from the Atlantic to the Pacific in 1973; 10 million tons, in the opposite direc-tion. The tankers provide substantial business for the Canal. Shipping much of this across the Isthmus by pipeline would relieve the Canal of that much traffic and cut down on one of the principal sources of large shipping. This appears to be a possibility if traffic becomes heavy enough.

Pipeline transportation of oil across the Isthmus could be a viable alternative. This would require segregating oil as to type and various products. Thus, there would have to be an infra-structure of tank farms and dealers to hold and consign the oil for particular refineries and localities.

The present average cost for moving oil through the Canal is 11.2 cents a barrel. If operating costs of a pipeline were to be 9 cents, a modest rate, apart from storage charges, there would be a small margin for profit. If high-volume transport should develop from oil found in Ecuador, the Upper Amazon basin, or elsewhere, this could become a profitable investment. If the oil companies should decide to use tankers of the 250,000-deadweight-plus classes for transporting Alaskan crude from Valdez to the Isthmus, pumping it across for refining at Caribbean refineries, or at the Isthmus itself, and then backhauling refined products to West Coast ports, this might make a pipeline a good investment. On the other hand, if the companies decide to construct a pipeline across the United States to the mid-Continent, Alaskan oil will probably travel via this line rather than be taken down to Panama.[18]

Meanwhile, the Canal offers a convenient, inexpensive way of transporting oil without the added cost of unloading, storing, pumping and reloading it at the opposite side, or the capital investment for a pipeline. Transiting oil is profitable business for the Canal. It would like to serve this business as long as it can do so competitively. The decisions are not in its hands, but in those of the oil companies and transporters. So long as it can do so, it will transit tankers that can be admitted to its locks.

Slurry and Moving Belt Transfer

Thought also springs to mind of the possibility of moving quantities of coal and ore across the Isthmus by slurry process from deepwater terminals at Colón and Balboa.[19] Problems can be seen in the costs of unloading cargoes at one side of the Isthmus, reducing them to slurries, storing them, reconsolidating them at the other end, and reloading them for shipment in the other ocean area.

Generally speaking, the commodities that could be transferred as a slurry or by moving belt can be gotten to destinations more cheaply and expeditiously by continuous ship movement rather than by transshipment. If there were no interoceanic canal, such a method might be more attractive. If the coal and ore carriers turn to very large vessels, transshipment may become preferable, in some instances, to diversion around the Capes.

Land- and Mini-Bridge Systems

The introduction of special unitized trains for carrying modular containers across the United States, with schedules keyed to arrival and departure dates of express containerships across the Atlantic and the

Pacific, with competing rate schedules, is offering fresh competition to the Panama Canal. European and Asian traders are being given an alternate means of moving high-priority cargoes to markets abroad.

The land-bridge system aims to improve delivery times to third continents on the far side of the Americas. This has not yet established a clear ascendancy over sea transport, however. Shipping companies have been meeting the challenge with new, faster containerships that can make the run between Europe and Asian ports in approximately equivalent times. Delays in ports, and the still relatively slow operation of through transcontinental freight trains, are impeding the progress of the land-bridge.

Mini-bridge trade by comparison, involving shipments between Japanese and East Coast United States ports, and between Europe and West Coast North American destinations, has been making some headway with delivery times two or more days faster than by all-water transportation. This innovation, coupled with the increase in trucking on the Interstate Highway system offers flexible opportunities for overseas commerce so long as rates are held comparable.[20]

This raises a query whether it would be to the nation's advantage to improve the rail system with Government subsidies for new roadbeds, rolling stock, and faster schedules rather than investing comparable dollars in further canal construction. In a sense, the Panama Canal has contributed to the demise of the railroads in the United States, just as it is now deterring the construction of large ships by imposing Panamax-size dimensions upon some builders.

A large investment of capital in the nation's rail system would strengthen the economy. It would provide jobs for the unemployed. It would improve the national transportation system. It would aid security in a time of emergency. A revitalized rail system could also help conserve energy supplies by stimulating more efficient means of transportation. The time may be ripe, therefore, for the injection of large amounts of capital not only in new port systems, but in the transcontinental rails as well.

Whatever is done, and this becomes a matter for national transportation policy, the United States will want to continue its support of the merchant marine to enable U.S.-flag shipping to compete with foreign companies, and to have an adequate fleet for use in time of national emergency. As long as the nation moves over 90 percent of its overseas commerce by water, it will be indispensable to have a large merchant fleet and an interoceanic canal. Considerations of saving energy also argue in favor of keeping a short water sea route in the picture of global transport.

Summary

Among the alternatives discussed in the preceding pages, we conclude that the United States should keep the existing lock canal functioning so long as this is practicable, pressing the improvements program in order to obtain the maximum usable capacity from the Canal.

We conclude secondly that the United States should keep a close watch on changes in the sizes and technology of shipping to determine when, if at all, it will become necessary to augment the present canal. To this end, we urge that periodic reviews be conducted with outside experts assisting the Government.

We believe it would be politically and militarily advantageous to build a sea-level canal rather than a Third Locks when there is need for further capacity, provided a clear grant can be obtained from the Republic of Panama, and questions over control, jurisdiction, and defense are amicably resolved. Although construction of Third Locks would be less expensive, a sea-level canal has the potential to provide greater capacity at less long-range cost, although further studies must be made to verify this. At this time, no economic necessity exists for a sea-level canal.

Towards a New Treaty Relationship

For some years Panama has been pressing for replacing the 1903 treaty with a new agreement. It objects to the grant "in perpetuity" to the United States of the right to "possess and exercise" power at the Canal Zone as if it were "the sovereign" there. [21]

Nationalists in Panama feel that these provisions, drawn a few days after their country gained its independence, are degrading. They wish to establish their sovereignty over the Zone and to fly their flag freely throughout the area. [22] They also wish to increase the payments to their country. Discontent over the situation was a factor in the riots that occurred near the Canal Zone in 1958 and 1964. [23]

Panama has benefited from the presence of the Canal in numerous ways. It has become a center for international banking, transport, and communications. Construction activity has been booming with the presence of foreign capital. More than 40 percent of the foreign exchange earnings and nearly one-third of its gross national product can be attributed to the existence of the Canal. Its national income has more than doubled in the past decade with a growth rate of close to 8 percent a year. [24] Gross investment as a percentage of gross domestic product is higher than that of Mexico. Its per capita income is one of the highest in Latin America. [25]

Following discussions of the situation in Panama at the Organization of American States and at the United Nations in 1964, as well as between the parties themselves, President Lyndon B. Johnson agreed to talks between the two countries to remove the "causes of conflict relative to the Panama Canal." [26]

An announcement of five "areas of agreement" on a new treaty by

President Johnson and President Robles of Panama, September 24, 1965, included: (1) abrogation of the 1903 treaty; (2) recognizing Panama's sovereignty over the Canal Zone on concluding a new treaty; (3) a fixed terminal date for a new treaty; (4) the Canal area to be integrated with the rest of Panama on an orderly basis; (5) fair and helpful treatment to all employees who have served the Canal.

The parties, in addition, stated that they were in agreement on maintaining United States armed forces and facilities at the Isthmus under a status-of-forces agreement; that studies should continue on a sea-level canal which shall be open at all times to the vessels of all nations on a nondiscriminatory basis; and a separate treaty to be concluded for a new sea-level canal.[27]

Three draft treaties came from the negotiators in 1967: one for the existing canal; a second for a sea-level canal; the third for mutual defense. The first called for joint administration of the Canal, increase in annuity payments, division of toll receipts, transfers of land to Panama, application of Panamanian law in the Zone under a progressive system, and termination of the new treaty in 1999. The second provided for construction and operation of a sea-level canal with joint administration for 60 years from completion of construction, followed by transfer to the Republic. The third document would have safeguarded United States rights to defend the Canal during the life of the treaties, but with Panamanian participation.[28]

The Government of Panama took no steps to ratify these drafts. Instead, it rejected them summarily.[29] When the contents became known in the Congressional Committee on Merchant Marine and Fisheries, it reported that the draft terms were "unworkable as well as contrary to the best interests of the United States." It added that:

It must be understood by all interested parties that the Congress looks with disfavor on such disruptive treaties and is adamant in its opposition to ceding United States sovereignty and jurisdiction over the Canal Zone . . . [30]

This plain-speaking signaled that, if the Executive were to submit a treaty along these lines to the Congress, it would face rough going. Although the Senate is the body with constitutional power to give consent to treaties, the members of this body would not overlook strong opposition in the other House.

Moves During the Nixon Administration

President Richard Nixon authorized negotiations to resume with the Republic of Panama when he came to office in 1968. These were continued until just before the 1972 presidential elections. In his 1972 Foreign Policy Report, the President indicated that the United States wished to develop a mature and stable partnership with its Latin American neighbors.[31] Little progress was made, however, during the ensuing year.

Changing International Scene

At a special meeting of the United Nations Security Council convened at Panama City in April 1973, United States Canal policy was criticized. The country was accused of colonialism in retaining control of the Zone. It was called upon to conclude a new treaty with Panama. When the vote was taken on a resolution criticizing United States policy, 13 of the 15 members voted with Panama. The United Kingdom abstained. The United States representative was forced to cast a veto to prevent adoption of the resolution. Although Ambassador Scali argued that the action was inappropriate in view of the continuing negotiations between the parties, and reaffirmed the desire for a new treaty, his views were brushed aside. In the closing moments of the meeting, the Panamanian delegate warned that his Government was prepared to go to the U.N. General Assembly where no veto could prevent the passage of a resolution.

Several representatives indicated privately that they were unhappy with what was taking place, and hoped the United States would maintain its administration of the waterway. But they felt obligated in principle to support the position of their host. The action was a diplomatic coup for the Republic.[32]

Shortly after being sworn into office, Secretary of State Kissinger signaled his desire to open a "new dialogue" with the countries of Latin America based upon "equality and on respect for mutual dignity." [33] Ambassador Ellsworth Bunker was designated to pick up the talks with the Republic of Panama.

Panama City Statement of Principles

A new attempt was made to make a show of progress when Secretary Kissinger journeyed to Panama City in February 1974 to sign with Foreign Minister Juan Tack a Statement of Principles to Serve as Guidelines for Negotiating a New Treaty. In an 8-point Statement, the United States promised to terminate the 1903 treaty and to replace it with a new instrument abolishing the concept of perpetuity. It agreed to Panamanian sovereignty at the Canal Zone, to joint participation in the operation and defense of the Canal, to assure just and equitable benefits to the Republic. It also agreed that at a terminal date full control would be transferred to Panama, although no date for this was specified. For its part, the Republic of Panama agreed to grant the United States the right to use land, water and air space needed for the operation of the Canal and for its protection, and to agree upon measures to enlarge the Canal's capacity.[34]

In remarks following the signing, the Secretary said that restoring territorial sovereignty was essential to Panama, while "preserving an indispensable international waterway" was vital to the United States. In such a spirit, he hoped that a "partnership" of the two countries would mark the "advent of a new era." Acknowledging that there was opposition that had to be overcome on both sides, the Secretary avowed "we will succeed—for our relations and our commitments to a new community in this hemisphere demand it." [35]

Comparing this statement with the Johnson-Robles announcement in 1965, it is difficult to see that much progress had been registered over the nine intervening years. The Kissinger-Tack Guidelines bear a close resemblance to the previous Areas of Agreement. Essentially, the 1974 Statement of Principles seems to have been made in order to make an appearance of progress; to head off restive elements in Panama; and to help the Government of the Republic save face before its own constituency.

The 1974 Statement stands in considerable opposition to the views expressed on Capitol Hill, a position said to have been conveyed to the Secretary before his departure for Panama City. [36] It is not in itself a binding treaty. It is, however, an Executive undertaking. The Congress may, if it sees fit, refuse to give its consent to a formal treaty concluded on such a basis or fail to implement its provisions. It does constitute a framework for further negotiations.

The Statement seems designed to make it embarrassing for opponents to reject a new treaty lest they be pointed to as enemies of progress. It further seems aimed at giving the Secretary of State elbow room for maneuver. If a treaty is signed and then turned down, the Government will be able to say it cannot control the Congress. At the same time, it is to be read in the context of the traditional rivalry between the Executive and the Congress over the country's foreign policy.

Failure to conclude a new treaty will be troublesome. Panamanian demands have pried open a lid to a Pandora's box. The United States Government has been put in a position where it can be condemned if it does not agree with these Principles. It can be faced with another confrontation in Panama or at the United Nations if it reneges on the terms of the Statement.

Thirty-five members of the United States Senate signed a joint resolution in the spring of 1974 declaring that the Panama City Principles constitute a "clear and present danger" to the rights and security of this country. [37] This more-than-one-third of the Senate placed the Government in a tight corner. Not all of the signers may remain in solid opposition to the Government if a new treaty is laid before the Senate. Some may shift positions if the President or his Secretary of State makes a strong case for a new arrangement. Nevertheless, the political lines are being drawn and notice has been served that many members of the

Congress do not like what they have seen. The diplomacy of Ambassador Bunker and the influence of Secretary Kissinger will be put to a serious test if a treaty emerges following the lines of the Statement of Principles of February 1974.

Observers in the Washington scene think the State and Defense Departments and the Congress are on a collision course. The military chiefs are said to be concerned over the erosion of defense rights and position at the Zone. There is also a question to what extent the President and Secretary of State are fully informed on the situation at the Isthmus. Considering the signals that have passed between Panama and the United States, a new treaty is clearly expected at the Isthmus.

Without access to the full record of what has passed between the Governments, it is impossible to know what promises have been made, what understandings have been reached, what things have been left in limbo to be worked out at another time. Not being privy to these things, we will focus upon the issues involved in reaching a new agreement.

Issues Relating to New Arrangement

There are fundamental differences over the control of the Panama Canal that need to be understood.

Control and Jurisdiction

It is beneficial to the commerce of this and other nations that the Panama Canal remain free, open and available to the passage of ocean shipping. Vessels passing through the Canal can fly the Panamanian flag out of respect to the Republic. Panamanians are now being employed and trained as pilots, and for other positions in pursuance of agreements made since 1955. The United States has proposed a program for orderly transfer of authority to Panama. The implications of the 1974 Principles are that this will be completed within a finite period.

The basic question is whether time will be allowed for mutual agreement to be concluded before nationalist sentiment within Panama takes matters out of the hands of diplomats. Statesmanship must find a formula that gives satisfaction and security to both parties so that the Canal will not become a football of power politics, as Suez was between 1967 and 1974.

Joint Administration

The principle of joint participation in the administration of the Canal provided for in the 1967 draft treaty was alluded to in the 1974 Statement of Principles. The parties have not come to agreement as yet, however, on precisely how responsibilities shall be handled. Administration of numerous civil functions can be placed in Panamanian hands fairly shortly. What seems not to have been resolved are such questions as police and taxing powers, the application of Panamanian law to disputes and liabilities concerning rights of passing vessels, and the like. Unless there is agreement upon these matters, incidents may flare into tests of strength. Good faith and bona fide efforts will be needed in the interim period.

The relationship between the Republic of Panama and the United States has fostered enrollment of Panamanian students in U.S. universities. This has contributed to the upgrading of Panamanian participation in the Canal organization as well as affecting the Republic's financial, business, and governmental operations. Looking toward the possibility of joint administration, it might be advisable to promote this interchange further.

Expansion of Capacity

At this point it is not clear what should be done to expand the capacity of the Canal. The United States is understood to have sought to retain an option to initiate a sea-level canal until the year 2000. Panama, on the other hand, is reported to have pressed for a firm commitment that work will be commenced on larger locks or a sea-level waterway within a short time, or that the United States shall forfeit its rights in this respect. With world shipping at its present stage of uncertainty, action cannot be taken until it is clearer how traffic will develop. From the present outlook, it appears to us that nothing further should be done at this time to expand the capacity of the Canal beyond its present limits. We incline to the view that the number of vessels seeking transit will not exceed the limits of its capacity before the turn of the century, if then.

Defense of the Canal

Panama's negotiators are reported to be seeking to have United States forces relegated to acting only when called upon by Panama to do so within the Isthmus, and to have their role limited to defending the Canal from external aggressors. With the Panamanian defense forces limited to the 6,000-man National Guard, it is feared that this may not be sufficient to deter a foreign invasion or to prevent acts of sabotage or guerrilla-type attacks upon the Canal. The Panamanian position is understandable from the point of view of a small independent power, jealous of its sovereignty, and eager to steer clear of great power rivalries. Much is at stake, nevertheless, in view of the global importance of the interoceanic link and its strategic placement. Utmost care must be exercised in this sphere lest a false step open the Canal to a Trojan horse vulnerability.

At the least, the principle of mutual defense, as embodied in the NATO agreements, is needed to safeguard the interests of both parties here.

Just and Equitable Benefits

Panama has asked for a larger share of benefits from the Canal in view of its Isthmian position. The United States is understood to be amenable to increasing the annual payment to Panama to approximately $25 million through a royalty on tonnages. The level of payments proposed is based upon the "estimated maximum net revenue that the Canal could produce as a result of toll increases which would not seriously limit traffic growth." [38]

We have two thoughts on this. Tolls should be devoted first to covering the cost of operations, paying off capital investment, and providing a fund covering necessary improvements. The United States investment in the Canal, in terms of real property, is somewhere on the order of $1 billion. The unrecovered costs today are $317 million of the original appropriations for Canal construction, plus $400 million interest costs borne by the United States Treasury on these funds prior to 1951 when the Canal was placed on a self-sustaining basis. The $400 million has now been written off in order to minimize the interest-bearing debt of the Canal Company.

Congressman Robert L. Leggett (Democrat, California), Chairman of the House of Representatives Subcommittee on the Panama Canal, said at the Hearing in July 1973: "My own view is that any payments to Panama respecting the canal, both in equity and in a good economic sense, ought to be generated out of the canal itself." [39]

Some increase in toll rates can be justified, not having been raised since 1914. The Canal Company is currently urging an increase for other purposes. But the Canal operates in the international marketplace. If its rates are raised too high, shipping will be encouraged to go in other directions. Traffic will drop off. There were objections raised to the 20 percent increase proposed in 1974 by some liner companies engaged in intercoastal and foreign commerce. Payments from Canal revenues thus have certain built-in limits.

The position taken by the United States has been a generous one. Secretary Kissinger's signature to the Panama City Statement is a benefit to the leaders of the Panamanian Government in view of the fact that the points made there have been among the principal goals of local nationalist elements. A monetary figure could be put upon them. We do not recommend that this be done. We do think, however, that the combination of the increase in payments offered and the signed Statement are in themselves a just and equitable share of the benefits.

Economic Value of the Canal

In the course of analyzing United States policy alternatives for the present canal, one should keep in mind that the economic value of the Panama Canal is finite. The economic value of major enterprises, according to contemporary thought, is that this is equal to the monopoly profits the enterprise could reap independent of what is actually charged. This is the value of service rendered by the Canal minus operating costs.

Recent studies sponsored by the Canal Company show that the net economic value of the Canal in 1975 will be approximately $80 million. Of this, about $32 million will accrue to United States consumers, the remainder being distributed among other Canal users.[40] Since the United States Gross National Product is approximately $1,000 billion, it is probable that the Panama Canal, while providing the United States large benefits in absolute terms, is not a crucial component of its economy.

If the Panama Canal were closed to the United States, domestic railroads, trucking operations, and air transport services would absorb much of the diverted traffic, reaping large profits in the process. The United States merchant marine would be seriously hurt by such an event. The effect of closure of the Panama Canal would ultimately be borne by consumers in the form of higher prices.

National Security and Other Aspects of the Canal

The ability of the United States military to act in World War II, the Korean War, and the Southeast Asian conflict was materially improved by transiting quantities of men, equipment, and supplies through the Canal. Washington sources have indicated that the role of the Canal could be significant if hostilities were to break out again. This aspect is not in the public domain, and has not been analyzed here, although it will doubtless be a factor in Government decisions.

The presence of U.S. personnel at the Zone with accompanying communications facilities gives the United States an eye and ear useful in monitoring Latin American affairs. Considerations of these facilities will also be of consequence in future decisions and this, too, has not been addressed here.

The United States should keep the treaty options open which it has with other countries for possible construction of an interoceanic canal in the event continued tenure of a canal at Panama becomes impossible for any reason.

The Panama Canal is valuable to the commerce of numerous countries, in addition to that of the United States. British, Japanese, Liberian, Norwegian, German, Greek, and Panamanian shipping, to mention but a few, are heavy users of the Canal. Some provision should be made for the interests and needs of these countries, as well as of those that are most heavily dependent upon the Canal for their imports and exports, to be represented on a regularized basis. We do not suggest that they should participate in the control of the Canal, but there should be ways in which their views can be heard.

In the event that agreement cannot be reached in respect to a new treaty, it might be valuable to unilaterally undertake many of the points now under negotiation. Raising the annuity payment and relinquishing lands and facilities would relieve pressure and lower the United States profile.

Conclusion

There are limits to how far concessions should be carried. By working to strengthen the effectiveness of Canal operations, while also agreeing to a modernization of the treaty provisions, the United States Government is seeking to forge a new policy that is responsive to international opinion.

Some of the demands made upon it have been made for bargaining purposes. Considerations of national interest must determine how far the nation will go in responding. The nation cannot be expected to sacrifice values that are basic to these interests. It is, however, also in the national interest to maintain cordial relations with Panama.

There will be those who may think the United States has already gone farther than it should have in conceding to others. We respect these opinions as being sincerely held. The views of many who are opposed to giving up rights acquired by treaty and purchased in the past are based upon an extensive knowledge of history.

A new arrangement for the Canal should be in the form of a treaty laid before the Senate of the United States for consent to ratification. The matter should not be treated as an Executive Agreement but rather be submitted to the Congress for ratification.

It is a matter for judgment whether, in being asked to give up the 1903 treaty, the nation will be getting enough in return. This must be answered by those who are privy to the details of negotiation and the understandings that have been reached between the Governments.

Looking to the year 2000, the United States shares with the people of Panama, as with those of other American republics, an aspiration to have a mature partnership of equals in a hemispheric system of mutual collaboration.

As a former President of the United States said in addressing the nations of the American hemisphere: ". . . our unfulfilled task is to demonstrate to the entire world that man's unsatisfied aspirations for economic progress and social justice can best be achieved by free men working within a framework of democratic institutions."

We have attempted in preceding pages to estimate the costs and benefits derived from the operation of the Panama Canal. Political benefits cannot be set down in dollars, but they are nevertheless real. Relationships with the Republic of Panama involve a complex linking of political, psychological and economic elements in the context of a Latin American political process.[41]

A partnership founded upon principles of equality, justice and fairness, and operating within the bounds of national, hemispheric and international interests, can afford an enduring link between the interests of the Panamanian people, the United States, and the community of nations interested in the interoceanic passage between the Atlantic and Pacific Oceans.

CHAPTER SEVEN FOOTNOTES

1. *Shipping and Canal Operations.* Hearing before Subcommittee on Panama Canal. Committee on Merchant Marine and Fisheries. House of Representatives. 93rd Congress, 1st Session, July 17, 1973, pp. 6-7.

2. *Improvement Program for the Panama Canal.* Prepared by A.T. Kearney & Co., Consultants. Panama Canal Company. Washington, 1969.

3. See statement of Albert E. May, Vice President, American Institute of Merchant Shipping. Hearings, *op. cit.,* pp. 46-47.

4. See testimony of Governor David S. Parker. *Ibid.,* pp. 33-34, 41-42.

5. See *Additional Interoceanic Canal Facilities,* Hearing before the Committee on Interoceanic Canals, United States Senate, 76th Congress, 1st Session, on S. 127 and S. 2229, May 16, 1939.

6. See *Proceedings* of the American Society of Civil Engineers, Vol. 73, No. 2, February 1947. Papers by Miles P. DuVal, "The Marine Operating Problems, Panama Canal, and the Solution," pp. 161-174; J.G. Claybourn, "Sea Level Plan for the Panama Canal to Provide Maximum Safety and Unlimited Capacity," pp. 175-196.

7. House Bill 1517. 93rd Congress, 1st Session. Bill to Increase Capacity and Improve Operations of the Panama Canal, January 9, 1973. See remarks of Congressman Flood on introduction of his bill in *Congressional Record,* January 29, 1973, p. H539. Senator Thurmond's bill, numbered S. 2330 was introduced into the Senate on August 2, 1973. See *Congressional Record,* Vol. 119, No. 125, August 2, 1973, pp. S15406-15408. The Deep Draft plan will be found in *Interoceanic Canal Studies, 1970,* pp. 75-78.

8. *Interoceanic Canal Studies,* 1970, p. V-134.

9. Hearing, *op. cit.,* p. 61.

10. See testimony of Alfred E. May, quoted above, p. 54.

11. The Panama Canal Pilots Association has supported the Third Locks plan and opposes a sea-level canal on the ground that the latter will eliminate a fresh water barrier between the oceans. See letter to the President of the United States, members of the Congress, and others inserted in the *Congressional Record,* November 15, 1973, 93rd Congress, 1st Session, Vol. 119, No. 176, p. H10092 by Congressman Daniel J. Flood.

12. Hearing, *cit. supra,* p. 87.

13. See hearing, cited above, p. 70. Governor Parker subsequently stated that he definitely favored the sea-level canal "at the appropriate time."

14. *Interoceanic Canal Studies, 1970,* p. 82.

15. Hearing, *op. cit.,* p. 47.

16. *Interoceanic Canal Studies—1970,* p. 107.

17. *Ibid.,* pp. 85, 87.

18. A pipeline now extends across the Canal Zone to serve Canal needs. This is not large enough to handle oil in commercial quantities. On the transportation of Alaskan oil, see J.B. Lassiter and J.W. Devanney III, "Economics of Arctic Oil Transportation." *Schiff und Haffen Sonderheft*, November 1970, p. 18. See also *Interoceanic Canal Studies—1970*, pp. IV-113 to IV-118.

19. See "Supertanker Loads Ore Slurry at Sea." *Ocean Industry*, August 1971.

20. See "Minibridge in Focus," "A Land Bridge—The Myth and the Reality," and "Mini-Bridge Forum," *Railway Management Review*, Vol. 72, No. 4, 1972. See also "The Mini-Land-Bridge and Panama Canal Traffic." Preliminary Draft Report No. 12, by Lim H. Tan, M.I.T. Sea Grant Program, Interoceanic Canal Project, Cambridge, Massachusetts, May 1974.

21. Text in 33 Stat. 2234. The treaty is analyzed along with later agreements in Norman J. Padelford, *The Panama Canal in Peace and War*. New York: Macmillan, 1942, Chapters 2 and 3.

22. See *The New York Times*, August 6, 1957; April 20, 1960; *Department of State Bulletin*, Vol. XLVIII, No. 1232, February 4, 1963, p. 171. Some efforts were made to promote a seizure of the Canal at the time of the Egyptian nationalization of Suez notwithstanding fundamental differences in the ownership of the two waterways. See Norman J. Padelford, "The Panama Canal and the Suez Crisis." *Proceedings of the American Society of International Law*, 1957, pp. 10-19.

23. See *The New York Times*, January 10-11, 1964. On political aspects of Canal, see Immanuel J. Klette, *From Atlantic to Pacific: A New Interoceanic Canal*. New York: Council on Foreign Relations, 1968, Chapter VII.

24. Inter-American Development Bank, *Economic and Social Progress in Latin America*. Annual Report, 1972. Washington, 1973. See chapter on Panama, pp. 263-271.

25. Agency for International Development (AID). *Gross National Product: Growth Rates and Trend Data*, May 10, 1972. Washington: AID, Office of Statistics and Reports, Table 3c.

26. *The New York Times*, January 10, 11, 1964. For an account of events during and after the Panama riots, see Lyndon Baines Johnson, *The Vantage Point: Perspectives on the Presidency, 1963-1969*. New York: Holt, Rinehart & Winston, 1971, pp. 181-184; *Public Papers of the Presidents - Lyndon B. Johnson*. Washington: Government Printing Office, 1964, Book I, pp. 121, 144; 219-220; 404-405; Book II, pp. 1163-1165.

27. Statement by President Lyndon B. Johnson on Progress of Treaty Negotiations with Panama. White House Press Release, September 24, 1965.

28. The texts of the instruments are found in *Report on the Problems Concerning the Panama Canal*. Committee on Merchant Marine and Fisheries. House of Representatives, 91st Congress, 2nd Session, 1970, Appendices IV-VI.

29. See statement published in *La Estrella de Panama*, September 5, 1970. Reprinted in *Reports on the Problems*, cited above, pp. 87-96. There was some debate on the meaning of the action taken. To some, it seemed in the nature of a "salida politica"—a defiant rejection on political grounds as serving no useful purpose.

30. *Report on Problems*, cited above, pp. 23-24.

31. Text in *Department of State Bulletin*, Vol. LXVI, No. 1707, March 13, 1972, p. 358. See address of Ambassador David H. Ward entitled "A Modern Treaty

for the Panama Canal." *Department of State Bulletin*, Vol. LXVI, No. 1730, June 12, 1972, pp. 818-822.

32. *United Nations Monthly Chronicle*, Vol. X, No. 4, April 1973, pp. 15-58. On background of meeting, see dispatches listed in *The New York Times Index*, March 13-15, 1973.

33. *Department of State Bulletin*, Vol. LXIX, No. 1792, October 29, 1973, pp. 542-543, Address to Latin American delegations to U.N. General Assembly.

34. The text of the Panama City Statement will be found in the *Department of State Bulletin*, Vol. LXX, No. 1809, February 25, 1974, pp. 184-185.

35. The text of the Secretary's remarks is contained in *Department of State Bulletin*, February 25, 1974, pp. 181-184.

36. See article by Senator Strom Thurmond (Republican, South Carolina) in *The New York Times*, May 7, 1974.

37. *Ibid.*

38. Department of State Release on Treaty Negotiations, *op. cit.*, p. 5.

39. *Shipping and Canal Operations.* Hearing cited above, p. 83.

40. James E. Howell and Ezra Solomon, *The Economic Value of the Panama Canal*, International Research Associates, prepared for the Panama Canal Company, December 1973, pp. 29, 32. The dollar values do not account for short-term effects which might result from a sudden large toll rate increase. For a discussion of these effects, see Ely M. Brandes, *The Economic Value of the Panama Canal: An Addendum Concerning the Short Term Value of the Canal*, also by International Research Associates for the Canal Company, March 1974.

41. Klette, *op. cit.*, p. 132.

CHAPTER EIGHT

CONCLUSIONS

This chapter will summarize the main conclusions of the study. No effort has been made to be all-inclusive. Only the major conclusions will be listed. In order to avoid misinterpretations and to prevent possible separation of recommendations from their arguments, recommendations are incorporated in the body of the volume itself.

Canal Advantages

1. The Panama Canal is a main thoroughfare of world commerce. The oceanborne commerce of the United States has long been the prime beneficiary of the existence of the Canal.

2. The Panama Canal provides important savings in distances for shipping bound between different ports in the Atlantic and the Pacific. These distances are translatable into time saved at sea, into savings in the consumption of fuel energy, and lowered transportation costs for shippers.

3. The cost saving advantages offered by the Panama Canal have been decreasing over time as other modes of commodity transport have been developed and improved. This trend has been counterbalanced by the increased use made of the Canal.

Trend to Large Vessels

4. The large liquid and dry bulk carriers now being produced by world shipyards are not currently competitive with standard size shipping that can transit the Panama Canal. A time is foreseen, however, when surplus tonnage may cause superships to compete for Panama Canal cargoes. Nevertheless, recent studies conclude that 90 percent of the vessels in the world fleet will be able to transit the Canal locks in the year 2000.

5. The development of deepwater ports in the United States will spur the use of superships. This will have an impact on Panama Canal traffic. Therefore, improvements in Canal capacity must be seen in light of national port policy.

6. The principal users of the Canal between now and 1985 will be intermediate size general cargo liners, containerships, refrigerator vessels, other specialized ships, liquid and dry bulk carriers able to fit within the locks.

7. As the numbers of Panamax-sized vessels increase, and the shipbuilding industry turns out more vessels exceeding the dimensions of

the Panama Canal locks, pressures will grow on commerce to employ larger vessels for the economies of scale these can offer. We expect the pressures to rise progressively after 1980.

Cargo Movement and Traffic Estimates

8. Cargo movement at the Canal is expected to rise from the present level of 121 million long tons to roughly 300-350,000,000 tons by the year 2000, assuming economic conditions remain generally favorable. Computer studies suggest that cargo movement will be on the orders of magnitude of the following amounts in intermediate years:

1975	134,000,000 long tons	1990	218,000,000 long tons
1980	156,000,000 long tons	1995	263,000,000 long tons
1985	182,000,000 long tons	2000	312,000,000 long tons

9. Based on estimated levels of cargo movement, we forecast ship traffic as being under 23,000 transits a year by the year 2000, with the following orders of magnitude in intervening years:

1975	14,800	1990	17,600
1980	15,400	1995	19,400
1985	16,100	2000	21,300

Limitations of Capacity

10. The fixed dimensions of the lock chambers impose limitations on the Canal. Ships larger than approximately 65,000 tons laden, or about 80,000 tons in ballast, cannot normally pass through the locks. The maximum dimensions that can be locked through are nominally 975 feet long by 106.9 feet beam by 39.5 feet draft.

11. The number of ships that can be put through the Canal in a year will ultimately be limited by human ability. Pilots, schedulers, and the remainder of the Canal work force make critical judgments with each transit. Judgments cannot be rushed. Moderate ship speeds are required in the sea level approaches, the Cut, Gatun Lake, and approaches to the locks. The number of factors affecting the scheduling of transits strains the limits of thought although there is some hope that computers may shoulder part of this task.

12. When the present improvements are completed, the Canal will have a rated capacity of approximately 26,800 transits a year, depending upon the mixtures of ship types and sizes that arrive for transit. As the numbers of vessels built to Panamax specifications increase, the rated capacity of the Canal may decline somewhat.

Cost of Canal Enterprise

13. The cost to the United States Government related to constructing, operating, maintaining and improving the Panama Canal over the years has amounted to over $2.5 billion. Recoveries from all

sources, including tolls on United States Government owned vessels, have been approximately $1.5 billion. The United States Government is thus running an unrecovered expenditure of nearly one billion dollars on the Canal enterprise. This needs to be borne in mind when considering the possible construction of additional facilities, or of turning the Canal over to others.

Toll Strategies

14. The present toll system has functioned well for the life of the Canal. The original policy of charging Canal users only the cost of providing service has been instrumental in furthering the usefulness and economic benefits of the Canal operation.

15. Recent inflation, coupled with desires to recover some of the original investment in the waterway, has necessitated a toll increase. The proposed 20 percent rise will not curtail use of the Canal by shipping. Inflation may make additional toll increases necessary.

16. A variable pricing system designed to meet the competition of alternate modes of transportation would generate additional revenues. But this would require more paper work to administer, tempt shippers to file false or incomplete reports of cargo, and be difficult to enforce.

Impact of Land- and Mini-Bridges

17. The land-bridge operation, employing unitized train-loads of containers on the transcontinental railroads across the United States synchronized with ship arrival and departure dates, offers a new competitive challenge to the Panama Canal. Thus far, this does not appear to be affecting Canal traffic.

18. The mini-bridge concept, involving shipment from an overseas continent to cities on the opposite coast of the United States, has up to now been more costly than all-water shipment. It can effect a small saving of time if connections are perfect. Rising ship operating costs and toll increases are improving the competitive position of the mini-bridge.

Third Locks Plan

19. We consider a project to construct a third set of locks economically unjustifiable. Their operation would require the pumping of sea water into Gatun Lake to provide adequate lockage water. The cost of pumping, coupled with the manning and maintenance costs, would necessitate a rise in tolls that would undermine possible economic advantages that could be drawn from the use of larger ships. Any lock type facility will ultimately impose limits on the size of ships capable of transiting. New locks would not make the Panama Canal any easier to defend. Since the locks would be too small to accommodate the very large aircraft carriers of the United States Navy, they would contribute little to national security.

Sea-Level Canal Plans

20. Recovering the costs of constructing a sea-level canal, and paying just and equitable compensation to the Republic of Panama out of tolls cannot be assured at this time, even with projected increased traffic. There are many unpredictable cost elements involved in such a course, including acquiring privately-owned lands, right-of-way payments to Panama, and others.

21. A saturated Panama Canal, or a massive shift to very large ships, will not in itself be proof that a sea-level canal will be economically justified. Governor David S. Parker anticipated this when he said a sea-level canal "sometime," when the time is right.

22. It is not clear that a sea-level canal will pay for itself if it is ready by the year 2000, although it is possible that by that time traffic demand will be sufficient to justify the investment.

23. It may be that a sea-level canal will turn out to be so expensive that it would be better not to attempt to build it, even when the Panama Canal has all the traffic it can transit. Meantime, we favor retaining the present Canal.

24. A sea-level canal will approximately equal in cost two nuclear aircraft carriers at today's prices, and might reduce somewhat the need for a two-ocean Navy. If the President or the Department of Defense were to say that a sea-level canal is needed on grounds of national security, this would carry impressive weight with the country.

25. The country may decide to build a sea-level canal even though it is not economically justified, but is required for defense purposes. The State and Defense Departments will have to determine if unrecoverable expenditures are balanced by political—i.e., prestige and influence—and defense considerations.

26. Should construction of a sea-level canal be undertaken, a track across the Isthmus just to the northwest of the present Zone appears to be most desirable. Building in this area will not interfere with the operation of the present Canal. A sea-level waterway built away from the present canal can be built without the necessity of achieving high capacity initially. It can be enlarged in stages to accommodate both more ships and larger ships. The present Canal would remain available during and after construction of the new facility as a backup in the event of slides or other engineering problems. The fresh water Gatun Lake need not be destroyed with all its recreational, electrical power, and municipal uses. A canal in this area will probably be less costly to construct than if built elsewhere.

27. A sea-level waterway separated from the original canal but near existing defense facilities will be relatively easy to defend and make it more difficult to disrupt transiting operations at both canals. Construc-

tion north of the Canal would entail acquiring more land, but in this area relatively little development has taken place. Furthermore, once a new facility is completed, operations can be consolidated in the island between the two canals, freeing territories on the east bank of the present Canal, which are of considerable economic value, for return to Panama, if this is deemed to be desirable.

Stay with the Present Canal Indefinitely

28. Construction cost estimates and forecasts of economic benefits obtainable from a sea-level canal are only approximate at this time. These imply that a sea-level canal may never be desirable. It is conceivable that no major new facility should ever be undertaken and that the present Canal should be maintained indefinitely, even if traffic demand exceeds its capacity.

A New Treaty

29. Treaty relationships with the Republic of Panama need to be modernized within the context of a new hemisphere relationship. A treaty along the general lines of the drafts referred to the governments in 1967 will cover legitimate aspirations of the Panamanian people while preserving the indispensable needs of the United States for a free and open canal available to the use of all nations on a non-discriminatory basis. The treaty should endorse the principle of the Canal being dedicated to the advancement of commerce.

30. Improved relations with Panama are likely to be achieved through an increased role for Panama in the Canal enterprise, as well as added economic benefits that are fair and equitable.

31. Some civil functions can be transferred to Panamanian administration shortly. Portions of the Zone not needed for the operation and defense of the Canal can be returned to the Republic on a piecemeal basis. Construction of a sea-level canal along an axis northwest of the present Zone would allow transfer of activities to what would amount to an island between the two waterways. This would permit most of the land, towns, ports and installations lying to the east of the existing Canal to be turned over to the Republic of Panama if this is desirable.

32. A joint council or commission to advise the governments on steps to extend the capacity of the Canal would afford a routine basis for consultation and exchange of views.

33. United States armed forces are needed for the defense of the waterway. A separate rights and status of forces agreement should be concluded that will assure freedom of action to take necessary steps to protect the Canal and to defend it against external attack.

34. Other prime user nations should be drawn into a treaty relationship to afford a regularized basis for the expression of their needs and interests in the use of the waterway.

35. A separate treaty will need to be concluded for construction of a sea-level canal, regardless of whether this is built inside or outside of the Zone.

Maintaining United States Leadership

36. The Congress in passing the Marine Resources and Engineering Development Act of 1966, declared its determination that the United States should remain a leader in ocean science, technology and engineering. In passing the Merchant Marine Act of 1970, it voiced its will that the United States rejuvenate its merchant marine in such a way that it would carry 30 percent of the nation's export trade in place of the then 7 percent. Realization of these goals can mean increased traffic for the Canal, rising toll receipts, improvement of the national economy, and further enhancement of the nation's position in relation to others.

37. We have tried to look at the Canal operation in a fair, independent manner, in harmony with United States national interests. We believe that the results vindicate the conscientious, efficient administration of the Canal and warrant pursuit of these policies.

38. The United States should keep its treaty options open for construction of an interoceanic canal elsewhere in the event that conditions at the Isthmus make retention of the existing Canal untenable.

39. Innovative techniques can be developed for excavation and construction of a sea-level waterway and their development should be pursued before they are needed for such a major undertaking.

40. The impact of political relationships on supplies of energy is changing the competitive position of the Canal for world shipping. Where this will lead is unknown, but the importance of energy supplies for keeping commerce moving does merit further investigation and close government attention.

41. The United States has sometimes been accused of refusing to change its position at the Canal to adapt to new conditions. Furthermore, instances of reaction to crises rather than initiative to produce changes in accordance with its will have sometimes been common to foreign policy. We have the capacity to lead. We have the men to do so, the talent and the experience. These should be put to the task of improving the interoceanic canal as an instrument for furthering world commerce.

42. In the course of this study the authors have come to appreciate how greatly the Panama Canal has facilitated world commerce, and with this international relations and understandings. It is essential that an outward looking view be preserved in handling Canal affairs in the future.

INDEX

INDEX

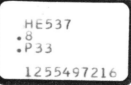